THE COLLECTED WORKS OF

ERIC VOEGELIN

VOLUME 31

HITLER AND THE GERMANS

PROJECTED VOLUMES IN THE COLLECTED WORKS

1. *On the Form of the American Mind*
2. *Race and State*
3. *The History of the Race Idea: From Ray to Carus*
4. *The Authoritarian State: An Essay on the Problem of the Austrian State*
5. *Political Religions; The New Science of Politics; and Science, Politics, and Gnosticism*
6. *Anamnesis*
7. *Published Essays, 1922–*
8. *Published Essays*
9. *Published Essays*
10. *Published Essays*
11. *Published Essays*
12. *Published Essays, 1966–1985*
13. *Selected Book Reviews*
14. *Order and History,* Volume I, *Israel and Revelation*
15. *Order and History,* Volume II, *The World of the Polis*
16. *Order and History,* Volume III, *Plato and Aristotle*
17. *Order and History,* Volume IV, *The Ecumenic Age*
18. *Order and History,* Volume V, *In Search of Order*
19. *History of Political Ideas,* Volume I, *Hellenism, Rome, and Early Christianity*
20. *History of Political Ideas,* Volume II, *The Middle Ages to Aquinas*
21. *History of Political Ideas,* Volume III, *The Later Middle Ages*
22. *History of Political Ideas,* Volume IV, *Renaissance and Reformation*
23. *History of Political Ideas,* Volume V, *Religion and the Rise of Modernity*
24. *History of Political Ideas,* Volume VI, *Revolution and the New Science*
25. *History of Political Ideas,* Volume VII, *The New Order and Last Orientation*
26. *History of Political Ideas,* Volume VIII, *Crisis and the Apocalypse of Man*
27. *The Nature of the Law, and Related Legal Writings*
28. *What Is History? And Other Late Unpublished Writings*
29. *Selected Correspondence*
30. *Selected Correspondence*
31. *Hitler and the Germans*
32. *Miscellaneous Papers*
33. *Autobiographical Reflections and Index*
34. *Index*

The Editorial Board wishes to give grateful acknowledgment to those who have contributed to support publication of this book and series, including the Foundation for Faith in Search of Understanding, the Liberty Fund, Inc., Robert J. Cihak, M.D., and John C. Jacobs Jr. A special thanks for support goes to the Charlotte and Walter Kohler Charitable Trust.

The University of Missouri Press offers its grateful acknowledgment for a generous contribution from the Eric Voegelin Institute.

THE COLLECTED WORKS OF

ERIC VOEGELIN

VOLUME 31

HITLER AND THE GERMANS

TRANSLATED, EDITED, AND
WITH AN INTRODUCTION BY

DETLEV CLEMENS
AND
BRENDAN PURCELL

UNIVERSITY OF MISSOURI PRESS

COLUMBIA AND LONDON

University of Missouri Press, Columbia, Missouri 65201
Printed and bound in the United States of America

5 4 3 2 1 03 02 01 00 99

Library of Congress Cataloging-in-Publication Data

Voegelin, Eric, 1901–
Hitler and the Germans / Eric Voegelin ; translated, edited, and with an introduction by Detlev Clemens and Brendan Purcell.
p. cm. — (The collected works of Eric Voegelin ; v. 31)
Lectures delivered in the summer of 1964 at the University of Munich.
Includes bibliographical references and index.
ISBN 0-8262-1216-6 (alk. paper)
1. Hitler, Adolf, 1889–1945. 2. Heads of state—Germany—Biography. 3. National socialism—Philosophy. 4. Germany—Politics and government—1933–1945. 5. Racism—Germany. I. Clemens, Detlev. II. Purcell, Brendan. III. Title. IV. Series: Voegelin, Eric, 1901– Works. 1989 : v. 31.
B3354.V88 vol. 31
[DD247.H5]
943.086'092—dc21 99-13973
CIP

∞ This paper meets the requirements of the American National Standard for Permanence of Paper for Printed Library Materials, Z39.48, 1984.

Designer: Albert Crochet
Typesetter: Bookcomp, Inc.
Printer and binder: Thomson-Shore, Inc.
Typeface: Trump Mediaeval

Contents

Editors' Introductions
Eric Voegelin's "Hitler and the Germans" Lectures in the Context of the Germans' Treatment of Their Nazi Past 1
Detlev Clemens
The Philosophical Context of the "Hitler and the Germans" Lectures 21
Brendan Purcell

Editors' Note 41

Part I. Descent into the Abyss

1. Introduction 51
(First Lecture 51)
2. Development of Diagnostic Tools 70
(Second Lecture 74)
(Third Lecture 96)
3. Descent into the Academic Abyss as Manifested by Schramm's "Anatomy of a Dictator" 110
(Fourth Lecture 123)
(Fifth Lecture 147)
4. Descent into the Ecclesiastical Abyss: The Evangelical Church 155
(Sixth Lecture 170)
5. Descent into the Ecclesiastical Abyss: The Catholic Church 184
(Seventh Lecture 184)
(Eighth Lecture 204)
6. Descent into the Legal Abyss 213
(Ninth Lecture 222)

Part II. Toward a Restoration of Order

7. First and Second Reality in Ancient, Post-medieval, and Modern Times of Crisis 239
(Tenth Lecture 251)

8. The Greatness of Max Weber 257
(Eleventh Lecture 257)

Index 275

HITLER AND THE GERMANS

Editors' Introductions

I. Eric Voegelin's "Hitler and the Germans" Lectures in the Context of the Germans' Treatment of Their Nazi Past

In the summer semester of 1964, Eric Voegelin's lectures on Hitler and the Germans were, without a doubt, the most spectacular course in the Arts Faculty of Munich University. Although announced as an introduction to political science, the lectures had aroused great expectations. Their publication as a book had been arranged even before they were held, and while only a few dozen students were enrolled in the political science department, every week the lectures attracted several hundred students and scholars from various other departments. This fact certainly corresponded to Voegelin's own understanding of classic political science as the key science in the field of the humanities. The audience's expectations were not disappointed. Voegelin's argument—and certainly also its pointed and at times polemical presentation—stirred up heated emotions whether in enthusiastic agreement or in angry rejection. On the one hand, the lectures increased the antipathy Voegelin met among some of his German colleagues at the University of Munich and provoked hostile press coverage[1] and even personal threats. On the other hand, for most of his students, they became what one of them in retrospect described as "the high point of their German

1. See "Deutschenhaß als 'neue Wissenschaft,' " in *Deutsche Nationale Zeitung und Soldatenzeitung*, June 26, 1964. This article, accompanied by a repulsive photograph falsely claiming to be of Voegelin, characterized him as an "arrogant sectarian" whose lectures reflected a "systematic hatred of the Germans."

education, for they had met no one else who had told them the truth more bluntly."[2]

This is the first reason Voegelin's lectures are published in a form that deliberately preserves the style of their presentation, conveying to the reader the special atmosphere where he combined an authoritative treatment of a highly controversial topic with the explanation of fundamental concepts of his political philosophy. While the "Hitler and the Germans" lectures undoubtedly mark the peak of Voegelin's work as an academic teacher in Germany, they also were his most elaborate and outspoken analysis of the spiritual level of contemporary German intellectual life and, in general, of German political culture. He certainly was not attempting to provide a thorough, balanced study of the origins and functioning of National Socialist rule in Germany based on the latest historical literature, and therefore he could conspicuously ignore some of the classic analyses of the Nazi dictatorship and its rise that were available at his time. Voegelin's topic was the Germans' complicity in Nazi rule and their current treatment of their National Socialist past. For him, the most important challenge for German society was not the "mastering of the past" (*Vergangenheitsbewältigung*)—the current and opaque German expression for this process—but rather a "mastering of the present."

Such a mastering of the present required the achievement of a consensus among Germans regarding the role and significance of the Nazi dictatorship and the Holocaust in the context both of German history and of German national identity in the postwar era. Consequently, in his lectures Voegelin dealt not only with the past but also with the presence of the past in the Federal Republic of Germany of the 1960s. He questioned whether the Germans had adequately reflected upon their Nazi past and gone through a revolution of the spirit, or whether the mentality that made possible Hitler's rise to power did not still dominate in Germany in unbroken continuity. Since the past cannot be altered after the event, the "mastering of the present," in Voegelin's eyes, was largely a problem of moral consciousness and therefore inevitably demanded a relentless spiritual self-examination of their past *and* present by the Germans. "Urged to do so by the young people in

2. Manfred Henningsen, "Eric Voegelin und die Deutschen," *Merkur: Deutsche Zeitschrift für europäisches Denken* 48, no. 8 (1994): 728.

the Department" of Political Science, as he wrote later,[3] Voegelin tried to show how this could be carried out, provided the analyst had sufficient command of the right diagnostic tools. In fact, by drawing from various relevant sources from 1964—new historical studies, public discussions, newspaper articles, and so on—and by judging them critically, Voegelin made his students realize that the way in which these sources dealt with the Germans in the Nazi empire revealed much about the mentality and political culture of the Germans in the Federal Republic, too. And this gave rise to the scathing critique of German intellectual and spiritual life both before and after the Second World War, which constitutes the lectures. Such a critique of the mentality and substance of an entire people was an enormous provocation and challenge to the contemporary attempts at "mastering the past," as becomes clear from a brief survey of the Germans' postwar treatment of their Nazi past.

Since 1943 the Allies of the anti-Hitler coalition had been in agreement that once Germany had been militarily defeated, the "Hitlerites and Huns" should stand trial and be held accountable for their war crimes.[4] The leading Nazis were to be interned and the entire German people made to understand that they themselves had brought chaos and misery on their country. Finally, all traces of National Socialism were to be eliminated by a "denazification" of the public sector and important private companies of all former active Nazi party members and by a democratic reeducation of the German people.[5] However, by the time the Federal Republic was constituted in West Germany in May 1949 and the responsibility for the further prosecution of war criminals and for denazification was formally transferred to the German authorities, the Allies had to recognize that their original aim of denazifying the Germans was unrealizable because of inescapable legal and political problems.

The Nuremberg trials against the main war criminals showed that it was impossible to effectively prosecute, through ordinary

3. Eric Voegelin, letter to Bishop Johannes Neuhäusler, January 18, 1965, Eric Voegelin Papers, Hoover Institution Archives, box 27, file 3.

4. See Moscow Four-Power declaration, November 1, 1943, in Helmut Rönnefarth, *Vertrags-Ploetz,* vol. 2 of *Konferenzen und Verträge* (Würzburg: Ploetz, 1959), 217.

5. See Yalta Four-Power declaration, February 12, 1945, ibid., 245 f.

criminal law, unspeakable crimes organized and perpetrated by or on behalf of irresponsible state authorities—what Hannah Arendt called "administrative massacres."[6] This insight was to be confirmed by numerous later trials of Nazi criminals and is extensively dealt with by Voegelin.[7] The conviction of the main war criminals in Nuremberg was possible only on the grounds of the ill-defined offenses of "crimes against peace" and "waging aggressive war," which at that time lacked an indisputable basis in international law, thus raising doubts whether the legal proposition *nulla poena sine lege* (no penalty without law) was not violated. Although the Allies were careful to avoid the impression of victors' justice, the trials to some extent had undesirable psychological effects on the Germans. It is true that the detailed evidence of the atrocities committed, which came to light during the trials, contributed to a shocked disillusionment of Germans with National Socialism and a tardy delegitimization of Nazi rule. It is equally true that in 1946 the vast majority of Germans interviewed considered the Nuremberg trials to be justified and fair.[8] Because the few top-ranking Nazis were held mainly responsible for the war crimes, however, the widespread loss of political, moral, and ethical sensitivity among Germans, which preceded the crimes, their readiness to obey, and their involvement in the crimes did not become an issue.[9] The blame could be laid on the Nazi élites, and the average German could feel exonerated.

But without a sense of guilt there could be no successful reeducation; denazification was a failure for the same reason. The purge of all former Nazi functionaries from the public sector was more easily proposed than implemented. For the Allies, the intended differentiation of Germans into major offenders, offenders, lesser

6. Hannah Arendt, *Eichmann in Jerusalem: A Report on the Banality of Evil* (New York: Penguin, 1994), 288, 294.

7. See below, 64 f., 230–36; see also Jürgen Weber and Peter Steinbach, eds., *Vergangenheitsbewältigung durch Strafverfahren? NS-Prozesse in der Bundesrepublik Deutschland* (Munich: Olzog, 1984), and Adalbert Rückerl, *Die Strafverfolgung von NS-Verbrechen, 1945–1978: Eine Dokumentation* (Heidelberg: Müller, 1979).

8. Anna J. and Richard L. Merritt, eds., *Public Opinion in Occupied Germany: The OMGUS Surveys, 1945–1949* (Urbana: University of Illinois Press, 1970), 93 f. In 1946, 78 percent of Germans judged the Nuremberg trials as fair; by October 1950 this number had fallen to 38 percent.

9. See Peter Steinbach, *Nationalsozialistische Gewaltverbrechen: Die Diskussion in der deutschen Öffentlichkeit nach 1945* (Berlin: Colloquium Verlag, 1981), 27.

offenders, followers, and exonerated persons by means of questionnaires and denazification tribunals demanded the willing and self-critical cooperation of the Germans themselves. Instead, they reacted with a "solidarity of general exculpation"[10] to the mass inquisition and internment. Those who had been incriminated "exonerated" and helped each other obtain whitewashing testimonials from the denazification tribunals—ironically called *Persil-Scheine,* after a well-known soap powder—that were required for the resumption of ordinary work and were thus a precondition for returning to civil society.[11] Once again, lying, fellow traveling, and opportunism were the normality, and secured political rehabilitation. Therefore, even those Germans who were in favor of holding the Nazis accountable for their crimes and who were willing to cooperate viewed these denazification procedures as unsuccessful and, above all, unfair.

Indeed, besides being marred by serious organizational problems, denazification showed blatant divergences among the four powers in each of their occupation zones with regard to its general conception, definition of concrete aims, and rigor of enforcement. German feelings of unjust treatment were also stirred up by the wholesale dismissals of Nazi party members from public office in the Soviet and American zones and compulsory questionnaires for all those older than eighteen in the Western zones with the legally dubious principle that the accused had to prove their innocence. These measures were rightly seen as resulting from the presumption of a German "collective guilt" (*Kollektivschuld*), with all Germans—whether good or bad—under suspicion of personally contributing to a criminal and murderous system.[12] However, since most Germans rejected denazification as inefficient and unfair and the notion

10. Peter Graf Kielmansegg, *Lange Schatten: Vom Umgang der Deutschen mit der nationalsozialistischen Vergangenheit* (Berlin: Siedler, 1989), 35.

11. In the American zone alone, 13 million questionnaires were handed in. In all three Western zones, 3.66 million Germans had to stand trial by 1949–50. Of these, more than 95 percent were classed as followers or as exonerated persons or the cases were dropped for other reasons. Among the rest, 1,667 persons were classed as major offenders, 23,060 as offenders, and 150,425 as lesser offenders. On Jan. 1, 1947, about 265,000 persons in the three Western zones either were interned or had been interned and already had been released. See Karl Dietrich Erdmann, *Das Ende des Reiches und die Neubildung deutscher Staaten* (Munich: Deutscher Taschenbuch Verlag, 1983), 114–17.

12. In the summer of 1945, the Allies publicly displayed horrifying posters and reports from the Dachau and Belsen concentration camps with the accusatory headline "Diese Schandtaten: Eure Schuld!" ("These atrocities: Your guilt!"). See

of collective guilt as too indiscriminate, they also suppressed the underlying fact that the crimes committed under the German National Socialist regime indeed called for an examination of conscience by each individual German. And those who on the basis of questionnaires or tribunals were declared denazified received quasi-official confirmation that they had had no role in the Nazi crimes. All in all, the Allied denazification process was an ill-conceived and unsuccessful attempt to confront the Germans with the question of their individual guilt in Nazi criminality and even paved the way toward the rehabilitation of the offenders. It remained a traumatic but unproductive experience for the Germans and contributed to a lasting silence, suppression, or dishonesty regarding their own involvement in the Third Reich.

In fact, the consequences of the denazification process ran counter to the expectations and hopes of prominent Germans—thinkers, writers, film makers—who understood the defeat and collapse of the Third Reich as a "zero hour," a special opportunity to reconstruct a politically and morally renewed Germany. They considered the self-critical coming to terms of the individual Germans with their personal position regarding inhumanity and tyranny to be a necessary precondition of this reconstruction. Publisher Eugen Kogon, a survivor of Buchenwald, understood his outstanding book about the atrocious reality of the "SS-state" in the concentration and extermination camps as "an *ecce homo* mirror . . . which does not show just some monsters, but *you and me* as soon as we have succumbed to the same spirit that those who created the system have succumbed to."[13] The title of a well-known film by Wolfgang Staudte from 1946 gave this reminder to the Germans: *The Murderers Are among Us.* And Karl Jaspers's famous refutation of a German collective guilt in 1946 was only partly a defense of the Germans against accusations from abroad. It was mainly an admonition that what was required was a coming to terms, not with an abstract "guilt of the German people," but with the question of personal guilt—whether criminal, political, or moral—of every

---

Christoph Kleßmann, *Die doppelte Staatsgründung: Deutsche Geschichte, 1945–1955* (Bonn: Bundeszentrale für politische Bildung, 1986), 308.

13. Eugen Kogon, *Der SS-Staat: Das System der deutschen Konzentrationslager* (Munich: Karl Alber, 1946), v [author's emphasis]. Published in English as *The Theory and Practice of Hell,* trans. Heinz Norden (New York: Farrar, Straus, 1950).

individual German.[14] Therefore, he called for an "unconditional self-examination" and "inner change of heart" to be accomplished alone by the individual in society. For Jaspers, this purification of the soul, understood as a "continuous becoming of oneself," was the precondition for the realization of personal and political freedom after the catastrophic experience of dictatorship.[15] In the same year, Hannah Arendt approached this problem from a different angle by asking what were the consequences, for German society, that one could not distinguish the criminals and mass murderers from the innocent and furtive heroes while still being compelled to live next door to them.[16]

Twenty years later, this was precisely one of Voegelin's central lessons in these lectures: that the acceptance of one's own past, the unsparingly self-critical assessment of individual guilt for crimes committed in the name of the German people, was the prerequisite for a truly free and democratic society of citizens free of mutual suspicion and mistrust.[17] Only such a society could also summon up the resolution to declare guilty those who perpetrated or abetted crimes, thus confirming that, as Jaspers had stated, guilt is always individual, never collective, even if it encompassed very large sections of a people.[18] One could even ask whether it was not precisely the Germans' refusal to openly deal with the question of individual guilt at its different levels according to Jaspers that made it possible to lay upon them the reproach of a collective guilt for National Socialist crimes.

Even if the uprooting and displacement of millions of people in the wake of the war enabled many of the offenders and supporters

14. Jaspers differentiated four categories of guilt—criminal, political, moral, and metaphysical—none of which could constitute a collective guilt. For him, guilt always remains attached to an individual, and only from political guilt could a "collective liability" be derived in the sense that the German people collectively had to bear the political consequences of German misdeeds during the Nazi past. This differentiation was most valuable as the basis for public discussion of German guilt. See Karl Jaspers, *Die Schuldfrage: Zur politischen Haltung Deutschlands* (Munich: Piper Verlag, 1987). Translated by E. B. Ashton as *The Question of German Guilt* (New York: Capricorn Books, 1947).

15. Jaspers, *Die Schuldfrage*, 61, 16, 82.

16. Hannah Arendt in *Die Wandlung* (April 1946), cited in Wilfried Röhrich, *Die Demokratie der Westdeutschen: Geschichte und politisches Klima einer Republik* (Munich: Beck, 1988), 17.

17. See below, 76.

18. See Voegelin's unmasking of the notion of "collective guilt" as a cliché, 75–82 below.

of the terror regime to assume new identities, thus escaping responsibility for personal involvement in crimes, at least in the local context everyone knew who the "hundred-percent convinced Nazis," the informers and collaborators, had been. And yet, instead of uncovering them and reporting them to the allied or, later, German authorities—which might have raised critical questions about one's own behavior under the dictatorship—an attitude of collective silence dominated Germans' dealing with each other's Nazi past. The reasons may have been various: the deep traumas caused by years of war and captivity; the impression of the ineffectiveness or even unfairness of the denazification procedures; preoccupation with one's own survival in the postwar plight; the sudden unmasking of long-held and state-approved convictions and their terrible consequences; disillusionment, fear of the future, and the determination to work for a better future; later, the frustration about the unwillingness of German authorities to act against former Nazi officials and their reinstatement in former positions. All of these reasons led many Germans in the "years of rubble," where the "mastering of the present" was a physical, not a spiritual, problem, to adopt an apolitical attitude and avoid any public discussion of the question of individual guilt for Nazi crimes. This experiential complex induced Germans, when faced with their past, to reactions ranging from shock, speechlessness, and repentance in word and deed to—very often—repression, but also to brazen opportunism and what Jaspers called "aggressive silence" regarding any attempt at denazification.[19] After all, in 1945 and 1946 a majority of the Germans held the opinion that National Socialism was a good idea but badly implemented, and until the mid-1950s it was equally widely held that without the war, Hitler would have been one of the greatest statesmen in German history.[20]

On the level of individual responsibility, most Germans lacked the strength for moral conversion, and denazification was not—and probably could not be—effectively imposed from outside. Collectively, however, the Germans all the more conscientiously faced the question of guilt and responsibility for the Nazi past. The newly

19. Jaspers, *Die Schuldfrage,* 76.

20. See Peter Reichel, "Vergangenheitsbewältigung als Problem unserer politischen Kultur," in *Vergangenheitsbewältigung durch Strafverfahren?* ed. Weber and Steinbach, 155 f.

founded West German state ostentatiously embodied dissociation from the Nazi regime. It defined itself as the democratic countermodel of the fallen dictatorship and at the same time situated itself within the continuity of German history. In accordance with its self-interpretation as the legal successor of the German Reich—and contrary to the German Democratic Republic in the east[21]—the Federal Republic of Germany was willing to accept responsibility and pay compensation to individual victims and to the state of Israel. Of course, this way the "state" had to do what its citizens were unable or unwilling to do. This corresponded to the tradition of German state-centered political philosophy since Hegel and showed that the cliché of collective guilt could serve as an alibi, averting the question of individual guilt each German would have to answer for him- or herself. Since German people as a whole were held responsible for Nazi crimes and since the German state accepted this responsibility and its financial consequences, the task of owning up to the Nazi past within one's own identity was left to the state:

> In principle, the condemnation of the Nazi past may have been determinedly adopted, as it were, as the state doctrine of the Federal Republic, but it remained abstract. The citizens were not expected to accept the general-abstract past as their own. From the beginning of the 1950s on, even the accomplices in the National Socialist crimes could count on the general tendency and readiness to forget.[22]

The prevailing attitude of the Germans to the Nazi past was further supported by the state of international politics, marked by the developing cold war. The containment of communism required a stabilized West Germany. It would not have served the Western Allies' interests if the Germans, as future allies, had to bear the stigma of being inveterate Nazis; nor would it have done so if the newly founded German state underwent a phase of internal weakness caused by a painful process of serious moral self-examination. This is one of the reasons why, from 1947 on, the Western Allies,

21. In the Soviet occupation zone, the National Socialist past was officially "mastered" by initial denazification of the public service as well as expropriation and land reform, which were expected to destroy the basis of fascism. Compensation payments by the GDR were never made. However, exposing the high number of former Nazis in leading positions in the Federal Republic became part of the East German ideological contest with the "class enemy."

22. Kielmansegg, *Lange Schatten*, 17.

especially the United States and Great Britain, toned down their attempts at denazification and were rather accommodating to the German government's attempts from as early as 1949 to reverse its results.[23] The gradual reintegration of the Federal Republic as an almost-equal partner within the Western camp was interpreted, at least by the Germans themselves, as a national rehabilitation, with regard to the Nazi past. Here, it proved advantageous that the Federal Republic was conceived as a countermodel, not only to the Nazi regime, but also to the East German state. Through their anticommunism, the West Germans could demonstrate that they had learned the lessons from the past and stood up against dictatorship in the present without having to prove their democratic values by reflection on their own previous acceptance of dictatorship. In the end, the West Germans' pride in mastering the initial difficulties of reconstruction and especially in the "economic miracle" of the 1950s fostered the development of their self-esteem and of a quasi-ahistorical national identity. They wanted to believe that their economic and political success had freed them from the shadows of the past. "We are somebody again" was the widespread slogan that best represented this feeling.

Historical research in the 1950s also reflected this tendency of avoiding the question of individual guilt and of making the task of coming to terms with the Nazi past a collective matter. "Contemporary history" was given a symbolic importance with the foundation in 1950 of the publicly funded Institute for Contemporary History in Munich, still today the German center for research into Germany's recent history. In the years immediately after the war, German historiography was marked by moral dissociation from the recent past. At the same time it attempted to define the historical and ideological roots of National Socialism and its place in the continuity of German history in order to find new moral ground after "the German catastrophe."[24] Next, historians directed their interest to the details and motivations of the political decisions leading

23. In the British and the American zones, denazification was declared completed in February and March 1948. The allied prosecution of war criminals was suspended in May 1949, although the last death sentences were carried out in June 1951. See Ulrich Brochhagen, *Nach Nürnberg: Vergangenheitsbewältigung und Westintegration in der Ära Adenauer* (Hamburg: Junius, 1994).

24. Thus the title of one of the most influential books of the time: Friedrich Meinecke, *Die deutsche Katastrophe: Betrachtungen und Erinnerungen* (Wiesbaden: Brockhaus, 1946).

to the fall of the Weimar republic as well as to the structure of the National Socialist regime and its role in the outbreak of the Second World War. In this early postwar research, National Socialism was clearly understood as "Hitlerism," and the historical developments in its rise were mostly related to—and explained by—Hitler's dark, criminal will to power and the machinations of a self-interested conservative political and economic élite. The more Hitler was demonized as the demagogic seducer of the Germans, the more their individual responsibility for the establishment and functioning of the National Socialist regime slipped into the background. This seemed to fit with the theory of totalitarianism fully developed in the 1950s by Carl J. Friedrich, Zbigniew K. Brzezinski, and Hannah Arendt,[25] which laid the basis for the image of the defenseless individual caught in the all-embracing dictatorial machine applying sophisticated mechanisms of manipulation and terroristic means of intimidation. From this perspective, National Socialism appeared as a violent national phenomenon that had overcome the Germans and made them the first victims of Hitler, followed after the war by their scapegoating through "unfair" denazification. Hitler, in fact, became an alibi for the Germans, a majority of whom in the 1950s and 1960s wished to draw the *Schlußstrich,* the bottom line, under the Nazi past.

When assessing the German "mastering of the past," a term used naturally and in the sense of a completed stocktaking and final judgment by the highest officials of the Federal Republic in the 1950s, there is the ambivalent picture we have already referred to. That picture shows nondiscussion of guilt on the individual level and, on the collective level of the West German state, recognition of responsibility and official reparation accompanied by a remarkably lax prosecution and mild sentencing of Nazi criminals or functionaries, who, if sentenced at all, were often speedily rehabilitated. Thus, former Nazi officials were reinstated up to the highest levels of the civil service, the law, or education.[26] Depending on which aspect of the picture is highlighted, there is a different judgment

25. Carl J. Friedrich and Zbigniew K. Brzezinski, *Totalitarian Dictatorship and Autocracy* (Cambridge: Harvard University Press, 1956); Hannah Arendt, *The Origins of Totalitarianism* (New York: Harcourt Brace Jovanovich, 1951).

26. Among very many cases, the most spectacular was Hans Globke, the secretary of state in the chancellor's office and Chancellor Konrad Adenauer's right-hand man (see below, 66 f.). But later, Chancellor Kurt Georg Kiesinger (1966–69) and president

about the German treatment of the Nazi past in the first decade after the war, and the need for making the German "mastering of the past" a topic for further historical research in its own right is obvious and undisputed.

On the one hand, recent attempts—which stem from the context of "revisionist" German historiography since the 1980s—to interpret the policy of the Adenauer government from 1949 as first of all driven by the effort to face up to the Nazi past seem more than a little forced.[27] On the other hand, the thesis of a general attitude of suppression in the German society of the 1950s certainly needs differentiation, and the verdict of Ralph Giordano, that the postwar Germans had loaded a "second guilt" on their shoulders by not confronting their past, seems overdrawn.[28] It has been convincingly argued that in 1949 the new German state had to be built up and gain legitimacy and acceptance with the same people who had been the people of the Third Reich. And it would most probably have been impossible to achieve this if those Germans burdened by their personal Nazi past had been condemned and ostracized on a mass scale.[29] Kogon had warned already in 1947 that pushing millions of former Nazis onto the sidelines of democracy would create the seedbed for antidemocratic conspiracy.[30] It was equally inconceivable that the administrative and economic reconstruction could succeed without making use of at least some of those experts who had had their formative experiences during the Third Reich. This was a dilemma, and it was also one of the greatest challenges for the young Federal Republic, which was thus almost necessarily tainted from its beginning. Of course, legitimate reference to the unavoidable need to reintegrate 8 million former Nazi party members, along with the fellow travelers, into the new democracy—a reintegration from which also numerous Nazi criminals profited—can be no general excuse for the German suppression of the Nazi

---

of the Federal Republic Karl Carstens (1979–84) were also attacked for their former membership in the Nazi party.

27. This is certainly the case for Manfred Kittel, *Die Legende von der "Zweiten Schuld": Vergangenheitsbewältigung in der Ära Adenauer* (Berlin: Ullstein, 1993).

28. Ralph Giordano, *Die zweite Schuld oder Von der Last Deutscher zu sein* (Hamburg: Rasch und Röhring, 1987).

29. See Hermann Lübbe, "Der Nationalsozialismus im deutschen Nachkriegsbewußtsein," *Historische Zeitschrift* 236 (1983): 579–99.

30. Eugen Kogon, "Das Recht auf den politischen Irrtum," *Frankfurter Hefte* (July 1947): 641–55.

past with regard to individual guilt and involvement. It would certainly not have done any harm to the new state if at least those guilty in the criminal sense had carefully been singled out and brought to justice. But again, the lesson taught by the unsuccessful denazification after 1945 was reaffirmed: that it was impossible to discern perpetrators from fellow travelers and bystanders without the readiness for moral conversion of those affected.

Instead, the Germans' attempts in the 1950s to come to terms with the Nazi heritage were not only dominated by a "collective silence" about the past; but far surpassing this, changing the general position of the Germans from the defensive to the offensive was the German government's "policy of the past" (*Vergangenheitspolitik*) starting as early as 1949.[31] Its aim was the rehabilitation of what it called the "victims of denazification," a process it branded as too undifferentiated and unfair. And this "policy of the past" was by no means kept secret or pursued discreetly. It was propagated with such astonishing openness in public discussion that it had to give rise to the question of an unbroken continuity in the mentality and political culture of the Germans from the Third Reich to the Federal Republic and overshadowed the credibility of the "new beginning" the Germans professed they were making. For Voegelin, this policy of laxity toward former Nazis was scandalous; it could not be excused by any considerations for the inner stability of the Federal Republic, and it brought him to ask whether the country had sunk to the level of an "operetta republic."[32]

And in fact, at the end of the 1950s, the Germans were made to understand that the bottom line under the "mastered" Nazi past was not so easily drawn. Several factors forced the crimes of the past and the question of individual guilt into the forefront of public discussion. First were spectacular trials, like the 1958 *Einsatzgruppen* trial in Ulm, which shed new light on the atrocities committed. In the same year, the Central Office of State Administrations for the Prosecution of National Socialist Crimes was established in

31. Norbert Frei, *Vergangenheitspolitik: Die Anfänge der Bundesrepublik und die NS-Vergangenheit* (Munich: Beck, 1996). In the German *Land* of Hesse, for example, 34 percent of all employed in the public service had been dismissed in 1945. By 1949 all but 2 percent had been reemployed in the public service. See Olaf Groehler, "Personenaustausch in der neuesten deutschen Geschichte," in *Vergangenheitsbewältigung 1945 und 1989: Ein unmöglicher Vergleich?* ed. Klaus Sühl (Berlin: Verlag Volk und Welt, 1994), 167–79, at 171 f.

32. See below, 69.

Ludwigsburg. Its achievement was not so much that there was greater determination and severity in prosecuting and sentencing Nazi war criminals, but that through criminal investigation, the crimes were prevented from falling into oblivion and new historical sources became available. Thus, an immense wealth of evidence was preserved for future research. Then, a new generation, which had not been educated under the Third Reich, had been growing up and were asking their parents critical questions. Although the *Einsatzgruppen* trials themselves could have focused on the role of "ordinary men" in the Nazi regime, it was above all the sensational trial of Adolf Eichmann in Jerusalem in 1960 that made the "banality of evil" visible and raised anew the question of the personal responsibility of bureaucrats and fellow travelers among the Germans. It is perhaps symptomatic of this renewed awareness that Jaspers' *Question of German Guilt* was reprinted in Germany in 1962.

Contrary to this were events that could be interpreted as signs of a recrudescence of National Socialism. On Christmas night in 1959, the Cologne synagogue was desecrated, marking the beginning of a wave of almost five hundred anti-Semitic occurrences in West Germany over a few weeks and raising serious doubts abroad about the stability and reliability of the Germans' democratic convictions. In 1964 the National Democratic Party (NPD), placing itself openly in the tradition of the National Socialist party, was founded and began to rapidly increase its votes, even gaining seats in some of the provincial parliaments. In the same year, only about half of the West Germans considered the National Socialist state to have been an unjust dictatorial regime, while in 1969, only 25 percent of the population was in favor of a further prosecution of Nazi crimes.[33]

Thus, by the mid-1960s, a social atmosphere had developed where the earlier consensus with regard to "mastering of the past" crumbled and the topic began to provoke passionate social conflicts. Historical research, too, now went beyond its initial approach, turned toward studies of local conditions and everyday life under Nazi rule, and, with the new questions of "structural history," explored social and economic structures and the actors' room for maneuver. In this context, Voegelin posed the central question that had not

33. Kielmansegg, *Lange Schatten,* 63, 54.

been deeply discussed among Germans: What was their role, first individually and then collectively, in making possible the National Socialist tyranny and its crimes, and how was that role continuing to be reflected in various aspects of the Federal Republic?

When seen against this historical background, the explosive effect of Voegelin's argument becomes fully understandable: He challenged, on several fronts, the Germans' dominating attitude regarding the Nazi past. As openly and sharply as possible he criticized the obvious biographical continuities between the Third Reich and the Federal Republic in large sectors of the public service, the law, and the economy, as well as the laxity of the administration of justice in prosecuting Nazi crimes. Of course, for Voegelin the insufficient denazification and prosecution of Nazi criminals were only symptoms of a far more serious syndrome: the suppression and avoidance of the question of whether there was continuity in the mentality and political culture of the Germans beyond the break of 1945, a continuity of moral and spiritual decline that had made possible the rise of National Socialism and that in the Federal Republic prevented a thorough dealing with individual guilt and responsibility for crimes committed. As the lectures show, Voegelin had clearly answered this question for himself in the affirmative. But in order to make his students understand and share his judgment, he had to destroy some of the delusions of the German society in which they had grown up.

In the first place stood the dominating image of Hitler as the demonic, thus enigmatic and therefore ultimately inexplicable, seducer of the Germans. In pointed contrast to this cliché, Voegelin showed the mediocre, half-educated, stubborn, self-assertive, petit bourgeois character of Hitler, whose real and only greatness lay in the brilliant exploitation of political opportunities for his own ends. With this character sketch, Voegelin turned the central question about Nazism—how a man like this could set himself up as the highest representative of a people and cause unspeakable crimes in its name—sharply back on the individual Germans, millions of whom had voted for Hitler and the really "grotesque, marginal figures"[34] around him and had willingly followed their Führer into war. At the same time, Voegelin's characterization of Hitler was

34. Eric Voegelin, *Autobiographical Reflections,* ed. Ellis Sandoz (1989; available Columbia: University of Missouri Press, 1999), 18.

an outspoken reproach to the inability of the diligent scholars of contemporary history to communicate an understanding of the past useful to the formulation of German identity in the present. The historical details they presented might be correct and important, but if the historians lacked the timeless criteria for a judgment upon the concrete historical details, their research would be worthless for the crucial questions of their time. Microscopic analysis of historical details could serve as a pretext for avoiding the kind of discussion of historical problems that would be most valuable—and painful—for the self-interpretation of contemporary German society. For Voegelin, it was a necessary correlative of the demystification of Hitler to recall and make accessible again the theoretical vocabulary whose loss had not only enabled Hitler's rise to power but also prevented any effective confrontation of the Nazi past in the present.

This also explains Voegelin's indignation with the helpless banality of Percy E. Schramm's characterization of Hitler in his edition of Hitler's *Table Talks.* If Schramm, of all persons, became the focus of Voegelin's mordant critique of German society, it was not because he suspected him of a secret affinity for National Socialism or of a deliberate playing down of Hitler.[35] Rather, he singles out Schramm, the eminent academic historian, chancellor of the illustrious Order *Pour le Mérite,* as an example of how the German intellectual élite lacked the elementary concepts for an adequate judgment of Hitler. It would have been neither controversial nor worthwhile to accuse an inveterate Nazi of loss of reality, of moral degeneration, or of dehumanization. But the fact that Voegelin criticized the "better" Germans, such as Schramm, and even those famous for their firm stand against National Socialism such as Cardinal Faulhaber, Bishop Neuhäusler, Pastor Niemöller, Rudolf Bultmann, and others, showed the radicality of his thesis of

35. Voegelin defends Schramm against this very accusation (see below, 110, 148). As a matter of fact, Schramm had been among some two dozen German historians who after the war had been dismissed from their university posts for being too close to the Nazi system before 1945. After his release from American captivity in the fall of 1946, Schramm was banned from teaching until 1948. During this time, he was on several occasions attacked by colleagues for his refusal to admit that German historians should reexamine their role in the Third Reich. See Wilfried Schulze, *Deutsche Geschichtswissenschaft nach 1945* (Munich: Oldenbourg, 1989), 126 f., 160, 208.

Germany's deep intellectual and moral decline before, during, and still after the Nazi period.

With this radical critique Voegelin exposed himself to the accusation of deep antipathy toward the Germans. And in fact, the lectures show traces of a personal requital with the milieu he held responsible for the rise of National Socialism and for his own forced emigration. Also, the distance from Germany he had gained during his two decades in the United States can clearly be felt. But however harsh and sweeping his judgment about Germany's spiritual decline, he never accused the Germans of a collective guilt for the atrocities committed, even if he—in accord with Jaspers—proclaimed the collective responsibility of a people for its past.[36] Equally, it did not occur to him to construct a historical determinism leading from a specific German mentality to the Holocaust. Again and again he emphasized the individual's freedom of action in the decision to act morally or immorally. Individuals serve Voegelin as examples of failure and guilt, and he portrays Thomas Mann, Karl Kraus, Heimito von Doderer, as representatives of an intact spirit and morality. And when he referred to rather young martyrs to National Socialism, like Alfred Delp or Dietrich Bonhoeffer, to exemplify that it takes only a few extraordinary individuals to ward off phenomena of moral and spiritual decline in a given society, this was certainly also meant as a challenge to his young students.[37] Nowhere else does it become more obvious that for Voegelin, "mastering the past" was above all a problem of the present and of the spiritual level of the Germans, and for this purpose he aimed at redeploying the classic philosophic vocabulary to the judgment of historically concrete political orders and disorders.

Regarding the effect of his lectures on his students, Voegelin in retrospect was not dissatisfied, although he remained quite skeptical of the spiritual quality of the German university after the bloodletting of twelve dark years.[38] However, he did not care to give his lectures a wider audience than that of the University of Munich and his students. His assistants prepared a typescript of the lectures for the Munich publishers Piper Verlag, and in October 1964, Voegelin in fact signed the contract for a book under the

36. See below, 76.
37. See below, 197.
38. See Voegelin, *Autobiographical Reflections*, 88, 91 f.

title "Hitler and the Germans."[39] But in spite of several pressing reminders from the publisher, who had already announced the manuscript's publication, Voegelin never completed it for publication. Several reasons for this must be taken into consideration. First there was the pressure of time. In the following winter semester, Voegelin taught at Harvard and Notre Dame Universities and he continued to work on volume 4 of his *Order and History.* It is also conceivable that the contract for a book on Hitler and the Germans only served as an inducement for Piper Verlag to publish his *Anamnesis* too, for which Voegelin could simultaneously sign a contract.[40] While for Piper the sensational book about this highly current and controversial topic was the more interesting project and also promised better sales, Voegelin valued *Anamnesis* far more highly[41] and later remarked that he thought he had sufficiently dealt with the topic of Hitler and Germans in his lectures and did not give their publication any greater priority.[42] Finally, Voegelin knew that if "Hitler and the Germans" were published, he would expose himself and his Institute of Political Science to fierce reactions—of which the audience reactions were only a foretaste—and would be publicly drawn into the discussion of "this most disagreeable of topics," as he called it,[43] which increasingly polarized and impassioned the German society. It probably would have involved him more than he wished in the atmosphere, as he saw it, of spiritual decline in Germany, from which he had gained an inner distance, and he would have been distracted from what he considered more important academic projects.[44]

The importance of Voegelin's lectures lies not only in their marking a clear break with the approaches toward "mastering the past" at that time but also in their raising questions that still characterize Germans' attempts at situating the Nazi period within their collective identity. A few points must suffice to underline this.

39. Voegelin to Walter Hinderer (Piper Verlag), August 25, 1964, Voegelin Papers, box 29, file 30.

40. Ibid.

41. Voegelin to Walter Hinderer (Piper Verlag), May 4, 1965, ibid.

42. In Eric Voegelin, "The German University and the Order of German Society: A Reconsideration of the Nazi Era," in *Published Essays, 1966–1985,* ed. Ellis Sandoz, vol. 12 of *The Collected Works of Eric Voegelin* (1990; available Columbia: University of Missouri Press, 1999), 1.

43. Ibid.

44. Henningsen, "Eric Voegelin und die Deutschen," 729.

Three years after Voegelin's lectures, Alexander and Margarete Mitscherlich published their book *The Inability to Mourn*,[45] which was hailed as "a first major reversal in the history of the recovery of memory in post-Nazi Germany,"[46] achieving from the psychoanalytical point of view what Voegelin had done from a philosophical standpoint:

> They identified the psychological mechanisms of memory suppression: Germans had refused to recognize what caused the "catastrophe" and what their own psychological involvement and their personal contributions had been; they created walls of self-protection against the experiences of the past.[47]

And the "unrealization" (*Derealisierung*) and "orientation toward the unreal,"[48] which the Mitscherlichs noted in the Germans, are different ways of expressing what Voegelin had categorized with the concept of "second reality."[49] "Unrealization" and, as a consequence, the inability to feel compassion are not overcome by dealing with the atrocities in terms of abstract numbers of victims, organizational structures, or demonization of perpetrators. Voegelin's critical remarks about the ability of contemporary historians to convey the results of their research to a wider public—and therefore their limited usefulness for "mastering of the present"—seem fully justified. It is revealing that wider public discussions about Nazi terror were triggered by the portrayal of individual fates, starting with the publication of *The Diary of Anne Frank* in 1957. When reinforced by the powerful visual and audio effects of productions like the Holocaust television series in 1978 and Steven Spielberg's *Schindler's List* in 1994, such characterizations gained mass appeal and through the depiction of the victims' suffering made evident the magnitude of the guilt. Voegelin's method of reading extensively from Karl Kraus's descriptions of life in the concentration camps certainly was an early attempt at achieving the same effect.

45. Alexander and Margarete Mitscherlich, *Die Unfähigkeit zu trauern: Grundlagen kollektiven Verhaltens* (Munich: Piper Verlag, 1967). Translated by Beverly R. Placzek as *The Inability to Mourn* (New York: Grove Press 1975).

46. Manfred Henningsen, "The Politics of Memory: Holocaust and Legitimacy in Post-Nazi Germany," *Holocaust and Genocide Studies* 4, no. 1 (1989): 15–26, at 22.

47. Ibid.

48. Mitscherlich, *Die Unfähigkeit zu trauern,* 43, 16.

49. See below, 239 ff.

In some way, even the extraordinary public success of Daniel J. Goldhagen's *Hitler's Willing Executioners* points to the same deficit. No other people involved in war crimes has put as much academic effort into the analysis of its own shadowed past as the Germans since the 1960s. But then a book that ignored or disparaged this research and accordingly received devastating criticism by the overwhelming majority of experts on both sides of the Atlantic became the biggest best-seller among historical books in recent years and stirred up a heated public discussion among an educated public in Germany. This can be explained only in part by its successful marketing or its simple and easily accessible main thesis. At least to some extent, its success can also be attributed to the moral distantiation from the past that it allowed the Germans of 1996.[50] Chastened—as they were in Goldhagen's view—by democratic conversion, they could take a shuddering but, in the end, uninvolved glimpse at the atrocities of those strange Germans of the Nazi empire and their obsession with "eliminative" and then "exterminative" anti-Semitism.[51] Goldhagen allows his willing audience to see themselves standing on the "better side" of history.

Both Goldhagen in his book and Voegelin in these lectures choose an approach to the Nazi past that deals with the mentality and psychological state of individual Germans and their collective acts. This generally seems effective for the further exploration of the collective German memory after historians have shed light on almost everything about Nazi Germany that can be grasped with historical methods. But whereas the limitedness of Goldhagen's interpretative categories and monocausal diagnosis allows contemporary Germans to remain inwardly untouched by, or at least uninvolved with, the Nazi past, Voegelin's application of classic concepts of humanity and dehumanization to the problem leaves the adequate reaction to the experience of the Holocaust as a continuously open task. In this context it seems symptomatic that the ongoing discussion about a gigantic Holocaust memorial planned for the center of Berlin within sight of the German parliament, despite ten years'

50. Johannes Heil and Rainer Erb, eds., *Geschichtswissenschaft und Öffentlichkeit: Der Streit um Daniel J. Goldhagen* (Frankfurt: Fischer, 1998), 171.

51. Daniel J. Goldhagen, *Hitler's Willing Executioners: Ordinary Germans and the Holocaust* (New York: Knopf, 1996), 69–79.

argument, has produced no decision. Voegelin's principal point is underlined: The remembrance of the past cannot once and for all be cast into one mold; there is no final "mastering of the past." Situating the National Socialist past and the Holocaust within the German identity remains an ever painful process in the present that every generation has to relive.

DETLEV CLEMENS

II. The Philosophical Context of the "Hitler and the Germans" Lectures

Voegelin's "Hitler and the Germans" lectures are his longest sustained attempt at understanding the Nazi epoch and its aftermath in philosophical terms. He had the greatest respect for the historical sciences. Still, historiographic development has not necessarily been accompanied by a deeper penetration of the questions that this phase in recent Western history poses to humanity. Unlike any other topic in modern history, interpretations of the Nazi regime and of the role of the Germans in that regime have the capacity to stir profound emotions and lead to apparently irresolvable counterpositions. Voegelin attempted in these lectures to face some of the questions arising from the history of the period that could not be answered within the context of normal historiographic conventions. This part of the introduction will explore the philosophical framework underlying the lectures: their context within Voegelin's attempt to develop a philosophy of history; a key element in his political philosophy, the anthropological principle; how he applies the anthropological principle to the historical data; and his attempt to restore the order of existence through a program of radical conversion.

§1. Universal Humanity versus a Closed, Racial Society

> The vast majority of all human beings alive on earth is affected in some measure by the totalitarian mass movements of our time. . . . What no religious founder, no philosopher, no imperial conqueror of the past has achieved—to create a community of mankind by creating a common concern for all men—has now been realized through the

community of suffering under the earthwide expansion of Western foulness.[52]

While Voegelin was giving his lectures to political science students in the summer of 1964, he was also working on *The Ecumenic Age,* which eventually became the fourth volume of *Order and History.* During that period in the early 1960s he was wrestling with the problem of historiography, with essays like "World Empire and the Unity of Mankind," "What Is History?" and "Eternal Being in Time" bearing the marks of that intellectual struggle.[53] What he referred to as the "break"[54] in his program for *Order and History* was the insight that once the dynamic in-between structure of human consciousness in its search for the divine ground had been articulated, he had formulated the underlying hermeneutic principle of each society's equivalent quest throughout history.

In those essays, Voegelin had already developed an understanding of the triad of spiritual outburst, ecumenic empire, and historiography. As he pointed out, there was, not a necessary connection, but an empirical connection between the occurrence of an ecumenic empire and historiography. If, as a matter of fact, in Israel, Hellas, and China a spiritual outburst had preceded the empire, there occurred an attempt at intellectually integrating the shock waves posed to its many victims by the world empire. And such an attempt at integration assumed the form of historiography. In all of these essays, Voegelin speaks of the modern equivalents of the ecumenic empire, which elsewhere he spoke of as ideological empires.[55] He does not go out of his way to draw upon his personal fate under the National Socialist regime as a source of his own historiographic work, yet his overwhelming experience was of belonging to the

52. Eric Voegelin, "The Origins of Totalitarianism," *Review of Politics* 15 (1953): 68–85, at 68.

53. Eric Voegelin, "World Empire and the Unity of Mankind," *International Affairs* 38, no. 2 (1962): 170–88; "What is History?" [1963] in *What Is History? and Other Late Unpublished Writings,* ed. Thomas Hollweck and Paul Caringella, vol. 28 of *The Collected Works of Eric Voegelin* (1990; available Columbia: University of Missouri Press, 1999), 1–51; "Eternal Being in Time" [1963], in *Anamnesis,* trans. and ed. Gerhart Niemeyer (Columbia: University of Missouri Press, 1990), 116–40.

54. See Eric Voegelin, *The Ecumenic Age,* vol. 4 of *Order and History* (1974; available Columbia: University of Missouri Press, 1999), 1–6.

55. Eric Voegelin, *Conversations with Eric Voegelin,* ed. R. Eric O'Connor (Montreal: Thomas More Institute, 1980), 117–18.

worldwide "community of suffering" resulting directly from that ideological empire.

In his lectures, Voegelin does not lead the audience directly into his still-inchoate reflections on ecumenic empires, nor into his response to them—namely, a philosophy of humanity in history—but there are echoes, where he discusses Aquinas' "universal conception of the *corpus mysticum*" and, later, the "universal formulations of humanity."[56] Nor does he directly discuss racism, which he had already investigated in two books in 1933 and in an extended article.[57] Yet it is precisely in relation to what in the final chapter of *The Ecumenic Age* he would speak of as "universal humanity"[58] that his earlier diagnoses of racism would now need to be situated. Because it could be suggested that Voegelin's intellectual response to the evil of the Holocaust could be formulated in terms of the lethal failure of a people, through their political representatives, to fully actualize their participation in universal humanity by denying that participation to any other group of their fellow humans on the basis of race.

Nazism never arrived at the claim to universality that, for example, Marxism did; yet however blatant the contradiction of a particular nationality somehow lording it over the rest of humanity, it too assumed the trappings of a claim to world order. So a remark of Voegelin's in 1961 could in part be applied to the Nazi empire. Diagnosing the foredoomed pathos of the world empires, he noted that "an affinity of meaning subtly connects a creation of empire which claims to represent mankind with a spiritual efflorescence which claims representative humanity."[59] And the "Luciferic" attractiveness[60] he discerned in Nazism was the attractiveness of an ideological order in which a purified German people could experience themselves as an intramundane perfect society, successfully closed both nationally and racially against the

56. See below, 203, 209.

57. Eric Voegelin, *Race and State,* ed. Klaus Vondung, trans. Ruth Hein, vol. 2 of *The Collected Works of Eric Voegelin* (1997; available Columbia: University of Missouri Press, 1999), and *The History of the Race Idea: From Ray to Carus,* ed. Klaus Vondung, trans. Ruth Hein, vol. 3 of *The Collected Works of Eric Voegelin* (1998; available Columbia: University of Missouri Press, 1999); "The Growth of the Race Idea," *Review of Politics* 2 (1940): 283–317.

58. Voegelin, *The Ecumenic Age,* 300–335.

59. Voegelin, "World Empire," 171.

60. Eric Voegelin, *Die politischen Religionen* (Stockholm: Hermann-Fischer, 1939), 9.

anxiety-inducing reign of evil posed by a tiny minority of Jews.[61] Speaking of Turgot, Voegelin, in words that can easily be applied to those who supported Hitler, notes that

> the intramundane tribalism of mankind implied in the *mass totale* holds a powerful appeal to spiritually and intellectually immature men who can reap the emotional benefits of being members of the tribe in good standing without submitting to the unpleasant discipline of spirit and intellect.[62]

In the same 1961 address on world empire, Voegelin linked Polybius' questioning of the senselessness of a merely world-immanent Roman empire and Matthew's requirement (in Mt. 24:14) that the ecumene be filled with the Gospel in order to gain its fulfillment:

> Between them they have gained the insight that the end of all human action does not lie within this world but beyond it; this insight, which had been secured for personal existence by Plato in his Judgment of the Dead, has now expanded to include the *telos* of society in history.[63]

He contrasted the spiritual realism of Plato, Polybius, and Paul with the immanent apocalypse of the various imperial constructions. In that ghastly farce of an inner-worldly apocalypse without a trans-worldly eschaton, "mankind has become a synonym for the inmates of an apocalyptic concentration camp."[64]

It is for this reason that Voegelin so profoundly criticizes the attempt at mastering the past, or at mastering history in any way. For such notions of mastery come from a similar world-immanent notion of the meaning of history as a thing to be dominated rather than as a mystery to be lived in full consciousness of its tragic capacity for fall and of the fact that its fulfillment is beyond time. Thus, in the lectures he counterposes the "presence under God" to any attempt at "mastering" history. This is his invitation to German historians to situate what he later calls "History I"—the history internal to a society's existence—within "History II"—the history in which a society comes into and goes out of existence.[65] History II recognizes the reality of that process of moving presence, in individuals and

61. For Fichte's specifically German version of the closed nation-state into which ideas of race will later flow, see Voegelin, *Race and State,* 142–53.

62. Voegelin, "World Empire," 183.

63. Ibid., 184.

64. Ibid., 186. See also Klaus Vondung, *Die Apokalypse in Deutschland* (Munich: Deutscher Taschenbuch Verlag, 1988), 207–25, 279–82, 486–88.

65. Voegelin, *The Ecumenic Age,* 173.

in societies, that is both in time and oriented beyond time. The German experiences of order and disorder during the Hitler period arrive at such an extreme that History I, or conventional world-immanent historiography, simply breaks down when it attempts to exclude the evident transfinite dimension of History II.

§2. The Anthropological Principle versus Radical Stupidity in Individuals and in Society

At the start of the first lecture, Voegelin refers to the political dimension, what he calls "the central German experiential problem of our time: Hitler's rise to power. How was it possible? What consequences does it have today?"[66] The lectures were intended as a study neither of Hitler nor of National Socialism but of how it was possible for someone like Hitler to gain ascendancy in Germany—that is to say, of how it was possible that an effective majority of Germans accepted a leader of Hitler's type. This goal of the lectures is a more complicated one than understanding either Hitler or the National Socialist period as such.

The "anthropological principle" is Voegelin's term for Plato's comment that the polis is man written large.[67] It holds that the quality of a society is determined by the moral character of its members. Plato deploys the principle as a diagnostic instrument for articulating the sequence of decline in a society, from older through middle to younger generation, in the *Gorgias* (from Gorgias to Polus to Callices) and the *Republic* (from Cephalus to Polemarchus to Thrasymachus). It is particularly in Voegelin's diagnosis of the middle generation, represented by Polus, that I would suggest the ideational thrust of the lectures can be found:

> He is the type of man who will piously praise the rule of law and condemn the tyrant—and who fervently envies the tyrant and would love nothing better than to be one himself. In a decadent society he is the representative of the great reservoir of common men who paralyze every effort at order and supply mass-connivance in the rise of the tyrant.[68]

66. See below, 52.

67. See Eric Voegelin, *The New Science of Politics: An Introduction* (Chicago: University of Chicago Press, 1952), 61–63.

68. Eric Voegelin, *Plato and Aristotle,* vol. 3 of *Order and History* (1957; available Columbia: University of Missouri Press, 1999), 26–27.

The specific form of spiritual decline Voegelin focuses on here is what he calls stupidity, understood as the radical refusal to actualize one's participation in the transcendent. The Hesiodian-Aristotelian principle to which he appeals to explain this indicates the appalling effect when the mass of men become immune to wise leadership, let alone are capable of themselves being wise.[69] And the "Buttermelcher Syndrome" to which he often refers is the twentieth-century version of Polus's hapless "Surely you must think as I do."[70] Polus simply cannot understand that anyone could rise above the social normality of his own spiritual contractedness, backed up as it is by that legion of decent citizens whose obedience to the secondary virtues[71] substitutes for serious moral effort at the level of the primary virtues of prudence, justice, and moral courage.

Thus we may understand why Voegelin seems hardest here on reasonably decent, if not even somewhat heroic, figures. The lack of intellectual and moral penetration demonstrated by Schramm's work is paradigmatic of a society stalled at Polus' level of mediocrity. The issue then is Hermann Broch's "guilt of the guiltless," the mystery of complicity in evil by those who seem not to be evil.[72]

But what is the experience in terms of which he will criticize this complicity among the mass of citizens to whom he applies the term used both by Kraus and Mann, "rabble"? It is exactly what is insufficiently actualized, their most human capacity, the quest for the truth of the right order of existence and for living justly in accord with that truth. In the lectures Voegelin takes up this failure to achieve one's humanity and, in terms of radical stupidity, develops it as a key diagnostic tool.[73] In fact, that diagnosis is the central explanation he offers for Hitler's accession to and remaining in power. It is interesting to see how closely Hannah Arendt's notion of "thoughtlessness" in *The Life of the Mind* corresponds to Voegelin's

69. See below, 88–89, 96.

70. See Plato, *Gorgias,* 471e, and Voegelin's commentary, *Plato and Aristotle,* 27.

71. See below, 000, on Amery's category of "propriety" and on the secondary virtues.

72. See Ernestine Schlant, *Hermann Broch* (Chicago: University of Chicago Press, 1986), 125–41. She notes of Broch's novel, *The Guiltless,* that "all the characters are guilty of the advent of Nazism because their indifference allowed Hitler's takeover to occur" (126).

73. See below, 88–91, and particularly his use of Musil's notion of the "higher stupidity," 98–102.

diagnosis of the collapse of spirit underlying National Socialism as an ideology:

> There was no sign in him [Eichmann] of firm ideological convictions or of specific evil motives, and the only notable characteristic one could detect in his past behavior as well as in his behavior during the trial . . . was something entirely negative: it was not stupidity but *thoughtlessness.*[74]

One must ask: Whence this systematic regression from the rationality of common sense? Voegelin's answer is that the fundamental stupidity is to put one's own will, libido, at the center of the universe, and that such dedivinization leads all too quickly to a dehumanization. This is the wilful resistance to creatureliness expressed in the quotation from Novalis: "The world shall be as I wish it!" And Voegelin comments: "There you already have in a nutshell the whole problem of Hitler, the central problem of the dedivinizing and dehumanizing."[75] The consequence of self-divinization's replacing the ejected divinity is dehumanization, in the sense that all other humans are reduced to material for my self-aggrandizement.[76]

It is left to the "German University" lecture to develop the experience contrary to this, in the light of which Voegelin is making his critique, that is, the shared actualization of the individual's quest for truth and its just realization in a genuine politics. In that address, he deploys Heraclitus' notion of the *xynon* as the key analytic tool:

> Through spirit man actualizes his potential to partake of the divine. He rises thereby to the *imago Dei* which it is his destiny to be. Spirit in this classical sense of nous, is that which all men have in common, the *xynon* as Heraclitus has called it. Through the life of the spirit, which is common to all, the existence of man becomes existence in community. In the openness of the common spirit there develops the public life of society. He, however, who closes himself against what is common, or who revolts against it, removes himself from the public life of human community. He becomes thereby a private man, or in the language of Heraclitus, an *idiotes.*[77]

74. Hannah Arendt, *The Life of the Mind* (New York: Harcourt, Brace, Jovanovich, 1978), 4–6.
75. See below, 88.
76. See below, 87, 96.
77. Voegelin, "The German University and the Order of Society," 7.

And it is precisely the socio-political implication of this failure to share an ethical life with others that Broch discussed in the characters of his stories in *The Guiltless*:

> None of them is directly "guilty" of the Hitler catastrophe. . . . Nevertheless it is precisely from such a state of mind and soul that Nazism derived its energies. For political indifference is ethical indifference, hence closely related to ethical perversity. . . . This guilty guiltlessness reaches upward into magical and metaphysical spheres and downward to the darkest realm of instinct.[78]

Directly deriving from the anthropological principle is what in *The New Science of Politics* Voegelin called the problem of representation—how in fact a people arrives at the kind of representation it has, and of what type. So, the title of the lectures, "Hitler and the Germans," also functions as conveying a theoretical insight into the structure of the National Socialist society. Once the type of person Heraclitus classed as an *idiotes* had reached a critical mass both among the voting public and in the controlling élites, a Hitler figure could be seen as representative of their shared radical stupidity; nor would his coming into and remaining in power have been possible were he not perceived as in harmony with their own closure to the transcendent.

§3. *Diagnosing Radical Stupidity: Application of Anthropological Principle to Historians, Churches, and the Law*

In the foreword to his 1966 *Anamnesis,* Voegelin gave a succinct account of his methodological approach:

> A philosophy of politics is empirical—in the pregnant sense of an inquiry into the experiences which penetrate the whole area of reality that we express by the symbol "man" with their order. The work of this philosophy requires . . . the constant interchange between studies on concrete cases of order and analyses of consciousness which make the human order in society and history intelligible.[79]

78. Herman Broch, *The Guiltless,* trans. Ralph Manheim (London: Quartet Books, 1990), 289.

79. Eric Voegelin, "Consciousness and Order: 'Foreword' to *Anamnesis* (1966)" [his own translation of the *Vorwort* to *Anamnesis: Zur Theorie der Geschichte und Politik* (Munich: Piper Verlag, 1966), 7–13], in *Logos: Philosophical Issues in Christian Perspective* 4 (1983): 18–19.

It is precisely this recall of those classic principles in the context of the Nazi materials that characterizes these lectures. Voegelin's citation from Doderer's *The Demons* explains well the need for the method he adopted there:

> The abandoned, highly concrete task of his own life . . . has of course to be consigned to oblivion, and along with it the capacity for remembering in general.[80]

So the method of the lectures is anamnetic in the sense of undertaking the task of overcoming an oblivion of "the origins, the beginnings, and the grounds of order in the present existence of man."[81] In the lectures, that anamnetic effort takes various forms: the recall of philosophical or revelational insights, the confrontation of essential forgetfulness (witting or unwitting), and the lifting up of the mass of newly ascertained historical materials to theoretical relevance. And that very interaction between principles and the data of disorder also and correlatively deepens the anamnetic meditation itself. Responding to recent publications on National Socialist Germany, Voegelin discussed Schramm's "Anatomy of a Dictator," along with studies of the churches and the legal profession.[82] His inquiry uncovered (i) a historiography that was substantially unhistoric; (ii) a German Evangelical Church that misinterpreted the Gospel; (iii) a German Catholic Church that denied universal humanity; (iv) a legal process enmeshed in criminal homicide; and (v) in that very inquiry itself, the concrete possibility of recovering the experiences of order whose forgetfulness is the disorder itself.

(i) We have already mentioned Voegelin's working on historiography while he was engaged in preparing these lectures. But that historiography was rooted in the anthropology of Plato and Aristotle, in the light of which Voegelin had a criterion for assessing the radical nonessentiality of a world-immanent approach toward history by which it could be "mastered." Less than six months later, in his "Immortality: Experience and Symbol" lecture at Harvard, he noted that "man while existing in time, experiences himself as

80. See below, 256.

81. Voegelin, "Consciousness and Order," 22.

82. Later standard studies available in English are John S. Conway, *The Nazi Persecution of the Churches* (London: Weidenfeld and Nicolson, 1968); Klaus Scholder, *The Churches and the Third Reich,* vols. 1 and 2, trans. John Bowden (London: SCM Press, 1988); Ingo Müller, *Hitler's Justice: The Courts of the Third Reich,* trans. Deborah Lucas Schneider (Cambridge: Harvard University Press, 1991).

participating in the timeless." In a gloss on T. S. Eliot's formulation in *Four Quartets,* that "history is a pattern of timeless moments," and "the point of intersection of the timeless with time," he remarked:

> I shall use the term *presence* to denote the point of intersection in man's existence, and the term *flow of presence* to denote the dimension of existence that is, and is not, time.[83]

What the world-immanentist history Voegelin is criticizing seems closed off from is an awareness of the spiritual failure, on the part of the German élites during the Nazi period, to actualize their essential human capacity of participating in the timeless. That missing dimension in academic historians—a dimension fully aware of the tragic drama being enacted in Germany and Austria—Voegelin finds in the German-language literature he cites throughout "Hitler and the Germans." For example, in the lectures, like a delayed-exposure night photograph of the stream of light from traffic weaving through a darkened city, Voegelin lets quotations from Karl Kraus's *Third Witches' Sabbath* shine through the Nazi night of the spirit. Kraus's title connects the Third Reich with the first witches' sabbath of the late medieval legends and the original *Faustbuch* and Goethe's reworking of the material in his *Faust.* Neither Kraus nor Voegelin develop the symbolism of the witches' sabbath, but the relationship between National Socialism and witchcraft returns in chapter seven.[84] In that chapter Voegelin also mentions Doderer's diagnosis, in his *Demons,* of characters in 1920s German-speaking culture that Doderer considered equivalent to Dostoevsky's ideological *Devils.* It is the forgetfulness of human participation in the timeless (something not forgotten in the writers' symbolizations), with its implication of self-condemnation for the stupidity of radical spiritual dullness, that Voegelin diagnoses as the fault of run-of-the-mill historiography in German. As he indicates in the 1965 "German University" lecture, Thomas Mann's reprise, in *Doctor Faustus,* of Jeremiah's Lamentation "as the great lamentation of a German over

83. Eric Voegelin, "Immortality: Experience and Symbol," in *Published Essays, 1966–1985,* 80, 77.

84. Not even Kraus could have anticipated that Hitler would commit suicide on Saint Walpurga's eve, April 30, the legendary date of the witches' sabbath when they consorted with demons on the top of the highest peak in the Harz mountains, the Brocken.

Germany" is a far more adequate judgment of the truth of the Nazi period than that of academic historians.[85]

(ii) The anamnetic core of his critique of the Evangelical Church's response to National Socialism is his analysis of chapter 13 of Saint Paul's letter to the Romans. There he has little difficulty in seeing that the Evangelical claim, in its various theological opinions regarding the race question, insofar as it affected its members, was not in fact based on Scripture at all. Rather it derived from the Romantic-nationalist understanding of figures like "father of gymnastics" Friedrich Jahn, whom, he sardonically notes, was elevated almost to the status of a church father. Studies like those of Klaus Scholder's will broaden the critique and perhaps lead at times to a less harsh judgment, but the substance of Voegelin's anamnetic diagnosis would seem to remain valid: that of an Evangelical Church inherently unfaithful to Scripture.

(iii) The point that Voegelin wishes to remember about the German Catholic Church's response to Nazism is precisely its failure to be catholic in the sense of universal. He focuses on Aquinas' comprehensive understanding of the notion of mystical body as potentially including all of humanity, from the first human being to the last. He then shows that this comprehensive reading, which should have led to an awareness that all, including Jewish, human beings were in some sense part of the Church of Christ, did not do so. Whatever the accuracy of his rather modernist understanding of the Christian sacrament of baptism, the basic thrust of his critique seems valid: that, on the whole, representatives of the Catholic Church in Germany were not moved by a spirit of service to all of humankind. And given that the self-definition of the Catholic Church is its universality, his critique of its institutional exclusiveness in Nazi Germany is a devastating anamnesis of its failure to live up to what it proclaimed itself to be.

(iv) What is Voegelin essentially reminding the legal profession of? While the discussion on the law may appear somewhat abstruse at times, what is central for Voegelin can be gleaned from his discussion of the *Rechtsstaat.* His criticism of the *Rechtsstaat* is that, because it was an abstraction, a second reality, it obscured or eclipsed entirely the first reality of common sense and of ethics,

85. Voegelin, "The German University and the Order of Society," 16–18.

making it easy for jurists and citizens to obey the law, no matter what its content. This Gödelian sense of the intrinsic derivativeness of the legal order is perhaps autobiographically one of Voegelin's most profound convictions, born from his many years of struggle with Hans Kelsen's positivism, and a key point in his *The Nature of the Law.*[86] Voegelin's anamnesis with regard to law in Nazi and post-Nazi Germany yields the insight that law in itself is never the ethically defining context. Rather, experiences of order, whether philosophical or revelational, alone provide the matrix within which the law is formulated and toward which it must primarily be responsible.

(v) One can hardly expect the therapy proposed in this series of lectures to be adequate. Apart from his first book, in 1928, every one of his volumes may be seen, in one way or another, as taken up with responding to the ideological empires of the twentieth century. The comprehensive answer is to be found where his work up to 1964 had led him: in a recovery of the originating experiences of classic philosophy and Judaeo-Christian revelation and their application to the new circumstances of these times. Still, part 2 begins with an examination of Doderer's ideological *Demons,* their refusal to perceive reality, and the substitute second reality they erect. Then he refers to Musil's qualities (in the sense of Himmler's secondary virtues) without a man, and goes on to the discussions in Rabelais and Cervantes of how an educated rabble-élite can play around with unreality, a game that can become murderous. Again, it can be suggested that the issue here is anamnetic, that at the core of ideology is the refusal to accept the structure of reality, including the mystery of its participation in the timeless. For Voegelin, the answer to that refusal is to reawaken the shared quest for truth, the Heraclitean *homologein,* which alone could ground the community of the *nous,* Aristotle's *homonoia.* However implicitly, for Voegelin, Max Weber, while affected by the wider cultural closure within which a Hitler came into power, went beyond it through his anguished recovery of the experience of transcendence and was thus a paradigm of the German recovery of order.

86. *The Nature of the Law and Related Legal Writings,* ed. Robert Anthony Pascal, James Lee Babin, and John William Corrington, vol. 27 of *The Collected Works of Eric Voegelin* (1991; available Columbia: University of Missouri Press, 1999), xxi, 26, 28, 42–48, 68–69.

§4. *Overcoming Radical Stupidity in the Present: Toward a Restoration of Order*

While most of the lectures have to do with what Voegelin calls his descent into the depths[87] of the moral and spiritual abyss of Nazism and its aftermath in postwar German society, they also point toward a restoration of order. How did Voegelin think the anamnetic ascent from the depths might be achieved? What did he expect his listeners to do now?

A year after the lectures, Voegelin returned to them in his "German University" address. To convey how his approach to the recent German past differed from current historiography, he referred to Nietzsche's *On the Advantage and Disadvantage of History for Life.* Nietzsche had classified history as monumental, antiquarian, or critical. Monumental history aimed at inspiration from the past, antiquarian history at restoring it. But, for Nietzsche, "only one who in a present emergency is in imminent danger of being crushed, and who seeks relief at any cost, has the need for critical, that is, evaluative and judgmental history." For Voegelin, what Nietzsche meant by critical history is not "the investigation of the events of the past in the modern academic sense of critical research," nor is it a matter of "the banality of so-called value judgments." Rather, it has to do with "the judgment of a past epoch that arises from a new spirit. In order to pursue critical history, therefore, it is not enough to *speak* differently—one must *be* differently."[88] Voegelin had experience of academic colleagues for whom the fall of National Socialism required of them pragmatic adjustments, but no more. Thus they responded by speaking and writing differently than they had during the Nazi period while remaining inwardly unchanged. Voegelin continued:

> *Being* differently, however, is not something which is brought about by foraging in the horrors of the past; rather, on the contrary, it is the revolution of the spirit which is the precondition for being able to judge the past critically.[89]

It is this revolution of the spirit, what he will refer to as the Platonic

87. See below, 184.
88. Voegelin, "The German University and the Order of German Society," 3, emphasis added. The translation has been slightly modified in this and the following citation.
89. Ibid., 3–4, emphasis added.

periagoge, the turning round or conversion of the soul,[90] precisely in answer to the aversion from truth and justice characterizing the epoch, that these lectures were concerned with and makes them a diagnosis of the National Socialist period like no other. But by what authority can Voegelin ask others to undergo this conversion?

If Viktor Klemperer's 1933–1945 diaries are rightly entitled *I Shall Bear Witness,*[91] Voegelin's status as a teacher of political philosophy may be seen as founded on his own life of bearing witness.[92] He maintains that "the character of consciousness" is "a process of augmenting insight into its own logos"[93] and his attitude to an ideology like National Socialism was something achieved through decades of reflection on the disruption it wreaked on, among others, himself. As he wrote in "Remembrance of Things Past,"

> An analysis of consciousness . . . has no instrument other than the concrete consciousness of the analyst. The quality of this instrument, and consequently the quality of the results, will depend on . . . the horizon of consciousness; and the quality of the horizon will depend on the analyst's . . . desire to know.[94]

And for Voegelin, this desire takes the form of the concrete quest for truth or the turning away from that quest he diagnoses as radical stupidity. In 1968, Voegelin asked of himself, "How can we, as human beings, get out of the socially dominant lie of existence (*Existenzlüge*)?" He answered that we must recognize

> that the phenomenon of the lie of existence is a phenomenon in history. . . . That existence in the *agnoia,* in the *alethos pseudos,* is *not* "the nature of man," but a pneumopathological situation. . . . That the phenomenon has emerged in the history of humanity more than once and has been thoroughly investigated. . . . [That] its contemporary social-dominance is bound up with [a] deliberate ignoring of history. . . . That everyone is personally responsible for the order of his existence—historical social-dominance does not have normative

90. See below, 270.

91. Viktor Klemperer, *Ich will Zeugnis ablegen bis zum letzten: Tagebücher 1933–1941,* and *Ich will Zeugnis ablegen bis zum letzten: Tagebücher 1942–1945* (Berlin: Aufbau Verlag, 1995).

92. Ellis Sandoz, in *The Voegelinian Revolution: A Biographical Introduction* (Baton Rouge: Louisiana State University Press, 1981), 47–70, gives the best available account of Voegelin's experience of Socialism; see also Voegelin's own remarks throughout his *Autobiographical Reflections.*

93. Voegelin, "Consciousness and Order," 18.

94. Eric Voegelin, "Remembrance of Things Past," in *Anamnesis,* trans. and ed. Niemeyer, 4.

> force, and cannot be used as an excuse for dishonest existence. . . . That the lie of existence is a social power which heavily burdens each of us and threatens each with lasting spiritual deformation (Plato, *Politeia* II: perversion of reality [from truth to lie]: the motivation for the dialogue). . . . That resistance to a social power of such great order demands a corresponding measure of spiritual passion, intellectual discipline, and hard study [and] that the recognition of these demands is the first step—but no more than the first step—in order to get out of the lie of existence. Recognition of the existential-ethical demands as an intellectual achievement is not enough—it must be followed by the passionate work of daily resistance against the lie of existence—the work is lifelong.[95]

These notes he prepared for students can be seen, in a sense, as the expression of his own response, throughout his life, to the Weberian call to "politics as a vocation" and as the basis for his moral authority with the younger generation. Without both of these aspects, it would not seem to have been possible to undertake the "Hitler and the Germans" lectures. The notes also spell out with embarrassing clarity just what the implementation of the *periagoge* would mean for each individual in a less or more corrupt society. But, as he remarked much later:

> If the story is to evoke authoritatively the order of a social field, the word must be spoken with an authority recognizable as such by the men to whom the appeal is addressed; the appeal will have no authority of truth unless it speaks with an authority commonly present in everybody's consciousness, however inarticulate, deformed, or suppressed the consciousness in the concrete case may be.[96]

So the story of Nazi Germany he tells in the lectures has authority only insofar as it is an expression of his quest for truth and appeals to and evokes the audience's equivalent quest. The story in question is the constitutive self-understanding of Western culture in its application to the specific case of the Nazi period in Germany. We can juxtapose the terminology of *In Search of Order,* where he speaks of the two aspects of story as "narrative" and "event,"[97] with the earlier terminology of *The Ecumenic Age.* Then History I may be conceived as articulating the narrative-dimension, and

95. Eric Voegelin, "Geschichtsphilosophie" [course outline] (1968, University of Munich), 7, Voegelin Papers, box 86, file 8.

96. Eric Voegelin, *In Search of Order,* vol. 5 of *Order and History* (1987; available Columbia: University of Missouri Press, 1999), 26.

97. Ibid.

History II as articulating the event-dimension of that period. At the level of History I, arguments and differences can be resolved by the normal methods of history. But it is at the level of History II, where individuals and a whole people were required—and often failed—to live at the level of tragic destiny,[98] that Voegelin's story may have for us the ring of truth.

Whence came Voegelin's own quest for truth, unfolding into a lifelong critique of ideological imperialism and his counterarticulation of universal humanity? It is not accidental, perhaps, that his intellectual struggle throughout the 1930s with National Socialism can be linked with a parallel concern for meditation in the Augustinian sense. That meditative exercise, evidenced for example in his unpublished "Herrschaftslehre" and in "Volksbildung, Wissenschaft und Politik," is what enables his diagnosis of National Socialism to be located primarily at the level of History II,[99] as an event he will categorize as "satanic," with the precise meaning of willed rejection of the structure of reality.[100] The diagnosis is given its clearest expression in the foreword to the second edition of his *Political Religions,* already banned in Nazi-occupied Vienna. The foreword was principally occasioned by a letter from Thomas Mann, who, while praising the book as a "very stimulating, instructive and informative work," remarked:

> What appears to me its disadvantage is that its objectivity sometimes attains such an uncritical, positively interested accent and starts having the effect of a defense of the scandalous pragmatism that is prevailing everywhere. One waits for the moral resistance and for some

98. In his discussion of Greek tragedy, Voegelin notes, "There may arise a tragic situation without a tragic actor," which is why he is inclined to regard farce rather than tragedy as the adequate mode for symbolizing the Nazi events. See Eric Voegelin, *The World of the Polis,* vol. 2 of *Order and History* (1957; available Columbia: University of Missouri Press, 1999), 251, and 100, 256, below.

99. Eric Voegelin, "Herrschaftslehre" [ca. 1930], in Voegelin Papers, box 53, file 5; "Volksbildung, Wissenschaft und Politik," *Monatsschrift für Kultur und Politik* 1, no. 7 (July 1936): 594–603. For further background on Voegelin's interest in "philosophical meditation," see Voegelin, *What Is History?* xxvii n. 19.

100. Phrases here such as "satanic" should, I would suggest, be understood strictly in the sense of the Frankfurt Theologian's *German Theology* of the late 1400s, quoted in Voegelin, *Die politischen Religionen,* 64–65: "If the creature apportions some good to itself, such as existence, life, intellect, knowledge, ability, briefly, all that must be called good, as if it were or had it, as if it owned or derived from it, then it is alienated from itself. Isn't this what the Devil did? Isn't this what his fall and alienation consisted of, that he arrogated to himself that he would be something; that he wanted to be a Who and have an Own? This presumption, and his 'I' and 'Me,' his 'My' and 'Mine,' was his alienation and his fall."

> reinforcement of the ethical Fronde, which indeed, as it seems to me, is beginning to develop throughout the world against the "Revolution of Nihilism."[101]

Voegelin takes up Mann's objections:

> . . . I do not wish to say that the struggle against National Socialism should not also be waged at an ethical level; only it will not—in my opinion—be carried out in a radical way, because the radix, the root in religiousness, is missing.
>
> A religious consideration of National Socialism must be allowed to proceed from the assumption that there is evil in the world. . . . Resistance to a not merely ethically bad but religiously evil satanic substance can be performed only by a similarly powerful, religiously good force. One cannot combat a satanic force with ethics and humanity alone.
>
> . . . It is awful to hear, again and again, that National Socialism is a relapse into barbarism . . . to the times before the modern progress toward humanity, where the speaker does not suspect that the secularizing of life, which the humanity-idea brought with it, is the very ground from which the anti-Christian movements such as National Socialism were able to grow.[102]

Voegelin's reflections on the background to National Socialism (what he could later categorize as an event in History II) are given a wider cultural framework in his 1944 essay "Nietzsche, the Crisis, and the War." Central to this defense of Nietzsche from the accusation of being somehow to blame for the advent of National Socialism is that Nietzsche was in fact diagnosing the core malady, not just of German, but of European culture: its aggressive despiritualized nihilism. For Voegelin, Nietzsche's greatness was to have achieved a position not unlike that of Plato's, where he saw that the only way beyond Europe's cultural suicide was through a conversion, if not the Christian *metanoia,* at least approximating to the Platonic *periagoge.*[103]

Just how the anamnetic diagnosis of the lectures, in terms of the anthropological principle, could be applied to later historiographical disputes may be gleaned from an earlier writing. Two points can be made: the first, regarding opposed methodologies; the second, regarding the Holocaust.

101. Thomas Mann, letter to Eric Voegelin, December 18, 1938, in Voegelin Papers, box 24, file 11.

102. Voegelin, *Die politischen Religionen,* 8–9.

103. Eric Voegelin, "Nietzsche, the Crisis, and the War," *Journal of Politics* 6 (1944): 177–212, esp. 185–86.

(i) Voegelin's article on Hannah Arendt's *Origin of Totalitarianism* suggests how the opposition between the intentionalist and the structuralist interpretations of the Nazi period might be resolved in terms of a philosophical anthropology.[104] Within that historiographic dispute, the intentionalist or biographic approach focused on Nazi history as primarily the work of Hitler, the powerful, evil dictator. The structuralist interpretations concentrated on social, political, and economic factors, with a weak or relatively unimportant Hitler more driven by the course of events than in control of them. Unwittingly anticipating the unresolved tension between both later historiographic disputes, Voegelin wrote in his review of *The Origins of Totalitarianism:*

> The treatment of movements of the totalitarian type on the level of social situations and change, as well as the type of conduct determined by them, is apt to endow historical causality with an aura of fatality. Situations and changes, to be sure, require, but they do not determine a response. The character of a man, the range and intensity of his passions, the controls exerted by his virtues, and his spiritual freedom, enter as further determinants.[105]

The whole thrust of the lectures takes seriously both issues, that of personal character in its various aspects of maturity, mediocrity, and corruption, and that of the historical construction and sedimentation of social structures, with their enabling or inhibiting effect on personal character. However, for Voegelin, the balance can never be conceded: The society should always be an expression of the morally mature persons within it. If, instead, the reverse holds, and "man is society written small,"[106] that should always be seen as an expression of moral and spiritual decline. The moral personality of the individual is not determined, however deeply influenced, corroded by, and fearful of, the social structures surrounding him or her. So, what have been called the intentional and structural—in other words, the personal and the socio-political—components are both essential, but personal achievement or failure to achieve moral and spiritual character would for Voegelin be the explanatory ground of the goodness or evil of socio-political structures.

104. Cf. Ian Kershaw, *The Nazi Dictatorship: Problems and Perspectives of Interpretation* (London: Edward Arnold, 1993), 1–16, 197–217; *Hitler, 1888–1936: Hybris* (London: Allen Lane, 1998), xi–xxx.
105. Voegelin, "The Origins of Totalitarianism," 72–73.
106. Eric Voegelin, "On Classical Studies," in *Published Essays, 1966–1985*, 258.

(ii) As with the inconclusiveness of the *Historikerstreit*'s methodological debate, there seems to be a similar and related unresolvability in opposed interpretations of the vilest series of evil acts committed by the Nazi regime: the Holocaust. On one side, there are attempts at mastering the past of the Holocaust such as Ernst Nolte's, suggesting, as Charles Meier notes, "that even though it was unique, the Final Solution was one terrible deed among others."[107] And this generalizing of the genocide of 6 million Jews seems to have the effect of lessening the responsibility of the perpetrators. On the other hand, Daniel Goldhagen's sweeping accusation of all Germans for "eliminative" if not "exterminative" anti-Semitism[108] runs the risk not only of a counterracism but of the historical determinism of a whole people that paradoxically would excuse from personal guilt those Nazi mass murderers who were German. However, Hannah Arendt, in a 1966 review of Bernd Naumann's *Auschwitz,* an account of the Frankfurt trials of Nazi camp functionaries, warned against indulging

> in sweeping statements about the evil nature of the human race, about original sin, about innate human "aggressiveness," etc., in general—and about the German national character in particular. . . . [But] in any event, one thing is sure, and this one had not dared to believe any more—namely, that everyone could decide for himself to be either good or evil in Auschwitz. . . . And this decision depended in no way on being a Jew or a Pole or a German; nor did it even depend on being a member of the SS.[109]

Surely Goldhagen and those opposed to Nolte's generalization thesis are right: Unspeakable deeds have been done, very large numbers of evildoers were involved, very many of these neither publicly repented nor made any kind of amendment for their deeds. Yet there seems something essential missing in the accusations, just as there is something essential missing in the strenuous attempts at mastering, if not of outright forgetting or denying, the past of the Holocaust. A descriptive sociological and historic account of the Holocaust, or of any particular aspect of it—whether from the side of a Nolte or of a Goldhagen—at best belongs to what Voegelin

107. Charles S. Meier, *The Unmasterable Past: History, Holocaust, and German National Identity* (Cambridge: Harvard University Press, 1988), 66.

108. See n. 51 above.

109. Quoted in Elisabeth Young-Bruehl, *Hannah Arendt: For the Love of the World* (New Haven: Yale University Press, 1982), 368.

called History I. But the criterion for a judgment needs to include an explicit consciousness of the nature of the human, in which perpetrators as well as victims can be dehumanized by the Holocaust or by any other genocide.[110] The "Hitler and the Germans" lectures are a powerful anamnesis of the humanity of each man and woman as *imago Dei,* as participating in "the biography of the flowing presence."[111] Only within the context of that presence can we ground a judgment regarding the absolute dignity of each victim and the awful guilt of each attempt at desecrating that image of God. Etty Hillesum (1914–1943), herself a Dutch Holocaust victim, while at Westerbork concentration camp spoke of her "love for all our neighbours, for everyone made in God's image."[112] And she reveals the source of the actualization of her participation in universal humanity to be her intense consciousness of the fact that each one is a you-for-God, when she writes, "My life has become an uninterrupted dialogue with you, my God, a great dialogue."[113] Voegelin's belonging, in its existential height and depth, to the worldwide "community of suffering" would not claim comparison with Etty Hillesum's. Yet, by his reminding us that our judgment of the Nazi period must be made within the perspective of her "great dialogue," he is inviting us too, not just to think or to speak differently, but to *be* differently.

BRENDAN PURCELL

110. Cf. Manfred Henningsen, "Die Regime des Terrors," *Merkur* 575 (1997): 105–16.

111. Voegelin, *Anamnesis,* 134.

112. Etty Hillesum, *Etty: De nagelaten geschriften van Etty Hillesum, 1941–1943,* ed. Klaas Smelik (Amsterdam: Balans, 1991), 671.

113. Ibid., 682. See also *Etty Hillesum: Letters from Westerbork,* trans. A . J. Pomerans (New York: Pantheon Books, 1986), 116.

Editors' Note

The 294-page typescript of Eric Voegelin's lectures on Hitler and the Germans, prepared from a tape recording by his assistants at the University of Munich's Institute of Political Science, is available in the Eric Voegelin Papers, Hoover Institution Archives, box 87, files 9–17, or as reel 90 in the Microfilm Collection. It encompasses what is here translated as the first through the ninth lectures. Since that typescript simply reproduces the recording of Voegelin's spoken words, all formatting had to be done by the editors. In the typescript, the division into lectures is generally indicated by the opening words "Ladies and Gentlemen." Thus, all headings (other than the title "Hitler und die Deutschen"), lecture numbering, paragraphing, footnoting, and references are by the editors. Quotations in the typescript often were not clearly indicated by quotation marks. Voegelin kept clippings in his files (Voegelin Papers, box 86, files 12–14, and box 87, files 1–8), which facilitated recognition and location of the newspaper and magazine articles referred to.

Given the *viva voce* nature of the lectures, uncorrected by Voegelin, the editors occasionally offer the closest approximation possible to the meaning of some unclearly formulated passages in the typescript. Eleven longer omissions from the typescript are indicated by ellipses in the main text. These are where Voegelin digresses from his argument, comments on matters of German usage unlikely to interest an English-speaking reader, quotes wordplays that fail to carry over in translation, or, in one case, lists a series of references prepared by his assistants. Silently omitted are some introductions (including administrative details) to lectures and some minor repetitions. A few minor factual errors and misattributions have been corrected.

Voegelin never gave the lectures he promised on Mann, or on Goethe and Novalis. The typescript does not contain the lecture on Musil, presumably because of a technical failure in tape recording. Klaus Vondung, one of Voegelin's students at the time, now professor of German and modern literature at the University of Siegen, has reassembled from his notes what is here translated as the tenth lecture. We are extremely indebted to him for giving us the gist of that last lecture in the series. While what we have translated as the eleventh lecture was given—after the sixth lecture—in commemoration of the centenary of Max Weber (a previous holder of Voegelin's chair in Munich), Voegelin considered it an integral part of the series.

We wish to thank all those who helped us in what has been a difficult task of reconstruction, particularly Theo Broersen, Paul Caringella, Eckhard Colberg, Elizabeth Crowe, Jürgen Gebhardt, Manfred Henningsen, Thomas Hollweck, Athanasios Moulakis, Máire O'Neill, Ellis Sandoz, Tilo Schabert, Julie Schorfheide, Klaus Vondung, and David Walsh. We take full credit for whatever translation or editorial errors we have made.

HITLER AND THE GERMANS

CONTENTS

Part I. Descent into the Abyss

1. Introduction 51

§1. Central Experiential Problem: Hitler's Rise to Power 51

§2. The Experiential Occasion of the Lectures: Schramm's "Anatomy of a Dictator" 53

§3. The Stupidity of a Whole People: The "Buttermelcher Syndrome" 55

§4. Present-day German Laxity toward Former Nazis 63

2. Development of Diagnostic Tools 70

§5. The Cliché of the "Unmastered Past" versus the "Presence under God" 70

§6. The Cliché of "Collective Guilt" and the Representation of a Society 75

§7. Clichés of "State" and "Democracy" 82

§8. Philosophical and Biblical Understanding of Humanity and of Radical Stupidity 85

§9. Karl Kraus's *Dritte Walpurgisnacht* on Lies and Propaganda 91

§10. Robert Musil on Simple and Intelligent Stupidity 98

§11. Carl Amery on Bourgeois "Propriety" as Secondary Virtue Eclipsing Primary Virtues 102

§12. Criminal Stupidity and Loss of Experience of Reality in a Disordered Society 105

3. Descent into the Academic Abyss as Manifested by Schramm's "Anatomy of a Dictator" 110

§13. Schramm's Conceptual and Stylistic Incomprehension of Hitler 110

§14. Hitler's "Aura" 114

§15. Hitler and Christianity 121

§16. Hitler's Views on Religion 124
§17. Hitler and Women 129
§18. Hitler and His Entourage 133
§19. Hitler and "The Art of Reading" 136
§20. Hitler's Social Darwinism 142
§21. Conclusion: Schramm's Spiritual Illiteracy Contrasted with Alan Bullock's Diagnosis of Hitler 147

4. Descent into the Ecclesiastical Abyss: The Evangelical Church 155

§22. Lack of a Theoretical Articulation of "Church" 155
§23. Intellectual and Spiritual Decline in the German Churches 157
§24. Evangelical Church's Participation in Nationalistic-*Völkisch* Ideology 162
§25. Theological Opinions Regarding Race Laws 165
§26. Anti-Semitic Tendencies in *Land* Bishop Wurm and Pastor Niemöller 171
§27. Anti-Semitic Residues in Present-day Evangelical Church 173
§28. Theoretical Inquiry into Romans 13 178

5. Descent into the Ecclesiastical Abyss: The Catholic Church 184

§29. Layout of the "Hitler and the Germans" Lectures 184
§30. Difference between Catholic and Evangelical Attitudes toward Nazism 185
§31. Dehumanized Response of Catholic Church to State Authority and to Persecution of Those outside the Church 188
§32. Karl Kraus on Concentration Camp Life 194
§33. Catholic Resistance to Dehumanization: Alfred Delp 196
§34. "Guidelines" for German Clerics and Theologians 199
§35. Tension between the Church as Social Institution and as Community of Universal Humanity under Christ 201
§36. Advances and Regressions in Differentiation of Knowledge of the Presence under God 204

§37. The Church's Representation of Universal Humanity: Its Duty and Its Failure 209

6. Descent into the Legal Abyss 213

§38. The *Rechtsstaat* as a Specifically German Concept 213
§39. Conflict between Hierarchical Legal Systems and Separation of Powers, as in the German Basic Law (*Grundgesetz*) 215
§40. Legal Positivism, Judge-made Law, and Authoritarian Rule 219
§41. Historical Background to Closed Legal Systems 223
§42. "Positive Law" and "Natural Law": Primacy of the Moral Substance of Society 225
§43. The Question of Morality in German War-Crime Trials 230

Part II. Toward a Restoration of Order

7. First and Second Reality in Ancient, Post-medieval, and Modern Times of Crisis 239

§44. Don Quixote's Second Reality as *Divertissement* 240
§45. *Divertissement*-character of Modern Logic 247
§46. Musil and Doderer on the Refusal to Apperceive Reality 252

8. The Greatness of Max Weber 257

§47. Unmasking of Passions of the Age by Marx, Nietzsche, Freud, and Weber 257
§48. Nonexperience of Transcendence Leading to Dehumanization 261
§49. Weber's Unresolved Tension toward Transcendence 264
§50. Weber as Intellectual Mystic 270

Part I
Descent into the Abyss

1

Introduction

§1. Central Experiential Problem: Hitler's Rise to Power

(First Lecture)

Ladies and Gentlemen,
In an introduction to political science, you can take the easy way. You can simply summarize well-known general principles, nicely set out as in a textbook, but this would really not be right. Because what is important for you, living in this country today, is how these general principles should be applied to the concrete political events you're familiar with. That application is what this introduction is about.

In an introduction to politics, you must also base your investigation on the political experiences and knowledge you have in daily life, in order to ascend from there to the theoretical problematic. The point of departure is topically and historically a matter of chance. There is in itself no scientific reason why we should begin with the German political experience, which is in fact yours. From the viewpoint of science we could just as well begin with the Chinese or the Indonesian experience.

So, a lecture course of this kind cannot be systematically constructed. Rather, we must start with specific political experiences, then analyze these and extrapolate from them to such an extent that we arrive at the scientific problems. That is to say, we find those categories of a rational interpretation of politics you must have a command of in order to be able to judge the political events you come across every day in your reading of the newspapers, in conversation, and so on. Consequently there will arise a continuous interplay between factual information and recourse to the experiences you all have, and these extrapolations. Only at the end of the lectures, in the final section, can I then explain systematically some theoretical problems, which will further point toward the other, more advanced lectures, to the theory of politics, to classic politics, and so on.

Where now shall our experiences begin? Last year I began with the directly interesting factual events of the so-called *Spiegel* affair.[1] That was all right, but it was still a very limited approach insofar as, at the center of the experiential facts I was able to describe there, all that was involved were problems of political legality. It seems more suitable to me now to approach a far more comprehensive experiential fact, namely, the central German experiential problem of our time: Hitler's rise to power. How was it possible? What consequences does it have today? and so on. Through this there comes into view the whole complex of political questions of a theoretical type. The immediate occasion for choosing as our experiential material the specific object—Hitler and the Germans—was again provided by certain actual events.

For in the last few years, especially in the last five years, I think, we have seen developing an extraordinarily rich literature on National Socialism, which means that today we have documentation on the problems of political legality, on the behavior of the churches, on the behavior of the writers of political history, and so on, that five years ago we did not yet have. When I say we did not have it yet, here again an experiential problematic is touched on, because, for example, I myself, since I belong to the witnesses of that time, naturally had it, but you did not. You know these things only from literary sources, from conversations, from accounts by those who lived at that time, and so on, and this experience is not a living one for you. So it will be one of the tasks of these lectures to make these experiences, now available in documentary

1. In October 1962, *Der Spiegel,* the leading German weekly news magazine, ran a cover story on Germany's defense preparedness highly critical of the policies of defense minister Franz Josef Strauss. In reaction, *Der Spiegel*'s offices in Bonn and Hamburg were raided and journalists arrested under suspicion of disclosing military secrets. This incident, seen as an attack on the liberty of the press, led to widespread protest throughout the Federal Republic and eventually to Strauss's resignation as defense minister. Voegelin's discussion is to be found in the unpublished "Einführung in die Politik" (transcript of his winter semester 1962–63 lectures, in Eric Voegelin Papers, Hoover Institution Archives, box 86, file 11), particularly pages 2–20.

form, alive. Thus, the rich development of materials is one of the reasons.

A second reason is that our coming to terms with the problematic has in general proven to be very inferior to our knowledge of the facts. And in introducing some of these matters I would now like to refer to only the last six or seven weeks, so that you can see where the problems are and where one must begin with the theoretical analyses. The immediate occasion that led us in the Institute [of Political Science] to decide definitely to hold these lectures during this summer semester was the outbreak of the Schramm affair. Percy E. Schramm[2] attempted to present a portrait of Hitler, which *Der Spiegel* published in a series of articles under the title "The Anatomy of a Dictator." This serialization has recently come out as an introduction to *Hitler's Table Talk,*[3] and its publication in *Der Spiegel* had already given rise to a fierce debate. There have been quite a number of reactions from, for example, Golo Mann; but especially interesting is the one from Albert Wucher[4] in the *Süddeutsche Zeitung,* to which again others reacted. There was this big discussion at the Congress for Cultural Freedom, in which Schramm participated and which provoked further reactions from the editor of *Der Spiegel.*

§2. The Experiential Occasion of the Lectures: Schramm's "Anatomy of a Dictator"

First, I would just like to present these materials to you, so that you can see what problems become topical, without treating these problems theoretically yet. I will later give an analysis of Schramm's work, probably in the lecture after next. For the moment we will just deal with the reactions, the concrete experiences, which you can pick up from the press, or from *Der Spiegel,* or other media, about the contemporary judgment of Hitler.

2. Percy Ernst Schramm (1894–1970) served in the First World War, was awarded his Ph.D. in Heidelberg in 1922, and was appointed professor of medieval and modern history at Göttingen in 1929, where he achieved fame in the 1930s for his medieval studies. He was assigned to the Wehrmacht's Supreme Command during the Second World War.

3. Henry Picker, *Hitlers Tischgespräche im Führerhauptquartier 1941–1942,* ed. Percy Ernst Schramm (Stuttgart: Seewald Verlag, 1963).

4. Dr. Albert Wucher (born ca. 1920), a journalist with the *Süddeutsche Zeitung,* was appointed professor of journalism at the University of Mainz in 1981. He wrote many historical books, particularly about the Nazi era.

The most interesting reaction to Schramm's work was Albert Wucher's in the *Süddeutsche Zeitung,* entitled "Hitler's Rather Delightful Reflection." Let me read out now some passages from this delightful reflection of Hitler, which will show you the directions we must take in pursuit of the problem. Wucher begins his questions like this:

> Who was Hitler? Every account of the Third Reich—there are a great number of them—which is in any way adequate, conveys a clear picture. By their deeds shall you know them—that is an axiom for the writing of history too. It is also to be found in original sources, beginning with *Mein Kampf* . . . [T]here are masses of Hitler's speeches, documents, files, etc. Not to mention the pictures, experiences of contemporaries, of party comrades and particularly of companions in the struggle. There is a legion of books on Hitler.
>
> But what does it mean? With a self-conscious gesture, the professor brushes the previous speaker aside, strides to the podium, with the pointer pulled out, in order to give, as he calls it, a "stocktaking that will maintain its value for years and years." The lecture begins: "I have deliberately refrained from dealing completely with the existing literature or further questioning surviving witnesses. . . . Even more have I resisted the attempt at daring to make a psychological interpretation." Rather, the scholar will present "useful facts," a discussion of "a documentary type."[5]

This characterization of Schramm's account is absolutely correct. So then, we see here a first problem, an oddity, and we will have to record a whole series of oddities before we can undertake an analysis. Here is a historian who enjoys the highest reputation among his colleagues, particularly as a medieval historian. He is proud of the fact that he is not cognizant of the entire literature and instead wants to produce "useful facts" and a discussion of a documentary nature. He does not explain why. Later we will come to why he does not take note of the entire literature and does not want to rely on the testimony of direct witnesses, although—as we will see—he does rely on some, but not on others. With that, a program is drawn up to exclude from the interpretation of Hitler all the levels relevant for the understanding of his personality and its impact and to characterize as "documentary facts" only those

5. Albert Wucher, "Hitlers gar liebliches *Spiegel*bild, oder: Mißglückte 'Anatomie eines Diktators,' " *Süddeutsche Zeitung,* March 7/8, 1964. There is a play on words here, since *Spiegelbild* means "reflection" but obviously refers to the portrait of Hitler in *Der Spiegel.* The Munich *Süddeutsche Zeitung* is a leading German, and the principal Bavarian, newspaper.

that can be ascertained by perception in space and time. What do "useful facts" look like?

Wucher now continues:

> Hitler had fascinating "deep blue," "radiant eyes," which he had so much "under control" that, when he wished, he knew how to make go cross-eyed. An ugly nose, but also a high forehead, well-formed ears, a girlish complexion, "no trace of baldness," strong growth of beard, well cared for teeth. "The head acted . . . as the controlling part; the trunk, arms, and legs, as it were, hung from it." [*He must have made a delightful appearance.*] "Hitler allowed his arms to fall down casually, but did not put them into his trouser pockets" (his arms?).[6]

Here we are coming across the first signs of the problematic. How is it possible that a highly regarded historian, whose medieval studies may in no way be looked down on, seeks with these odd methods to approach a phenomenon like Hitler by excluding all that is relevant for understanding him? Who, indeed, explicitly asserts that the concepts for treating Hitler's personality are lacking, that the expressions are not available, even though there is a rich literature that is by no means short of expressions for characterizing Hitler. And who says that one should hand this problem over to psychopathology, although the investigations into Hitler and the extensive literature on Hitler's personality show that Hitler's case is not a psychopathological phenomenon at all but something quite different.

§3. The Stupidity of a Whole People: The "Buttermelcher Syndrome"

There then occurred a whole series of reactions to Wucher's characterization that are very interesting. I will choose from the letters sent to the *Süddeutsche Zeitung,* a few of which indicate where the resistances lie. First, a letter from a member of the older generation, then from a member of the younger generation, presumably from your age group. First the older generation:

> I have read this failed "Anatomy of a Dictator" in the *Spiegel* and was horrified! Horrified exactly in the sense of Dr. Wucher's reflection in the *SZ.* And I may assure you that I have spoken with many, with

6. Ibid. Throughout these lectures, Voegelin's interpolations in his own citations are italicized within square brackets.

> important personalities, all of whom were like myself horrified with Mr. Schramm's "Anatomy." What is the matter with this professor that he evaluates Hitler in such a positive manner? What a dangerous game for our youth, who did not know this character, to set before them such an "Anatomy" in book form. One could say that you were quite right, even more than fair, to be amazed that the *Spiegel* as well as Schramm should be so naive. How Hitler was, as a human being and as a person, we who experienced him indeed know best, and truly no one needed any special spiritual and moral quality in order to recognize from the beginning who this man is, inwardly and outwardly. It remains indeed an eternal disgrace for the German people that there were any votes at all for this fellow.[7]

Please note the recognition of the fact that the problem of Hitler must not be isolated, but that it is a problem of "Hitler and the Germans" that arises here. The man got votes. But now another one, also from the older generation:

> There are a whole lot of very reasonable people among those who lost everything under Hitler, for whom the war destroyed everything and who no longer want this time to return in this form. But it is exactly these people who—restraining all hatred and diagnosing dispassionately—also include the positive sides of the Hitler regime in their personal mastering of this time. [*Please note this "mastering"! We will have to speak more fully about the question of the unmastered past.*]
>
> I do not believe that the German people is made up of millions of imbeciles, blinded and intoxicated by words, behind which in fact there was nothing! Then there would today still have to be very many imbeciles going around in Germany, whose intelligence, by the way, is quite willingly made use of when their votes are needed in an election. Whoever voted for Hitler must then [*from Wucher's viewpoint*] have been stupid, fanatical, and possessed of racial delusion. . . . Please refute the argument that instead of Hitler something better might have come.[8]

So, the conclusion: If Hitler was stupid or a criminal, and the people voted for him in droves, then they too must have been stupid and criminal. But that is not possible, so Hitler was not stupid and no criminal. The other possibility, the point that is being resisted, is that perhaps a very great number of Germans, perhaps the overwhelming majority, were in fact extraordinarily stupid, that in political matters a very great number still are, and that what we

7. Letter of Hilde Seitz, *Süddeutsche Zeitung*, March 21/22, 1964.
8. Letter of Wilfried Wiegand, ibid.

see here is a situation of intellectual and ethical rottenness, which in fact supported the rise of the phenomenon of Hitler. It is not only a German problem. It is an international problem. And now a younger man writes, "Something doesn't make sense":

> Certainly I am a young man, and my impression of Hitler comes from books and reports. But I realize, and want to say this to your Albert Wucher, that what he writes there seems less credibly convincing than Professor Dr. Schramm in *Der Spiegel.*

Perhaps you cannot appreciate this "Professor Dr. Schramm" as much as I can, because I lived through the National Socialist period and saw how extraordinarily respectful the National Socialists were to titles. From the National Socialist side among the ordinary people, Goebbels was never spoken of as "Goebbels"; it was always "Dr. Goebbels." If someone is a doctor, then that must be something fine; if someone is a professor, then all the more so. Therefore: "Professor Dr. Schramm."

> This Professor, whom he tries in a polemical way to correct ironically, is obviously more objective. If someone pulls Adolf Hitler to pieces in such a manner, then this sounds like "the revenge of the little man."
>
> One automatically asks, if one reads what an amateur Hitler must have been, this "below average man," how he was capable of giving shape to an epoch. [*Which he definitely did.*] He was a "gambler," I admit that, but one who outshone the others. How can that be explained, Mr. Wucher? Apparently he does not bear in mind that he classifies this man so basely that he must, according to the same measure, deny a whole generation's spiritual qualities. [*Then this precious concluding sentence:*] National Socialists did not consist only of some primitive workers.

Rightly diagnosed, the truth of the degeneracy of the German middle classes is not admitted. Therefore Hitler cannot have been what he was. Still in conclusion:

> Hitler's only crime was that he was a gambler who lost, and chained a whole people to himself, so that it went down with him. However, all politics is a gamble and the winnings increase when the stakes are higher. Today we cannot and will not gamble any more; therefore it is impossible for us to win anything either—except the much-quoted standard of living. But we could still lose more even without Hitler.[9]

9. Letter of Gerhard Hess (of Buttermelcherstrasse), *Süddeutsche Zeitung,* March 14/15, 1964.

When we look at a letter like this, we assume that it is by a young man of about twenty who, one could say on the basis of these last paragraphs, will still lose plenty of money in the lottery. But the other remark—that Hitler cannot have been as dubious as he was, since then the entire generation would have been just as dubious—and the clear realization that this has to do specifically with a problematic of the middle class (as the primitive workers were not so much involved in what was going on) is again an instance of this point of resistance that I referred to already in the other letter. We must have some name or other for this, and since this gentleman, whose name I will not mention, lives in Buttermelcher Street, perhaps I will call this phenomenon of resistance (which is a contemporary problem and will come up again and again) the "Buttermelcher Syndrome," so that we shall have an expression for further analyzing this problematic.

Now this flood of letters, which continued for three weeks, was followed by the holding of a public forum of the Congress for Cultural Freedom, in which Mr. Schramm, Mr. Besson, the political scientist from Erlangen, Gisevius, and Krausnick participated.[10] And Wucher also wrote a report on this public function held in the Scholastika Hall.[11] I was not there myself; but I was informed, from people who were there, that what Wucher wrote is accurate. Let us now see what comes out of such a discussion and where the problems lie. Above all, the title: "Hitler—An Alibi for the Germans." Please note the expression "alibi." We still have to speak in detail about the expression "alibi" and the lie.

> The panel discussion organized by the Congress for Cultural Freedom chose "Hitler as Alibi" as its theme. So this was not in fact Schramm's particular formulation of the question, but the more general problem, whether Hitler should be understood as an "accident," as a demonic and exceptional personality, which takes from us the responsibility, on which we can shift all the guilt.

10. Waldemar Besson (1929–71) was professor of political science at Erlangen, 1961–66, and at Konstanz, 1966–71. Helmut Krausnick (1905–90), historian, was director of the Institut für Zeitgeschichte, Munich, 1959–72. Hans Bernd Gisevius (1904–74), was a Prussian civil servant who became indirectly involved in the July 20, 1944, attempted assassination of Hitler. He was the author of *Adolf Hitler: Versuch einer Deutung* (Munich: Rütten and Loening, 1963).

11. Albert Wucher, "Hitler—ein Alibi für die Deutschen?" *Süddeutsche Zeitung*, March 20, 1964.

So, Hitler as a demonic manifestation; again we have a new expression. We shall have to speak in detail about the problem of demonism, what meaning it has and whether an expression like "demonic" can be applied to Hitler.

> Only indirectly was the crux of the matter approached: Does a picture playing Hitler down, which Schramm is accused of, not very much contribute to such misunderstandings? In order to see Hitler correctly, must we not distinguish between unimportant things in him (for example, Schramm's remark that Hitler shaved himself and seldom cut himself) and important characteristics? Must we not start with the central qualities, or else in the end overestimate numerous trivialities? [*As Krausnick then said:*] "The disposition of the German people toward Hitler is more important than Hitler himself."[12]

So here this great problem is acknowledged: Was Hitler a leader, or was he a man who was able to take advantage of a situation in time and of the corruption of the people, so that he could arrive at the top with very great political skill? Therefore one cannot in any way isolate Hitler and analyze him as a single personality. Instead one can see the phenomenon of his rise to power only in connection with a disposition of the German people, which brought Hitler into power. Expressions such as the "disposition of the German people" say nothing at all, of course. The question is, what constitutes this disposition? Concretely, what happened in the different classes of the population?

Now the next scene:

> Finally, the objection of the moderator, Dr. Hupka, as to whether Hitler had been really so mysterious that it was worth making such a fuss about this today. It should be sufficient to rediscover Hitler as he presented himself then. Anyway, if Hitler were considered merely as a scientific object, merely as a historic figure, then one would inevitably play him down.
>
> That was as wide and sharp as the criticism of Schramm got. But even that was enough to provoke a displeased hiss in the hall.[13]

Please note what is a very important phenomenon of our time. If, even in this discreet and general way, something that looks like an attempt to play Hitler down is criticized, resistance is already triggered. On this occasion, the hissing in the hall.

12. Ibid.
13. Ibid.

> The mildly attacked [*Schramm*] made light of the objections. He waved his book around and called it a scholarly work. Among scholars, however, it is usual that one first fully reads such a book. Critics who accused him of turning Hitler into a "petit bourgeois" had not really read it all. Had they done so they would have known that "this Hitler could disguise himself," could be nice to children, and could fascinate all kinds of people. He was "no idiot." [*Besson said that in the discussion.*] That would have to be [*here comes the Buttermelcher Syndrome again*] a "frightening" realization for the German people, Schramm said, who would have followed an idiot.
>
> [*Now Wucher on this:*] The remark that suddenly slipped out from the scholar immediately illuminated why so many false judgments about Hitler circulate, why after 1945 he was for the first time thoroughly demonized. It would, interjected Krausnick, indeed be for the people today more painful to have been taken in by an "idiot" than by a criminal. Schramm's portrait offers itself as a way out [*giving exact documentation of irrelevant facts*].
>
> . . . In the end the discussion led to recommendations for the younger generation. Schramm wishes to thoroughly "impregnate" or "vaccinate" them, and he believes that to achieve that, one can "never contemplate Hitler enough." Gisevius [*answered*] that there would be no better means for us to prevent a "possible return of a Hitler" than "to come to terms with the German Hitler." What is basically evil with all debates of this kind is that we would be nowhere near grasping the man from Braunau, this man of flesh and blood. "With the Nazis it was a devilishly human affair."[14]

That's enough to describe to you the level of discussion. You can see that all these formulas that were used really say nothing but are a confession that none of the participants knows how to investigate a phenomenon like Hitler or in what manner he should be discussed. That holds for all of them, not just for Schramm, whom I will later analyze more fully. The only satisfying thing perhaps was the remark of Waldemar Besson, the political scientist from Erlangen, who put the straight question: How was it possible that a people of 70 million were so taken in by an "idiot"? Now I shall in no way make propaganda for the word "idiot." It is far too sweeping, and obviously Hitler had a quite outstanding intelligence, by which he was able to fool other people. But there's still something in it. For this problem of the idiot ultimately is related to the problem of the *stultus,* of the fool in the technical sense, which we will later speak about. And apart from his pragmatic intelligence in taking in

14. Ibid.

opponents, Hitler in his objectives and his principles was in fact a *stultus,* a fool. This popular rendering as the *stultus,* as an idiot, is by no means to be completely looked down on, even if it is also far too undifferentiated. One could indeed almost go so far as to say that in that evening discussion the observation that Hitler was an idiot was, after all, still ethically and intellectually superior to the other clichés, which not even once got the point that a man can at the same time be intelligent and a *stultus,* a fool. We shall also have to discuss this question of stupidity, of folly, and of intelligence, which is bound up with it. All these events have deeply disturbed Mr. Augstein, the editor of *Der Spiegel.* As a result he found it necessary in a recent edition to set out his reasons for carrying this "Anatomy of a Dictator." To conclude, a few passages from this reply of Augstein. He has seen many things clearer than the professors.

> It may indeed for us budding or mature historians be rather distressing that there has been no success yet with a portrait of Hitler that is broadly accessible and still serious. But why do we blame Schramm? Surely the answer to the questions that are put to us lies "first and foremost in the person of the Führer."[15]

Please note this sentence of Augstein. It is regrettable, distressing, that we still do not possess a serious portrait of Hitler, that there has been no success with this yet, but why do we blame Schramm? The implication is that there is no suitable depiction of Hitler available. There are, of course, and they are accessible, even in paperback editions—for example, the large biography of Hitler by Alan Bullock, the English historian, which up to now is the intellectually most significant interpretation of Hitler. But this literature is obviously known neither by Schramm, nor Augstein, nor by anyone else with whom these people talk. They've not yet heard anything about it. This is a very remarkable fact. There is a very considerable literature of the discussion of Hitler, of which I have just given a representative example, not the very latest, but the discussion naturally has been going on since the '20s, and no notice is taken of all this enormous literature.

The question now is whether all that we know about Hitler—since there is an outstanding literature and there are outstanding

15. Rudolf Augstein, open letter to his readers, *Der Spiegel* 13 (1964): 17.

analyses of Hitler—is being deliberately concealed. Or—which I consider much more likely, as I'm not inclined to presume deceit in general unless very compelling proof is available—is the spiritual level of the persons involved, including Schramm and Augstein, so miserable that they themselves, if they read a good work on Hitler, cannot at all understand that it is good and cannot learn something from it?

Here there arises again the problem of spiritual illiteracy, which we shall have to speak explicitly about under the heading of illiteracy. I believe that this second explanation is the case here. In this connection it is not deceit but has to do with a particular symptom of intellectual and spiritual decay that renders the persons affected incapable of reading, grasping, and assimilating good literature in general.

Another argument from Augstein now, which is much more interesting:

> Wucher finds fault with the fact that Schramm clearly considers Hitler to have been a significant character. But Hitler was a significant character, uneducated, half- and quarter-educated, of raw cruelty, repellent in his vulgar brutality, completely and extremely inhuman, but still a significant character. You don't get three great powers to lay Europe at your feet, as Hitler managed to do in the Munich agreement, without political genius.[16]

Augstein again is correct here. The fact that Hitler was a more than undesirable figure should not lead one to overlook that he was successful. And no one who had such success is utterly contemptible. There must have been something in him that made this success possible. That is exactly what is embarrassing about this matter, that here appears a great politician, a brilliant politician, who yet lacks other qualities. Whether he is therefore to be seen as a significant character, that again is another question. You see, every word must be meticulously examined. When later, under the heading of the question of stupidity, we examine Robert Musil's essay "On Stupidity," we will there find a meaning of the term "significance" that is carefully analyzed and that precisely excludes Hitler as possessing significance. Hitler was not significant, even if he was a brilliant politician. Significance consists of something other than the talent of a medium, who is able to exploit the stupidity and

16. Ibid.

ethical degeneracy of other people for his purposes. Another passage from Augstein, who has indeed decidedly pedagogical intentions:

> What, probably, is the reason that the schools do not deal with Hitler adequately? They do not know how to offer the material in a form acceptable to young people, because they themselves are unable to organize and assess it. Schramm has shown one method as a help for the teachers.[17]

Again, a remarkable mixture of true and false. That Hitler presumably is not correctly depicted in schools we can well believe. For the school staff naturally does not have at its disposal the facilities we have available here for working through the problems. However, it is quite another matter to say that Schramm's portrait of Hitler shows a possible way of portraying him. For, as I have already said, there is literature on Hitler, and one could perhaps go so far as to say that school staffs too could inform themselves about descriptions of Hitler, since these can be found in paperback form on every street corner, without having to fall back on Schramm.

§4. Present-day German Laxity toward Former Nazis

The Schramm affair, insofar as it happened in public, is thus concluded. It properly belongs to a later lecture, for only then do the really interesting problems, which did not emerge in the public debate, arise.

When, on the occasion of the Schramm affair, we decided to hold the lectures on Hitler and the Germans in this summer semester, a whole series of newspaper reports relevant to these problems turned up, on a daily basis you could say. So, quite unsystematically, without looking for anything, just what one read in the paper at breakfast, I took out a few clippings. Belonging to these issues above all are the current Auschwitz trials and the Limburg euthanasia trial.[18] In the Auschwitz trials the interesting thing for us was by no means the sufferings of the victims, not because the sufferings of the

17. Ibid, 18.

18. The Frankfurt Auschwitz trials, from December 1963 to August 1965, were the longest and most extensive trials of Nazi crimes in Germany. Of twenty-two accused, six received life sentences, three were acquitted, and the rest were jailed for three to ten years. The Limburg trial, of medical personnel involved in euthanasia, took place in the spring of 1964.

victims can be neglected—they were horrifying. But the politically interesting thing is the character structure of the perpetrators. The victims are of political interest only insofar as they cooperated in their own extermination.[19] This is a problem that especially Hannah Arendt treated in great detail in her book on the Eichmann trial and on account of which she was then subjected to ferocious attack.[20] Again we have, at a more brutal level, the Buttermelcher Syndrome: The persons who are murdered even lend a hand in their own murder—that goes a bit too far, that must never be admitted. But the principal matter is the character of the murderers and how it is reacted to today. And now in the report of March 24 on the Auschwitz trial we find a very interesting item:

> The cry "murderer" rang out on Monday in the Auschwitz trial at Frankfurt through the courthouse. The fifty-six-year-old former concentration camp prisoner Hugo Breiden from Stuttgart lost control in the witness stand when he was shown a model of the notorious Boger "swing" on which, according to his testimony, he was beaten into a cripple by the accused Boger. Boger, who is one of the most incriminated of the former members of the camp Gestapo, stared apathetically into the room during this witness's testimony.[21]

I am reading out this passage because the journalist here reports that the victim lost control when he was confronted with this murderer, whom he saw killing others—he himself escaped death and was beaten into a cripple. It is due to a loss of self-control that he now cries "murderer." Please note the enormity of this report, for what it is saying is that one should peacefully allow oneself to be killed and shouldn't in any way shout "murderer." That is exacerbated further through later reprimands of the presiding judge to another witness, who spoke of the "murderers." The presiding judge majestically explained that according to German law a murderer could only be referred to as such if he is proven guilty. If you put these remarks together, then it follows: As long as I have not been killed, I must not say that the other person is a murderer. If I see that this other

19. Voegelin does not return to it in these lectures, but his judgment on that second issue is available in his review article of Hannah Arendt's *The Origins of Totalitarianism* in *Review of Politics* 15, no. 1 (1953): 68–85.

20. See Elisabeth Young-Bruehl, *Hannah Arendt: For Love of the World* (New Haven: Yale University Press, 1982), 337–78, and the postscript to the revised edition of Hannah Arendt's *Eichmann in Jerusalem: A Report on the Banality of Evil* (New York: Penguin, 1994), 282–84.

21. *Süddeutsche Zeitung*, March 24, 1964.

one is committing murder, I still may not say "murderer!" before he has been convicted in a proper court.

Link this to the fact that in this specific murderous situation in Auschwitz there were no proper court proceedings; for the *Rechtsstaat*[22] has disappeared when murder is not committed in the normal sense of criminal law but is carried out on a mass scale and precisely by those who should have punished murder—in other words, when the government, in this case the Reich chancellor, his ministers, the administrative authorities subordinate to him, his generals, etc., all cooperate in organized mass murder. So that Hannah Arendt, for example, in her Eichmann book, says that there was no German institution of that period that was not criminally involved in the murders[23]—none, including the army and the church, that there was *none*! From this it follows that the categories of the *Rechtsstaat,* which are drawn on here when someone says, "The witness is losing self-control" or "He should not call that man a murderer before he has been judged," have become meaningless. Thus we have a contemporary problem, not of the Nazi period in the past: that is, that problems that go beyond the scope of the *Rechtsstaat* are handled with the inadequate categories of the *Rechtsstaat.* We will have to spend a whole hour on a detailed examination of the problem of the *Rechtsstaat* under the particular conditions of the German situation.

So, the victim is reproached for losing his self-control when he calls the man a murderer, and in the same newspaper you can read how one should behave when one has to deal with murder and how one does not lose one's self-control. This is a report on the Limburg trial:

> Dr. Hans Hefelman, the fifty-eight-year-old defendant in the Limburg euthanasia trial, raised strong accusations on Monday against the judiciary in the Third Reich. The former department head of the "euthanasia" campaign said that at an April 1941 judiciary conference in Berlin all the chief public prosecutors and presidents of the Courts of Appeals had declared their support for the euthanasia program. The defendant, who is accused of complicity in the death of 73,000 allegedly mentally ill people, reported that the state secretary in the Ministry of Justice, Dr. Franz Schlegelberger [*the man is still living peacefully*

22. Chapter 6 below, on the *Rechtsstaat,* will make clear why it is preferable to leave this term, sometimes rendered "constitutional state," untranslated.

23. Arendt, *Eichmann in Jerusalem,* 18.

> *today in Schleswig-Holstein*], held a lecture at the conference in which he declared the "T 4" action was legal. None of the more than one hundred senior legal personnel, among whom was the president of the Supreme Court, Erwin Bumke, expressed objections.
>
> The details of the "T 4" campaign—which claimed about 100,000 allegedly mentally ill and incurably sick people as victims—were submitted to the lawyers. It was further explained that Hitler did not desire a law for the euthanasia measures, but that they would continue on the basis of his personal legal decree. The campaign, the lawyers were notified, was carried out as a "secret matter of the Reich."[24]

Legal proceedings are now being held against all these lawyers. And those who today reprimand the victim when he calls out "murderer" are the members of the same legal profession.

We have reports on that very meeting. It is a matter of fact that these assembled lawyers, among them the Supreme Court president Bumke, were informed that this campaign was planned, in fact without legal basis, merely on the grounds of a decree of the Führer that was to remain secret. The lawyers were informed that the campaign was to proceed as a secret matter of the Reich. That means all the highest German judges knew that this whole undertaking lacked any legal basis and they said nothing. Witnesses of this scene describe how all those appeal court presidents looked at Bumke—what will Bumke say next?—and Bumke said nothing! And then they too said nothing—and the whole thing started to move. That's what it looks like in practice.

In this connection, there is another interesting detail: the secret matter of the Reich. At that time, no one was ever punished or faced any disadvantage for refusing to take part in this euthanasia campaign. But anyone who betrayed this secret matter of the Reich or spoke about it in public was prosecuted with a heavy penalty. What is this secret matter of the Reich about? It is not something that occurred for the first time in 1941. The earliest case of such a "secret matter of the Reich" that I know of dates from December 1932. A very controversial person is involved, Hans Globke,[25] who became Adenauer's state secretary. In December 1932, Globke

24. *Süddeutsche Zeitung,* March 24, 1964.

25. Hans Globke (1898–1973) was deputy president of the Aachen police in 1925; in 1932 he became a principal officer in the Prussian Ministry of the Interior and then in the Reich Ministry of the Interior. From 1949, he was undersecretary of state in the federal chancellery, and from 1953 was secretary of state, functioning as Chancellor Konrad Adenauer's right-hand man.

circulated a note, in the Ministry of the Interior, to the effect that in the procedure for changing one's name, a proof of ancestry was to be produced, so that Jews could not change their names. That was in December 1932, before Hitler had come to power but when one could perhaps already speculate that he would come to power. And added to this circular of Globke's was the note that it should remain secret. That is to say, here you have the first case of the persecutions of the Jews by means of such an illegal circular, to be treated as secret, which anticipates the later events. I want to add this specifically to the characterization of Globke, how far back all this goes and how deeply it is rooted; Hitler was not the first to come up with this. That is something bureaucrats in the Ministry of the Interior were well able to think up on their own—even though later Globke was, you could say, whitewashed by clerical authorities. But he could not be whitewashed. It was always maintained that he had in various ways alleviated the enforcement of the anti-Semitic Nuremberg Laws. He alleviated nothing: They were all killed.

There is only one demonstrable case of alleviation, which perhaps despite its grotesque nature I would still like to recount. It was in 1942, I believe. Then he arranged, again through a similar internal decree to his subordinates, that German soldiers who wished to marry Czech girls—which occurred after the conquest of Czechoslovakia—had to produce a photograph of the girl in a swimsuit in order to receive permission to marry. When asked why this was an alleviation, he replied that it was an enormous alleviation, since until that decree nude photographs had to be produced.[26] This alleviation is the only one in Globke's career that can be provided with documentary proof.

And then, cheerful scenes are not lacking in our newspapers. Again in the last four weeks we have had the kind of amusing phenomenon like that of Mr. Bütefisch, an industrial magnate, upon whom was conferred the Federal Cross of Merit, First Class. By accident, someone from the Munich *Abendzeitung* remembered that Mr. Bütefisch was one of those industrialists who were sentenced at the Nuremberg trials to several years' imprisonment because they used prisoners for slave labor in Auschwitz. As a result the Federal Cross of Merit, First Class, was withdrawn from him. The case is

26. Arendt, *Eichmann in Jerusalem,* 18–19, 128.

interesting. Obviously the authorities in the various interior ministries who deal with the conferral of such decorations are not aware that German society is riddled with former Nazis and extremely disreputable people in high positions and that such things come out into the open by pure chance—just because someone remembered that Mr. Bütefisch was involved in the Nuremberg trial—for we do indeed know who these people were.

For example, in Hilberg's large study, *The Destruction of the European Jews,* which appeared in 1961, there is an extensive, twenty-page-long list, in double columns, of people who were involved in Auschwitz and other Jewish matters, among which there is also the complete list of the German industrialists, in IG-Farben, Krupp, Siemens, etc., who were involved in this slave labor and took advantage of it. In Auschwitz, industrial installations had been set up in order to fully exploit the people before they were completely worked to death and then incinerated. And if you glance through that list, among the industrialists you will find in the first place a Mr. Ambros, in the second place Mr. Bütefisch.[27] Then follows the whole list of the others who today are all still directors of large industrial companies and members of supervisory boards. So that can be established. And since I am a kindhearted man, I can say our Institute is happily prepared at any time to make lists, even printed out, available to unsuspecting interior ministers of the various *Länder,* and of the Federal Republic, of all those people who perhaps should not receive a Federal Cross of Merit—unless the Federal Cross is earmarked precisely for such people.

This was not the only case. Only a couple of years ago there was a similar "slip-up." There was in Brunswick a very influential local industrial magnate named Heims, by trade a coffee distributor and owner of the Park Hotel in Brunswick. This was the man by whose influence Hitler received German citizenship, so that he could be elected as Reich chancellor. He received not only the Cross of Merit, First Class, but as far as I can make out here from the photograph, the Grand Cross, with Distinction.

Another entertainment we have is the Zech-Nenntwich affair. A stouthearted SS cavalryman who murdered a few people is caught at last, and even locked up, and he has hardly been sentenced to four

27. Raul Hilberg, *The Destruction of the European Jews* (Chicago: Quadrangle Books, 1961), 705.

years in jail or penal servitude, I don't know which, when he strolls out, flees with a nice-looking girl to Basle, already has his passport, that is to say, a visa for the United Arab Republic—which naturally was not taken from him, you don't do that to a gentleman. He flies on to Egypt and is doing fine now in Cairo.[28] When you see such things as these remarkable conferrals of Crosses of Merit, the ease with which one can stroll out of German prisons if one is a former SS man, etc., you can again ask yourself various questions. First: Does it not look like an operetta republic if things like that happen here? Second, a more serious question: Up to what level is our whole federal-republican society still so riddled in an organized form with National Socialists that it is almost impossible to overcome such things, especially in the judiciary and in the police service? These then are the curiosities we shall have to deal with. For the moment I only picked them out as examples, in order to show you how great is the range of problems we must concern ourselves with.

28. Munich *Abendzeitung,* April 25/26, July 3, 1964.

2

Development of Diagnostic Tools

§5. The Cliché of the "Unmastered Past" versus the "Presence under God"

Let us now enter into the matter itself. I must draw up and analyze a whole series of concepts before we can treat materials objectively. The first concept is the concept of the unmastered past, about which, as you well know, there has been an extraordinary amount of discussion. When we hear the expression "the unmastered past," a series of questions immediately crops up: What does that really mean, in the first place? For whom is this past unmastered, assuming that we know at all what "mastering" means: for all, or for only a few people? Because it indeed was mastered by very many while it was still the present, since by no means did all the people who experienced the period of National Socialism cheerfully cooperate with it. Some were against it instinctively, because of tradition, etc. But some also knew precisely what was going on. That is to say, what is today the unmastered past, for people at the level of a Schramm or an Augstein, was a completely masterable present for the people who lived at that time. I mastered Hitler even before he came to power, and many others did too. So for whom is that an unmastered past?

And if it is not mastered, what does that really mean—that it is not mastered as past? Again one can ask, Why should it be mastered? For it has indeed passed. And consequently if there is somehow the feeling that there is still something to master in the past, then we are coming to what I have continually pointed toward in all these examples, that we live in an unmastered *present*. Here is the first thesis for our analysis of the problem of the unmastered past: It really is an unmastered present.

What now is the unmastered present? First, what is the present? The present can mean two things. In the first place, one can speak today of the ideologically and socially usual idea of the present as a point in the present (*Gegenwartspunkt*) lying between past and future. So the time of history is represented as going in a line from the past to the future through a point in the present, and from this viewpoint one understands the present. Thus contemporary events are events that occur in the year 1964; past events occurred in the year 1930. Against this linear conception of the present, which has existed only since the eighteenth century in this form as a thoroughly ideological notion, there is that other meaning of the present, in which the present is always related to the existence of man in his presence (*Präsenz*) under God. Insofar as—while existing and acting in immanent time—man exists under God, he has presence. And the meaning of the past and the future will become generally interpretable only when starting out from this presence. For otherwise everything would proceed irrelevantly in an external stream of time. What now does mastering the present mean? Under mastering the present there is a virtue to be understood, the virtue of placing the present of immanent time under the judgment of the presence under God. This kind of mastering, then, is a general human problem, not something of the modern era, not something for Germans only, but for everyman: to place the immanent present within the immanent process under the judgment of the presence.

These questions were clarified and formulated for the first time in classic politics, by Plato in the *Politeia* and in the *Gorgias.* To place oneself under the presence, under the presence of God, and according to that to adjudicate what one does as man and how one forms the order of one's own existence and the existence of society, that for Plato is an act of judgment. That means that man is always under judgment; hence the myths of judgment in the *Gorgias* and the *Politeia.* And because he is always under judgment, under the presence of God, in the sense of this "being-under-judgment" he must adjudicate how he acts and how others act and how this action brings about an order of society. For Plato, therefore, the judgment is above all the investigation of the not-being-present of the sophists as individual persons, and a not-being-present in the sense of the presence of the entire society insofar as it allows itself to be led and ordered—that means disordered—by sophistic ideas. So, what will be called political science arises in the critique of time in the sense of the empirically immanent society that does not place itself under the judgment in the presence of God. That is to say, the science of the order of man in society arises from the reaction against not existing in the present. We can say of Plato that he mastered the past of sophistry in a paradigmatic fashion, insofar as it reached into his time, *and* that he thereby mastered his own present and highlighted what the present, in the sense of this presence under God, meant. All science of politics begins with this. This mastering of the past, which is always a mastering of the present, was relatively simple in Plato's situation, for he had only to deal with the internal historical processes of the Hellenistic polis.

For us in the present situation the matter is much more complicated. We have a particular difficulty in mastering our present, since our society is dominated by different kinds of ideological principles and views—not only Marxist or National Socialist but also positivist, progressivist, secular-liberal, etc.—that erect the prevention of the mastering of the present into a principle. And this principle of prevention is already so old—it goes back at least two hundred years—that it has affected the entire Western, but particularly the German, situation and lays the greatest obstacles in the way of this very mastering, which has to be carried out again and again. So, if we wish to master the past in the sense of mastering the present, we are confronted with the task of clearing out all the ideological junk in order to make the *conditio humana* visible once again.

How can this be done? Again there are difficulties. For naturally one can only clear things out by becoming conscious of the presence and by having at one's disposal the expressions adequate for making it conscious. These adequate expressions are of course to be found in classical philosophy, in the whole history of Christianity, of scholasticism, etc., in humanistic philosophy up to the eighteenth century; they are absolutely the dominant ones. But under the influence of the development of the ideologies, which took over the classic and Christian vocabulary for understanding presence and reinterpreted it as an instrument for the prevention of knowledge of the presence under God, the words have simply changed their meanings. Therefore it is not easy even to speak about what is at issue here—for example, about the truth of existence, or freedom of existence under God—nor to speak about reason as the organ sensitive for the reception of transcendent being, or about the spirit, etc., for all these expressions have become ideologized. And this is an international, not only a German, problem.

However, the Western peoples are in a more favorable situation, even though all the ideological dirt has piled up there too. But still, traditionally in the institutions, in the universities, in literary works, the classic, humanistic, and Christian tradition has remained preserved in a way of which you, if you live only in Germany, can have absolutely no idea. There is such a tremendous reserve of tradition in existence, of such strength, that although these ideological phenomena certainly do emerge and are felt as phenomena of disorder and corruption in the social body, there is still enough healthy substance there to make it possible to be understood when one speaks of such things.

In Germany now, for certain historical reasons, that is not the case, for the German philosophical language that we use here was first developed in the eighteenth century. The man who coined most of the German philosophical vocabulary was Christian Wolff, and after him, Kant. These were the two most important figures. Only from that time on do we have a German vocabulary for the treatment of the problems, developed during the period of the ideologies and therefore loaded from the beginning with the meanings of the Enlightenment and of Romantic gnosis. As a result, one cannot, as is possible for example in England and America or in France, still use expressions such as "intellect" or "spirit" or "reason" and assume that—at least by the educated section of the population, which is very numerous in these countries—these words will be understood as a Plato understood them, or a Saint Thomas or a Bodin, or seventeenth- and eigthteenth-century authors, or as how up to now English-speaking poets like T. S. Eliot understand them. This entire dimension of meaning, where these expressions were indeed created in order to elucidate and express the presence under God, has been essentially suppressed in the German language. So that when you are speaking of "reason" in public, it is extraordinarily difficult to get across that you mean something other than, for example, the "reason" occurring in the *Critique of Pure Reason.* Or if you are speaking of "spirit," that something other than what Hegel understood by "spirit" is meant, or than what after him the epigonic human sciences understood by "spirit." Or to get across that you understand by it, for example, what Aristotle or Plato understood by *nous,* or what was understood in the tradition of revelation by *pneuma*. For such things are indeed not sufficiently known to a socially relevant extent.

So these are essential complications, which in Germany are attenuated only because we still have—up to a certain level—churches as places of retreat for classic culture, too. But the churches in Germany can contribute very little to this, partly because the Protestant ones are indeed much too much linked with the formation of ideology through existentialism and the like, and the Catholic side adheres too strongly to the traditional language of theology, which is not adapted to the modern problematic. So here we have unavoidable difficulties, which we must gradually overcome.

(Second Lecture)

Ladies and Gentlemen,
In the first lecture I began by presenting to you some materials that made it seem advisable to deal more fully with the question of Hitler and the Germans. Toward the end of the previous lecture I then indicated the difficulties lying in the way of such an enterprise. The difficulties arise from the predominance of a whole series of clichés. Our first task is to get rid of these clichés—and in doing so a lot can already be said about Hitler, for those very clichés are related to his ascent to power—and to discover the criteria for judgment.

The first cliché that had to be eliminated was the so-called unmastered past. There is no unmastered past: What is past, is past. There are only unmastered presents. There can indeed have been unmastered presents in the past, too; and inasmuch as the past, being the present in its time, was unmastered, this not being mastered reaches into the unmastered present, in historical continuity. Hence the survival of clichés, which now have to be eliminated. By the "present" there are two different things to be understood: first, the present in the sense of transition from the past to the future on the line of time in the world; and second, the present in the sense of presence under God. That means that action is always to be judged as action in the world under the orientation of its presence to God. Where that does not happen, the present is unmastered, and even if it sinks into the past, it remains still unmastered; and insofar as this worldly past influences the present in historical continuity, then also the contemporary present remains unmastered. So we must rather come to address the problem of the mastering of the present.

§6. The Cliché of "Collective Guilt" and the Representation of a Society

A second cliché now, which is directly connected with the first one of the unmastered past, is the famous problem of collective guilt. Let us divide this problem into a series of aspects, all of which are to be considered: the personal, the social, and the historical. In general, it has to be said that a collective guilt does not exist, especially not at the personal level, for guilt is always something that can be attributed to a person. This insight is by now rather an old one. To explain how old it is, let me quote a passage from the prophet Ezekiel, chapter 18. It reads:

> The word of the Lord came to me again: "What do you mean by repeating this proverb concerning the land of Israel, 'The fathers have eaten sour grapes, and the children's teeth are set on edge'? As I live, says the Lord God, this proverb shall no more be used by you in Israel. Behold, all souls are mine; the soul of the father as well as the soul of the son is mine: the soul that sins shall die. If a man is righteous . . . he shall surely live." (Ezek. 18:1–5, 9 RSV)

Here you have the classic case of what it means to master the present, in the transition from the older cliché of a collective liability, where the sins of the fathers are avenged on the following generation.

In Ezekiel's time, that is, about 580 B.C., this transition takes place with the insight that everyone is responsible only for what he does himself—but that he is indeed responsible for that. So, personally there is no liability for something that was done in the past by other people; but the fact that one is not responsible for what a previous generation did does not mean that one is now guiltless and has a right to be up to all sorts of mischief. Rather, each one of us is also obliged to be just.

Here then arises the second aspect of the collective guilt. Behind this consciousness of a collective guilt is hidden a completely different empirical fact. That is the fact that we all live in society, that the society acts through its representatives, that, insofar as it has representatives, it has a social structure, and that, if the representatives do not function, all members of the society, even those who have nothing to do with the representatives' misdeeds, have to bear, along with them, the consequences of these misdeeds, whether they are guilty or not. So, if a society is of such a type that it chooses criminal imbeciles and crooks as representatives, then the society as a whole is in a very unpleasant situation, because those who were not prepared to elect criminal imbeciles and crooks as their representatives are still caught together and hanged together. The society as a whole is therefore in a dangerous situation insofar as disaster will ensue inside and outside, as in the case of German society in the National Socialist period, with millions of murders and the causing of a world war.

Third, a society of such a type arrives at the historically unpleasant situation of not being trustworthy. This means that those who live in this society and do not take part in the criminal mischief do not trust their fellow citizens. There will be a situation of general mistrust. And naturally, those societies that suffer the consequences of these criminal mischiefs maintain for generations the greatest mistrust for a society that did such things. These are consequences that must be borne. So if you think, for example, of a phenomenon like the partitioning of Germany, and if there is continual discussion about reunification, it must be clear that this is not a matter of guilt; but rather, that no responsible statesman in the East, whether Polish, Czech, or Russian, can, after all that this country has done, contemplate with equanimity that Germany should again become a great power, and that in any foreseeable time we have no chance of any kind of reunification, except through again instigating a new world war. These are the consequences that must be borne historically.

But all of that has nothing to do with personal guilt. It is unpleasant to find oneself in such a situation, but that cannot be changed. Much more painful than the whole problematic of collective guilt is the emergence of the cliché as such and its use in order to prevent precisely what should happen, that is, the mastering of the present. The cliché of collective guilt becomes an alibi in two respects. First, one can accept the cliché of collective guilt, which then expresses itself in an extremely obliging burrowing into the past, in the investigation of all the atrocities that have occurred. This is carried out under the heading of contemporary history, which is another of these clichés, since there is no such thing as contemporary history. There is only an ordinary history.

What is going on under the heading of contemporary history is a kind of exhibitionism with the emotional aim of an exoneration by means of a generous exhibiting of past atrocities—that is, through a mastering in the sense of the cliché, which means then that the unearthing of all that happened under National Socialism is by no means a mastering of the past. It is quite the contrary: the attempt not to master the present by always talking only of those things that have already happened and that cannot be changed anyway, whereas what should be changed is our attitude in the present. So the excessively detailed investigation of the past is one of the alibi procedures in order not to master the present because one blames the past with the guilt one really should deal with in the present.

The other method is the rejection of a collective guilt for the past, again with the ulterior motive of refusing to master the present: One is not responsible for what happened in the past but is, however, by no means prepared to do what one should do in order to master the present. Now, what is this present, which must be mastered here?

I have given this course of lectures the title "Hitler and the Germans" and specifically not "On National Socialism," for, as I have just said, great mischief is being done with the portrayal of the historical details of National Socialism. You can consider the ideology of impartial historicism as one of the methods by which one shirks responsibility. The cliché of National Socialism, which indeed was a political movement that gave itself a name but was not a concept of political science, becomes an instrument for concealing the problem. What we have to deal with is not the National Socialists and their heinous crimes, nor the atrocities, not the unearthing of the past, nor the justified indignation of the victims—these are all phenomena situated in the continuity and causality of history; but our problem is the spiritual condition of a society in which the National Socialists could come into power. So it is not the National Socialists who are the problem but the Germans, among whom personalities of the National Socialist type can become socially representative and can function as representatives, as politicians, as Reich chancellors, etc.

For National Socialism is indeed preceded by a society in which it came into power, and the spiritual condition of a society in which National Socialism came into power is not offset by the fact that a National Socialist government was militarily defeated. Rather, this situation remains after the military defeat, as it existed before. And if it should change, one must produce very convincing symptoms for such a change. You can appreciate that not all that much has changed when you take a look at what appears in the newspapers every day. Consider that we have a regime in the eastern zone that is not only a communist regime but is ruled by a unity party,[1] in which not only communists—who indeed are Germans too—but also the other parties happily participate.

And as for the Federal Republic, just think about what happened last Pentecost Sunday, when a federal minister called Seebohm[2] gave speeches to the effect that the 1938 treaty by which Hitler used political blackmail to gain the Sudetenland should still be in force now and that on this basis there exist German claims on the Sudetenland. Now naturally one could play the matter down and say that a man like Seebohm is already well known for his notorious stupidity and that the matter should not be taken so seriously. But after all, that a notoriously stupid man like Seebohm is a federal minister and is not chucked out after his Pentecost speech casts a very indicative light on the state of affairs in the Federal Republic.

With that, a general problem is touched on, which must be taken into account when judging the relation of the Germans to Hitler: Since the national unification under the Bismarck empire, German society moved politically in the shadow of power politics but was not itself politically active. The attempts at arriving at an independent national movement from 1848 foundered, and after that the more intelligent people withdrew from politics. The unification came about through Bismarck's power politics, and the first victim of this power politics was the nationalistic and chauvinistic deformation of liberalism in the Bismarck empire. After 1918, in the shadow of defeat, a democracy again developed, the Weimar republic, which also was unable to flourish. So in this shadow of defeat and threat from outside, again, a free society could not develop. When I say that it could not develop, I do not mean that in a causal sense, but that as a matter of fact it did not develop. Naturally it could have developed if the people had been a bit more intelligent than they were.

1. This refers to the Socialist Unity Party of Germany (*Sozialistische Einheitspartei Deutschlands*).

2. Hans-Christoph Seebohm (1903–67), leader of the German Party (*Deutsche Partei*), served as federal transport minister, 1949–66.

And now after the Second World War we have indeed a Federal Republic, but its cohesion stands in the shadow of the occupation by the American and Russian armies. Empirically, we have no knowledge of what a free Germany, in the sense of a Germany that gave itself a representation without being in the shadow of power politics, would look like. It is an unknown quantity. And I do not know what would happen if the shadow of this threatening power of the American and Russian armies were to disappear. No one can predict that today. So now, for judging the present, the following is to be considered: National Socialism belongs to the past, it is no danger, even when there are again and again National Socialist manifestations from the past, which disagreeably make themselves noticed. The old National Socialists are gradually dying out or no longer possess an all too disagreeable political importance.

Where now do the resistances to the so-called mastering of the past come from? Where does this willingness to shunt onto an alternative track—like acknowledging the guilt of the past without undertaking anything in the present—come from? These motives have to do with the contemptible nature of the events and with shame about lost dignity during the National Socialist period. To understand this problem, we must first go, in greater detail, into the question of the representation of a society and then into questions of authority.

By the representation of a society is to be understood that a society exists insofar as it can give representatives to itself who act responsibly for it. If these representatives are dubious individuals, as they were during the National Socialist period, then the society as a whole is contemptible. That means, it does not function rightly. What now is contemptible about it? There are various methods for characterizing this contemptible nature.

We can fall back on Justinian's conception of authority. Justinian formulated the authority of the ruler as resting on three factors. He must be the emperor, in order to maintain internal order and to defend the empire externally. That is the power factor as source of authority for the ruler. But second (I am still referring to Justinian), the ruler must be the *religiosissimus iuris,*[3] the man who administers

3. Voegelin is extrapolating from the proemium to the *Institutes of Justinian* with its invocation of Christ and its reference to political order as maintained both by the physical force of the emperor's armies and the moral force of his being *religiosissimus*

the law with religious conscientiousness, whereby "law" is understood as law in the classical sense, that is, the justice of action in society—that is to say, substantial justice, not the content of positive law, which can be extremely unjust. That is the [second] source: reason. This formulation always has its origin in *justitia,* that is, an intellectual virtue, and in the *ius,* as a practical virtue of the ruler's. The third source of authority is the spirit—for Justinian, in the form of revelation—and the ruler must be the *defensor fidei,* the defender of the faith. Power, reason, and spirit are the three sources of authority that have become historically differentiated as such.

In my investigations in *The New Science of Politics* I introduced a somewhat different terminology to deal with the same problem. I spoke there of existential and of transcendental representation.[4] That meant that every ruler of a society represents in a twofold manner.

First—this would be the power factor in Justinian—he must existentially be the ruler; that is, the society depends for its existence on there being a representative who is able to act for it in both internal and external matters. Second, the qualities of this representative then further depend on the degree to which he represents the transcendent order of the divine, whether that of reason or of spirit. And now it is possible that power and transcendental representation, existential representation and reason and spirit, fall apart, that a society finds itself in a condition in which it can indeed produce an existential representative of the highest effectiveness, who at the same time represents neither reason nor spirit. That is the problem of Hitler.[5] Here one can formulate it precisely. From this classification of the sources of authority there arise three propositions, which are in contradiction with one another. Still from this very contradictoriness there arise the resistances against the mastering. The first proposition runs like this: Whoever has the power to shake the world, as Hitler did, is not contemptible.

---

iuris, most solicitous with regard to the law. See J. A. C. Thomas, *The Institutes of Justinian* (Amsterdam: North-Holland, 1975), 1.

4. See Eric Voegelin, *The New Science of Politics: An Introduction* (1953; Chicago: University of Chicago Press, 1987), 37, 49–50, 75.

5. See *The Nature of the Law and Related Legal Writings,* ed. Robert Anthony Pascal, James Lee Babin, and John William Corrington, vol. 27 of *The Collected Works of Eric Voegelin* (1991; available Columbia: University of Missouri Press, 1999), 55, 68–69.

Power is a true source of authority. Sometimes that is not willingly admitted or on the contrary is persistently maintained. The second proposition: Whoever shakes the world, even though or because he is irrational, is contemptible. And the third, the most painful of these propositions: A world that allows itself to be shaken by an irrational man is contemptible. The contradictoriness of these three propositions determines the emotional conflicts.

The first consequence of this contradictoriness is what I then called the Buttermelcher Syndrome—that is, that all who cooperated would have to admit that if the man was rationally and spiritually contemptible then they too were contemptible. If he were criminal and crazy then they too were stupid, criminal, and crazy. They do not willingly admit that, particularly not because it concerns indeed the entire representative level of German society: the poets and thinkers, the philosophers and writers, the pastors and professors, the industrial leaders and prelates, the politicians and diplomats, the judges and civil servants, and, not least, the generals. That means that all among the German élites were involved in the criminality and stupidity of the National Socialist regime and are burdened with this involvement up to today; for those people are indeed still alive and do not want to admit that what happened was criminal and mad, because then they too would have to admit that they themselves are criminals and madmen. That is the first consequence of what we called the Buttermelcher Syndrome.

The second point is the one to pay attention to. Precisely because of this resistance one shrinks from admitting that Hitler arrived at an eminent achievement in world history: By the success of his contemptibility he has unambiguously proved the contemptibility of the world in which he had success. That is an eminent achievement. No pessimistic cultural criticism could prove so clearly that the German society, and up to a certain degree also the surrounding Western democracies, have begun to rot spiritually and rationally in such a way that they are taken in by a man like Hitler and make possible his success. At the core, naturally, there remains the German problem. Hitler was himself always surprised at his success. Not that he was of the opinion that he was contemptible and that therefore the others were contemptible, too, when they were taken in by him. But he was always surprised at the fact that inside Germany, as well as in the external relations of the first years of the regime, everything worked out even when he did and desired the most fantastic things. And on the other hand, these lucky circumstances had again favored Hitler's success to such a high degree because he was always reinforced in his belief that he was right when all yielded to him—whether it was the remilitarization of the Rhineland, or at home the pastors and generals, etc.

These instances of caving in to irrationality and spiritlessness formed Hitler's own well-documented attitude toward Germans and foreigners; he saw through their contemptibility and unambiguously made it manifest. Hence, for example, Hitler's table talks, which we must discuss the next time, are of extraordinary interest, because they reveal in a completely open way his contempt for the people he had to deal with. Empirically, these manifestations of contempt matched the social reality. That is why Hitler's remarks on this very point are of the highest value in a critical analysis of the period; and it is just for that reason that they are not welcome. From that there now arises a task for us, which is precisely not to allow this achievement of Hitler's to be lost but to make conscious the contemptibility that he highlighted, the contemptibility of the others, to describe it exactly in precise detail and to know it, in order to prevent oneself in the future from becoming as contemptible as the people Hitler dealt with and to whom he owed his success.

And that is the mastering of the present that you are called to and that one cannot escape by taking up the atrocities of the past. For what is at issue, I emphasize once again, is not that atrocities were committed. What is at issue is, not the horrors, but the men who cooperated in these things and their spiritual structure, which up to now has not changed in a convincing way. Now, how do we get hold of the matter? What are the categories by which we must deal with the problem? I have already spoken quite often of the political clichés. Let us approach these clichés systematically.

§7. Clichés of "State" and "Democracy"

First, the cliché of the state and of democracy, a cliché that must be removed if we wish to get hold of any kind of political problem at all. "The state" has had a quite particular meaning in Germany since the Romantic period, and particularly through Hegel's philosophy of law and of the state. I will therefore quote the key passage from Hegel's *Philosophy of Law* in which the state is defined, so that you may see how one cannot and should not carry out political science. This is what §257 says:

> The state is the actuality of the ethical Idea. It is ethical mind *qua* the substantial will manifest and revealed to itself, knowing and thinking itself, accomplishing what it knows and in so far as it knows it. The state exists immediately in custom, mediately in individual self-consciousness, knowledge, and activity, while self-consciousness in virtue of its sentiment towards the state finds in the state, as its essence and the end and product of its activity, its substantive freedom.

And then still another sentence from the following paragraph:

> The state is absolutely rational inasmuch as it is the actuality of the substantial will which it possesses in the particular self-consciousness once that consciousness has been raised to consciousness of its universality. This substantial unity is an absolute unmoved end in itself, in which freedom comes into its supreme right. On the other hand this final end has supreme right against the individual, whose supreme duty is to be a member of the state.[6]

Now in no way do I intend to dispute that these sentences make good sense within the Hegelian gnosis. And if one is a professional Hegelian, one may be edified by them. But what we in politics wish to know is whether Mr. Minister X understands his business, whether he has initiative, whether he is informed, whether he steals more than is absolutely necessary, whether he lies more than is publicly beneficial, and so on, but not that the state is the reality of the moral idea. That is completely uninteresting in politics. So in politics we have to do with human things, and if in place of the men who are the representatives we put the state as cliché in this way, as Hegel does here, then we have already got completely away from political reflection. . . .

The second of these clichés is democracy. Here we must go into more detail. One can do nothing at all with a textbook definition of democracy, which again is only a cliché. It is no use to you to know that there are three forms of government, a monarchy, an aristocracy, and a democracy, and that in a monarchy one is at the head, that in an aristocracy several rule, and that in a democracy all rule. It is also no use to you if you know that in the democracy

6. Georg W. F. Hegel, *Philosophy of Right,* trans. T. M. Knox (New York: Oxford University Press, 1967), 155–56.

the people rules and that there is the great principle of popular sovereignty. All of that is of no use at all for a human understanding of democracy. One must draw upon other definitions of democracy, which are not intended as definitions in the textbook sense but as empirical observations of intelligent human beings.

I will now give three such definitions. The first is from George Santayana, the American philosopher: Democracy is the unrealizable dream of a society of patrician plebeians.[7] If men were all patricians, which however they are not, then a democracy could work. But since the majority is made up of plebeians, the greatest objections can be raised against the practicability of a democracy.

You see that this definition is geared to the human problem, but it is no textbook definition. You cannot write it down and take it home as a dogma about democracy. But there are still other views on democracy that complement this one, without their thus being false. Churchill once defined democracy as the worst form of government with the exception of all the others.[8] All forms of government are bad, because they have to take account of the human factor of imperfection. Democracy is a wretched form of government simply for the reasons Santayana mentioned in the first definition. What is really needed is a society of patrician plebeians, and we do not have that. But we nevertheless have to put up with democracy, for the other forms of state are even worse. A third such definition is from the American humorist Mark Twain, whom I quote with particular fondness, since I am myself a member of the Mark Twain Society, just like Churchill. Mark Twain says democracy rests on three factors: "freedom of speech, freedom of conscience, and the prudence never to practice either of them."[9]

With that you now have an interpretation of the first definition by Santayana; for what matters here is that freedom of speech and freedom of conscience belong to the free society but that a democracy cannot work if its members have principles and want

7. Voegelin is summarizing the discussion on democracy in George Santayana, *The Life of Reason: Reason in Society* (New York: Scribners, 1936), 321–24.

8. The actual quotation is: "Indeed it has been said that democracy is the worst form of Government except all of those other forms that have been tried from time to time" (Winston Churchill, *W. S. Churchill: His Complete Speeches, 1897–1963*, vol. 7, ed. Robert Rhodes James [New York: Chelsea House Publishers, 1974], 7,566).

9. The actual quotation is: "It is by the grace of God that in our country we have those three unspeakably precious things: freedom of speech, freedom of conscience, and the prudence never to practice either of them" (Joseph R. Conlin, ed., *The Morrow Book of Quotations in American History* [New York: McMorrow, 1984], 294).

to realize them. This insight of Mark Twain is a commonplace of democratic politics that you can read in every English or American textbook of politics.

Every society that works, a society of patricians, is based on courtesy, on compromises, on concession to the other people. Whoever has a fixed idea and wants this to be carried into effect, that is to say, whoever interprets freedom of speech and freedom of conscience to the effect that the society should behave in the way that he considers right, is not qualified to be citizen of a democracy. The political interplay of every society, of every patrician and functioning society, is patrician. It is based on the fact that one thinks a lot about what the others do, but does not say it; that one is always aware that in the society there is more than one good to achieve, not only the good of freedom, but also the good of security, the good of welfare, and that if I specialize in one or other of these goods, I could thereby bring the whole society into disorder, because I could destroy the balance between the realization of goods on which the society is based. I could even destroy it if I kept advocating the good that is my hobbyhorse and I want to get accepted and realized at this time and if I continually forced it on the others, for they will then become recalcitrant and pigheaded. That is the problem that Aristotle treated under the heading of *stasis.*[10] If I harden myself with a particular idea and pursue only this goal, this one good, then in reaction there arises the counterstasis, the counterhardening, and with this the impossibility of social cooperation. Now we are excellently equipped with freedom of speech and freedom of conscience in this Federal Republic, but with respect to the third factor that Mark Twain emphasized, the wisdom or cleverness not to make unconditional use of these rights, there is still an ominous shortage. And a democracy will not function as long as there is a lack of this wisdom.

§8. Philosophical and Biblical Understanding of Humanity and of Radical Stupidity

In the series of definitions of democracy I have just given you, I have focused on the question of being human or of not being human. Now we must become clear about a number of concepts: first, What is

10. See Eric Voegelin, *Plato and Aristotle,* vol. 3 of *Order and History* (1957; available Columbia: University of Missouri Press, 1999), 322, 349.

man? and second, What are the symptoms of the falling down and the derailment of man? For they all play a big role in the decline of a society and made it possible for a type like Hitler to come to the top. The idea of man is not a question of arbitrary definitions; rather, man is discovered in quite specific historic places and in quite concrete situations. We have two such points where what man is was experienced, and from the experience of man in the concrete case, the idea of man was then generalized as binding on all men. I say this as a methodological introduction, so that you do not come up with the objection that man can be defined in one or the other way, and that human nature may be such and such but that it changes, and so on.

We are dealing here with strictly empirical questions: When was man as such discovered? and What was he discovered to be? These discoveries have taken place respectively in the Hellenic and in the Israelite societies. In the Hellenic society, man was experienced by the philosophers of the classical period as a being who is constituted by the *nous*, by reason. In the Israelite society man is experienced as the being to whom God speaks his word, that is, as a pneumatic being who is open to God's word. Reason and spirit are the two modes of constitution of man, which were generalized as the idea of man. We have not gone beyond these contents of the idea of man, that is, his constitution by reason and spirit. That seems to be the definitive discovery.

What does it mean to exist as constituted by reason and spirit? The experiences of reason and spirit agree on the point that man experiences himself as a being who does not exist from himself. He exists in an already given world. This world itself exists by reason of a mystery, and the name for the mystery, for the cause of this being of the world, of which man is a component, is referred to as "God." So, dependence of existence (*Dasein*) on the divine causation of existence (*Existenz*) has remained the basic question of philosophy up to today.

This was formulated by Leibniz in the classic proposition that metaphysics has to deal with two questions: Why is there something, why not nothing? and the second question, Why is the something as it is? These why-questions place at the beginning of all reflections on man what we can call, with a classic philosophical expression, the etiological problem of the existence of man and world. There is a ground of being in the sense of a first cause, a *prima causa* or a *proton aition,* to which we remain in relation philosophically through the seeking, the *zetema* in the Platonic sense, and pneumatically through hearing the word in the sense of revelation.

In both manners, through the seeking for the divine, the loving reaching out beyond ourselves toward the divine in the philosophical experience and the loving encounter through the word in the pneumatic experience, man participates in the divine. The concepts are *methexis* in Greek, *participatio* in Latin, participation in the divine. Insofar as man shares in the divine, insofar, that is to say, as he can experience it, man is "theomorphic," in the Greek term, or the image of God, the *imago Dei,* in the pneumatic sphere. The specific dignity of man is based on this, on his nature as theomorphic, as in the form and in the image of God. This is a basic complex of ideas we must start out with in order to critically investigate the defection from this complex.

The defection at its core always takes the form of a loss of dignity. The loss of dignity comes about through the denial of the participation in the divine, that is, through the dedivinizing of man. But since it is precisely this participation in the divine, this being theomorphic, that essentially constitutes man, the dedivinizing is always followed by a dehumanizing. One cannot dedivinize oneself without dehumanizing oneself—with all the consequences of dehumanization that we shall still have to deal with. Such dedivinization is the consequence of a deliberate closing of oneself to the divine, whether to the rationally divine or the pneumatically divine, that is, the philosophical or the revelational divine. In both cases there occurs a loss of reality, insofar as this divine being, this ground of being, is indeed reality too; and if one closes oneself to this reality, one possesses in one's range of experience less of this part of reality, this decisive part that constitutes man.

In this sense we speak of a loss of reality. Please understand that I am now giving only a series of concepts; their application will follow. We must then employ them so that we understand what it is we are really speaking of. Thus we can speak of loss of reality through dedivinizing and dehumanizing. The typical manifestations of this loss of reality are that the reality of man is put in the place of the lost divine reality, which alone grounds the reality of man, so that in place of the ground of being as the cause of being, man as the cause of being advances to the point of exaggeration in the idea that man must be the creator of the world. We will later deal with this special German problem of rebellion, which has its roots in the Romantics. But I will here quote this one sentence of Novalis: "The world shall be as I wish it!"[11] There you already have in a nutshell the whole problem of Hitler, the central problem of the dedivinizing and dehumanizing. However, with that the phenomenology of the defection from full humanity is not experienced. This is a problem that has always occupied human beings. How are these defections to be classified? How do they appear?

Let us first take the classical attitude toward the question, that not all men are fully man in Aristotle's terms.[12] In the *Nicomachean Ethics* [1095b10–13] Aristotle falls back on Hesiod, that means, to the eighth century. For Hesiod, these insights still derive from what can be called commonsense experience. I will quote this passage from Hesiod, which Aristotle later develops. In the *Works and Days,* from verses 293 f., Hesiod classifies men into three groups: First, that man is the best, *pan aristos,* who himself considers or thinks through all things, who can advise himself, *noese:* The *nous* plays a part here. The second type is also good, an *esthlos,* who listens to the best, to the *pan aristos.* The one, however, who neither thinks, *noe,* nor listens is a useless man.

So here you already have three types of men: the man who is in full possession of the *nous* and can advise himself, where, by *nous,* is meant openness toward the divine ground of being; the one who, in case of doubt, has at least enough reason to listen to him who is in full possession of it; and the one who has neither the one nor the other and therefore is a useless fellow, who can also become a dangerous fellow.

The Aristotelian divisions follow this Hesiodian classification. The man in full possession of freedom is the man who has authority and lets himself be led by his own *nous,* by reason. Then there are the others, some who are still being educated, others who never get beyond certain educational levels, but at least are still approachable,

11. "Logologische Fragmente," Fragment 124, in Novalis [Friedrich von Hardenberg], *Schriften,* ed. Richard Samuel, Hans-Joachim Mähl, and Gerhard Schulz, vol. 2, *Das philosophische Werk I* (Darmstadt: Wissenschaftliche Buchgesellschaft, 1965), 554.

12. Voegelin discusses these texts in *The World of the Polis,* vol. 2 of *Order and History* (1957; available Columbia: University of Missouri Press, 1999), 140, and in *Plato and Aristotle,* 301–2.

insofar as they listen when a wiser man tells them what is right and what is wrong. And then there is the third class, which he called the slaves by nature. Now what are we doing with this classification? An expression such as the Aristotelian "slaves by nature" can hardly be used for our purposes, for we no longer have slavery as a formal legal institution. The Hesiodian expression of the useless man, the *achreios,* is not all that useful either. Aristotle's slave by nature and Hesiod's useless man belong—the latter at least partly—to a kind of social substratum, while our problem is that the useless man exists at all levels of society up to its highest ranks, including pastors, prelates, generals, industrialists, and so on.

So I would suggest the neutral expression "rabble" for this. There are men who are rabble in the sense that they neither have the authority of spirit or of reason, nor are they able to respond to reason or spirit, if it emerges advising or reminding them. Here we again approach the Buttermelcher Syndrome: that it is extremely difficult to understand that the élite of a society can consist of a rabble. But it really does consist of a rabble.

That of course is only the division derived from classical politics. We must now supplement this division—of those who have human authority, those who can follow authority, and rabble—with a whole series of other phenomena belonging specifically to the German National Socialist period. These phenomena are:

First, the stupidity that we have already repeatedly adduced. Stupidity shall mean here that a man, because of his loss of reality, is not in a position to rightly orient his action in the world, in which he lives. So when the central organ for guiding his action, his theomorphic nature and openness toward reason and spirit, has ceased functioning, then man will act stupidly. You will remember that Professor Besson spoke of Hitler as an idiot, and I said that that is not entirely unjustified, if one understands by "idiot" the *stultus* in the technical sense.

This phenomenon was always recognized in ancient civilizations. The fool, in Hebrew the *nabal,* who because of his folly, *nebala,* creates disorder in the society, is the man who is not a believer, in the Israelite terms of revelation. The *amathes,* the irrationally ignorant man, is for Plato the man who just does not have the authority of reason or who cannot bow to it. The *stultus* for Thomas is the fool, in the same sense as the *amathia* of Plato and the *nebala* of the Israelite prophets. This *stultus* now has suffered loss of reality and acts on the basis of a defective image of reality and thereby creates disorder. For the moment, that is all on the question of stupidity. We will have more to say about it later.

A second point is closely connected with this stupidity: If I have lost certain sectors of reality from my range of experience, I will also be lacking the language for appropriately characterizing them. That means that parallel to the loss of reality and to stupidity there is always the phenomenon of illiteracy.

In statistics we speak of illiterates as persons who cannot read or write. And the word has this meaning in other languages, too. But in English, better than in German, we have worked out that a man can possibly read and write at the primary school level but still may be a totally stupid guy who cannot express himself with regard to very wide ranges of reality, especially matters of reason and the spirit, and is incapable of understanding them. Such a man is an illiterate. The question is now, can one simply introduce the word "illiteracy" into German as *Illiteratentum*? I would hesitate to do so and would rather use the established German word *Analphabetentum*, extending this expression *Analphabet* to stupidity and to the deficient command of language through loss of reality, in terms of the English meaning of "illiteracy." So there is illiteracy among people who are able to read and write very well, but who, as soon as it is a matter of understanding a problem of reason or of spirit, or questions about right action, of justice, are completely uncomprehending, because they do not get it. There the loss of reality can be noticed, which then also expresses itself in the deficient command of language.

There is also the very interesting case of Aldous Huxley, who expressly speaks of people who can read and write as the "Alphas" and "Betas."[13] They know the alphabet, but that is all. In Germany, in contrast to other Western societies, illiteracy—in this sense of the deficient command of language for the fields centrally important for action—runs through the élite. Not in the sense that all of the élite are illiterate—there are also in Germany very cultured people who have command of the German language; but the socially dominant popular literature that appears in public, including that by certain

13. See Aldous Huxley, *Brave New World* (London: Granada, 1983), passim, on "Alphas" and "Betas," the most intelligent of the still thoroughly controlled operatives in Huxley's anti-Utopian novel, as contrasted with "Epsilons," the selectively bred proletariat, suitable only for manual labor.

professors, is written by illiterates. In the next lecture, I shall give you a detailed analysis of illiteracy in Schramm's case.

§9. Karl Kraus's *Dritte Walpurgisnacht* on Lies and Propaganda

But now the actual experiences. I would like to quote a few passages from Karl Kraus's *Die Dritte Walpurgisnacht,* which has for us the extraordinary advantage that it was written in the year 1933, immediately after the Nazi seizure of power.[14] It shows you what a man of reason and spirit already knew at that time about National Socialism just from reading the newspapers.

I want to unmask the whole alibi swindle: that of course at that time, one could not yet know. One could, if one were intelligent enough. Whoever was stupid and had suffered loss of reality, naturally, could not know it. So, examples from *Die Dritte Walpurgisnacht.*[15]

> National Socialist thought fascinates through its capacity to make the one who tells the truth once credible for all future lies, and the theft, which for once he has not committed, to become the alibi for a thousand murders.[16]

Here the expression "alibi" emerges. We will later have to deal with the alibi in greater detail. That refers to Goebbel's well-known mischief, for example in spreading propaganda lies, throughout the world, that this or that has happened, in order to issue a denial of it two days later. Then one can see that people are always telling lies about the good National Socialists. Just like the uncommitted theft as alibi for the thousand murders.

> Who knows, perhaps even seeing that case would not be a hindrance for its confirmation. But often for finding out the truth the radio is enough. For me, for example, who heard a broadcast of "an informal conversation with people held in protective custody," who

14. Karl Kraus (1874–1936), Austrian critic and poet, edited and almost singlehandedly wrote the satirical magazine *Die Fackel* (*The Torch*) from 1899 to 1936. He composed an epic tragedy on the First World War, *The Last Days of Mankind* (1923). His work may be seen as an immense labor of creative recovery, both of the experience of reality and its linguistic expression, from ideological unreality.

15. Karl Kraus, *Dritte Walpurgisnacht* (Frankfurt: Suhrkamp, 1989). This latest edition, used here, reverts to Kraus's original title; Voegelin uses the title of the first, posthumous edition of 1952, *Die Dritte Walpurgisnacht.*

16. Kraus, *Dritte Walpurgisnacht,* 228.

personally gave all the information desired. It was a broadcast that was truly so entitled and already because of that was counteracting the suspicion of being something obtained by force. "In defense of the lies spread abroad," there were conversations between the police superintendent—a man who unmistakably had just attained the whip hand, with which he rhythmically distributed blows—a representative of the press office, and genuine, in no way acting, prisoners, most of them former ministers of the Baden Government, on whom, as it would be convincingly established in front of the ears of millions,

external traces of injury were *not detected.*

The prisoners—defenseless as the listeners, comrades in suffering of the prisoners, who up to then had been physically examined merely on behalf of readers—answered in turn that they had nothing to complain about, a formula as stereotyped as the state radio's addressing [its listeners] with "November greatness"[17] and the use of the title "the Jew X." The direction was not always completely successful and sometimes the answer had to be rather forcefully produced, so that one could hear the direction being administered. In the last dialogue a failure could be detected, followed by a terrible break in the sound, not caused by the airwaves, and after this a stammering by the interviewer, whose manner of speaking up to then was recognizable as professionally illiterate. That unfortunate prisoner, when asked whether he had been mistreated, as the lying propaganda had asserted, had broken out with sobbing words:

No, no one cut my ears off—but my existence—has been annihilated—

The informal conversation seemed suddenly broken off. However, afflicted with all the deficiencies of improvisation, it was repeated on records; and it was just this replaying that I heard. It exceeded all power of comprehension, as plan and deed, but before everything else, as the thought that such a horror, such monstrous propaganda should indeed function as a refutation, and one can only stagger at this attempt to persuade the mass mind through a godforsaken voice, whether such speculation was just satanically shameless or even immeasurably stupid.[18]

That now is one of the passages. May I add that in the '30s there was a saying, in constant use, that the National Socialists had never touched a hair on anyone. No one ever had a hair touched. But that is about the only thing that they did not do. And now another continuation of this passage:

17. Kraus says "*Novembergröße,*" possibly referring to the "heroes" of the November 1923 Munich putsch.

18. Kraus, *Dritte Walpurgisnacht,* 228–29. Indentations in citations from *Dritte Walpurgisnacht* indicate Kraus's quotation from contemporary media reports. Emphases are Kraus's own.

> A demon hunts these rulers from one false move to another. And through such clarification there has really occurred a change in the foreign propaganda they fought against. It does not seize upon the horror itself any more but upon this clarification, and the clarification does not let a single prominent spokesperson escape without their reestablishing the prejudice they are eradicating root and branch. By doing so it relies on the assurance given on the radio that they are the "standard-bearers of the truth," which has just now made a breakthrough. Today, as the proverb says, a man's speech means two things, which is why one must listen to both. And truly, as far as the German forked-tongue resounds, the listening world is convinced even more than is required. But Frank II,[19] who has this title already and who shouted this conviction:
>
> > National Socialism declares its support for the thought of mankind!
>
> deserves his *altera pars* to be heard too, by further continuing:
>
> > All Jews must completely clear out of every form of legal life![20]

So you find here the critical point in a very peculiar phenomenon of National Socialism, a propaganda that wishes to refute horror by continually producing new horrors. It is not all that easy to analyze. Here we are returning in detail to stupidity and illiteracy. A second case:

> The world was surprised at the people: [*please note, all 1933*] no wonder that the people were surprised at the world. If it confronted the culprits with the deed, they opened their children-eyes wide like the wolf listening to the fairy tale about the wolf. For what bad they did was done with such good intentions, and they cannot understand why they are so seriously misjudged. Despite the danger of appearing disloyal to their creed, whose slogan "Jew croak!" [*Juda verrecke!*] was at least interpreted as a wish, they protested that nothing of the sort had happened.[21]

You will not understand the allusion. The *Juda verrecke!* was at that time always written as I am saying it, without a comma between the words. So, a grammatical mistake. If *verrecke* were to be the imperative, then there would have to be a comma after *Juda.* Otherwise, indeed, it would be only a wish and not an imperative.[22]

19. Kraus is referring to Hans Frank, Bavarian justice minister and later Reichsminister and governor general in Poland.

20. Kraus, *Dritte Walpurgisnacht,* 230.

21. Ibid., 183.

22. Here Voegelin is summarizing Kraus, *Dritte Walpurgisnacht,* 125.

> It was a lie; now they are telling the truth. Certainly, it must be a misunderstanding, and perhaps it would be removed through the knowledge that here speaks with boundless openness a being which by nature is not bad, only with specific sensory tools performing and taking responsibility for what it does. That the comrade (*Volksgenosse*) does not believe the things he maybe just hears about may still be explained through the barrier that has proved necessary in the vicissitudes of life's circumstances. However, that he also does not believe the things he sees, indeed not even the things he does: that he does not know what he does and therefore immediately forgives himself, that testifies to a soul without falsity, which those differently constituted should well avoid but not mistrust. For his was the gift of not being able to lie, and because it would still also be impossible to lie as much as the actual situation would require, the ability of a medium must be in play, which helps such beings to come to terms through illusion with the things created by illusion.[23]

So again you see the extremely complicated psychological problems that we must later grasp with more conceptual accuracy than they are grasped in this language. And in conclusion just this passage here:

> And then again this touching inconsistency, not only in the guidelines but also in their observance: when, for example, a Jew is beaten on the Spandauer Bridge because he did not salute the flag, and another Jew in Neue Friedrichstrasse is beaten because through his salute he insulted the German character. What is consistent is only the amazement that no matter what one does, it is not right. An SA man beats up someone in another country too:
>
>> The culprit was immediately taken hold of and put into prison. When the police arrested him he was *absolutely astonished,* since, after all, he had *behaved no differently from what was usual in Germany.*[24]

We will come back to this point again.

Now we must speak of the *Rechtsstaat,* because since 1950 we have had a series of German legal judgments, according to which various concentration camp murderers and the like were excused on the grounds that under the given conditions of German society it was not possible for a man to recognize a crime as a crime. After the war, now, German courts!

> At home, diplomats are beaten and asked "what they as foreigners were doing in Germany." It is motivated by emotional drives, not

23. Ibid., 183–84.
24. Ibid., 184.

> planned. Indeed it would be a primitive psychology to imply that the dream life, which shifts the standards, is calculating. [*Now you see the consequences of the loss of reality that are characterized here.*] Through the whole series of apparitions that turned up like that, from the Reichstag fire to Rosenberg's and Habicht's successful missions in the attempts to win over England and conquer Austria, every day left the impression of something strange rather than frightful, for the explanation of which nothing remained except: honesty.

We shall also have to investigate this question of honesty. How does a man bring himself to commit crimes, and at the same time dispute he ever committed them, and still be honest? An extremely interesting psychological condition.

> If the surrounding world, which remembers the Armenian atrocities it could have intervened against, takes offense at tortures, whose thinking up required far more fantasy than would have been necessary for imputing them [to the Germans], it now gets to hear:
>
>> Believe us, *such lack of understanding* that *our measures* sometimes meet *saddens us all.*
>
> They don't mean it like this; but always otherwise. They feel it as a violation if they are thought capable of the actions they commit. Then they usually describe such actions as "alleged," a brief but good formula for the decision absolutely never to get involved in such matters, a formula that stems from the indisputability of a political morality based on telling tales about things that never happened. In order to give the incompetent a function, the pickpockets accuse the former functionaries of being materialistic. And by preferring a transfer into the concentration camps to a conviction in court, the suspicion will have hardened that just as the former functionary was capable of filling that post, he was capable of anything. So the alleged becomes real and the real alleged, and exactly that is the meaning of the great breakthrough to the "new civilizational type" [*another concept we will have to speak about. Gottfried Benn*[25] *has brought it out in a very interesting way, and also Heidegger.*], which literati make available: that the murderer, if he lies about it enough, has not murdered and that the cowardice of the murder bestows on him the stature of a hero. It is the principal camouflage that occurs by means of the little word "alleged," which we will see cropping up again and again in the commentary on the events. The world of course has known for a long time that there is horror, whose smell reaches

25. Gottfried Benn (1886–1956) was a medical doctor and writer in Berlin who showed a short-lived sympathy for National Socialism in 1933–34, then became its disgusted opponent. In 1938 further publication by him was prohibited. He was awarded the Georg-Büchner prize, the Federal Republic of Germany's highest literary award, in 1951.

> heaven, and puts up with this knowledge. But it obviously enjoys the spectacle of a moralistic endurance too, which even today offers it "alleged horror" without receiving the answer: Enough! Get away! Off the planet![26]

So these are the exciting propositions and the immediate reaction to them, and I ask you to notice that. Immediate reaction. Those are the experiential facts we must now analyze conceptually in selected examples. So, next time, something further on stupidity and illiteracy, and then the analysis of Schramm.

(Third Lecture)

Ladies and Gentlemen,
Let me remind you briefly where we stopped the last time. In relation to the problems of the unmastered past, of collective guilt and related clichés, I dealt with the general political clichés of the state and of democracy and with the problem of man: what constitutes a man and what is the problem of dehumanization, which always occurs when the constitution of man, that is, his attachment to God, is undone through resistance, resulting in dedivinization. The dedivinization and the dehumanization of man belong together.

I then said that this categorizing of dehumanization and dedivinization is, however, insufficient for grasping the problems as they occur in social reality. And therefore thinkers in the various political cultures have again and again, on the basis of the current situation, concerned themselves with classifying more concretely the development of disturbances of personality and consequently of social order. Thus, I dealt first with the Aristotelian classification, in which all men are the same in potency but not in actuality, so that one has three types: the man who has full authority, full stature, because he lives in the openness of reason and the spirit; the one who is not so adequate but still heeds authority; and the third type, who neither masters himself nor is himself an authority, nor even heeds the authority of others.

With the naming of this third type we had a certain difficulty, because the older types are still so bound to social classes that in contrast to the full man, the *spoudaios*, Aristotle described the ethically undeveloped man of the lowest level as the slave by nature.

26. Kraus, *Dritte Walpurgisnacht*, 185–86.

Today, that is no longer possible, for two reasons. The first is because Aristotle understands "slaves" to be by nature a lower class, while in the modern conditions of personal and social disturbances of order it is precisely not the lower classes who are the most essentially disturbing factor, but the élites. So we cannot with good conscience speak of the people or the lower classes, when the problem applies precisely to the upper classes. And second, we cannot properly call them slaves, because the legal institution of slavery no longer has any meaning in the modern context. We do not have it. We must refer, rather, to this general atrophy of man with the relatively neutral expression of "rabble," which penetrates right through all social levels and functions.

In connection with this Aristotelian vision, I then drew attention to the fact that there are further problems of characterization that were dealt with and discussed a first, general characterization of the pair stupidity and illiteracy. In the general characterization, I said that stupidity had to do with the loss of reality, where this loss referred to determinate sectors of reality, for example, the relationship of man to God. To this loss there also corresponds a loss of the linguistic expression for the description and treatment of this sector of reality, so that distortions in the representation of reality occur.

I can expand the linguistic failure from this spiritual sphere to all other spheres. This is what can be called spiritual illiteracy, caused by the loss of contact with determinate sectors of reality, again giving rise to stupidity in thinking and in action. As instances of such stupidity and illiteracy I gave you the very agitating experiences immediately after the National Socialist seizure of power in 1933 and read out some examples from *Die Dritte Walpurgisnacht* by Karl Kraus. Now, all the terms we must operate with occur in these passages—terms like "stupidity," "astounding honesty," "honesty" in the sense that the lie is not recognized as lie but honestly denied, "the lie" itself as opposed to the lie that is so compact that it is once again honesty, "inconsistency in argument," the various forms of "alibi," and also the expression "illiteracy." All these expressions occur, and I must now warn you not to slip into some kind of petit bourgeois ideas and assert or think that they are terms of abuse. They are not, but belong to the classic vocabulary and, in the continuation of the classic vocabulary, to the modern vocabulary of social analysis. Stupidity, ignorance, illiteracy, laziness, inertia, slothfulness of different kinds, and so on, are eminently important forces in the social process, and we must use those expressions to describe the structures of the social processes that are determined precisely through these factors. In classic philosophy we speak of irrationality, of *amathia;* in scholastic philosophy we speak correspondingly of *stultitia,* and further modifications of these vices. That is as far as we got the last time.

§10. Robert Musil on Simple and Intelligent Stupidity

And now we shall go into the modern concretizations. I will first present to you on the very interesting study by the novelist Robert Musil, who wrote, among other things, *The Man without Qualities.* It is an essay, "On Stupidity," which was given as a lecture in Vienna in 1937.[27] Here, our subject is being discussed: What is understood by stupidity, and what kinds of stupidity are there? The essay does not deal with all the kinds of stupidity. I will later have to go into kinds of stupidity other than those Musil dealt with here, but this is a very good point of departure.

Musil does not start talking about dehumanization and dedivinization, but begins with the commonsense sphere, first speaking of stupidity and defining it in the sense of psychopathology—for example, in the case of clinical stupidity, whether the man is still accountable or too stupid to carry out these tasks or to understand that, and so on. Stupidity can be defined in this sense. Musil took the definition from some psychological textbook that said, "We call 'stupid' behavior that does not carry out something for which all the conditions except the individual ones are given."[28] So, only the personal factor impedes the resolution of a task that would usually be regarded as resolvable in a social situation. Such incapacity to perform is stupidity. Every stupidity is therefore always related to the normality of a determinate social behavior. What in one society and one historical situation has to be considered as stupid, in another situation may perhaps be described as clever.

27. Robert Musil, "Über die Dummheit," in *Gesammelte Werke,* vol. 8, *Essays und Reden,* ed. Adolf Frisé (Hamburg: Rowohlt, 1978), 1,270–91. The translation used here is Robert Musil, "On Stupidity," in *Precision and Soul: Essays and Addresses,* trans. and ed. Burton Pike and David S. Luft (Chicago: University of Chicago Press, 1990), 268–86. See also David S. Luft, *Robert Musil and the Crisis of European Culture 1880–1942* (Berkeley: University of California Press, 1980), 283–86.

28. Musil, "On Stupidity," 284.

In a situation of disorder and chaos, qualities such as cunning, craftiness, and violence are indeed necessary in order to preserve one's life and to prevail, and whoever lacks them is incompetent and perhaps may perish. Under ordered conditions, however, precisely this craftiness, violence, misuse of trust, and so on, is a symptom of stupidity, because a man who behaves in this way will be socially boycotted. So, stupidity is always to be understood in relation to the social and historical context. The opposite of stupidity, then, would be the cleverness of the behavior in question, the performance, so that it would now arise that every type of performance had a type of stupidity corresponding to it. Thus one must differentiate stupidity according to the types of performance that are normally required in the society. One cannot speak of what is stupid in general, but there are stupidities, types of stupid behavior, that would correspond to the performances actually required by the situation.

However, can "stupidity" also, because it generally signifies an incompetence in performance, occasionally substitute for each differentiating word that should denote a particular kind of stupidity? Just as perhaps "vileness" is a general expression for moral violation, without going into the differentiations of the specific ethical violations. So we have wide-ranging expressions, along with the special expressions, for stupidity and vileness as violations of the capacity for performance and of morality.

The third variation in the meaning of "stupidity" is when "stupidity" is used as a term of abuse. If it is used as a term of abuse, then it is a matter of a panic situation, which is supposed to sweepingly make up for, so to speak, an outburst of angry abuse. There are conditions that we characterize by saying that "a person 'almost suffocates' on his anger," or "one is 'at a loss for words,'" or "one must 'gain breathing space,'" and then one begins to grumble in a general way: that is vile, that is stupid. So that would be the abusive intention. That would now be a condition of speechlessness and mindlessness, a violent outburst, and Musil characterizes this condition as "an oppressive condition of insufficiency." It is a kind of outburst into violence when one says, "'something has finally become just *too* stupid' for one to take"; for "this something" that has become too stupid for me and that gives rise to an act of violence, "this something is oneself."[29]

29. Ibid., 280.

So when stupidity occurs as an act of abuse and the differentiating articulation of the problematic is no longer mastered, then there appears a panic-like behavior in which it is precisely oneself who is stupid, because one no longer masters the situation, nor can articulate it. Musil adds—bear in mind that this was written in 1937—

> In periods when energetic, sweeping action is highly esteemed [*with clear eyes on the events in Germany*], it is essential to also be reminded of what sometimes resembles action to the point of being mistaken for it.[30]

So that means that the great energy, the taking of firm action, the forcefulness, is a panic-like failure in the face of reality, which is a form of stupidity.

Later investigations have taken up these insights of Musil, particularly the investigations into the denial of reality caused by the possession of worldviews or, in the extreme case, as expressed in fits of rage described by Doderer. We shall have to speak again in greater detail about Doderer, who especially in *Die Merowinger* has more closely pursued Musil's problem of stupidity as synonymous with the fit of rage and has chosen the literary form of the farce as the corresponding representational form for stupidity, which is equivalent to a failure in the face of reality. We shall also have to speak about this problem of the farce later, as National Socialism is no tragedy; for a tragedy can play only at the level of the spirit, not at the level of the undifferentiated fit of rage. At this level of vulgarity there is then only the farce, even if the farce is a bloody murderous farce. So, from a literary viewpoint, farce, not tragedy, would be the representational form that is appropriate for the National Socialist problematic.

By the way, Frisch also expressed a very decisive rejection of this problem of tragedy in his *Biedermann und die Brandstifter*. In that play the chorus recites this speech in classic choral form: "It is unworthy . . . to call an imbecility Fate simply because it has happened."[31] The word "imbecility" occurs also in Doderer, who on the last page of his book deals with this problem of imbecility through examples selected from Heidegger's works.[32]

30. Ibid.

31. Max Frisch, *Biedermann und die Brandstifter* (Frankfurt: Suhrkamp, 1958), 9. The translation used here, with slight modification, is from Max Frisch, *The Fire Raisers*, in *Three Plays*, trans. Michael Bullock (London: Methuen, 1962), 4.

32. Heimito von Doderer, *Die Merowinger oder Die totale Familie* (Munich: Deutscher Taschenbuch Verlag, 1981), 307.

Now further types. Musil distinguishes between the honorable, or simple, stupidity and the higher, or intelligent, stupidity. This is a very important distinction, as we will see in a moment. By "honorable" or "simple stupidity"[33] is meant what one could call a lack of understanding. One speaks of people who are slow on the uptake. Now simple people of this sort, who are completely honorable, possibly have valuable qualities such as loyalty, reliability, purity of feeling, good manners, and more of the same kind; and these virtues emerge unadulterated and give rise to the picture of a very attractive character, as Musil emphasizes. Later we will further qualify that by saying that they do so because the competition from other qualities of a higher order, like efficiency or ability, is lacking. So, with the simple man we are in a sphere of stupidity that is not immediately vicious but, on the contrary, can be possibly very attractive, indeed has a certain purity of appearance—but precisely because more complicating factors of this higher, spiritual sphere are completely lacking.

In contrast to this simple stupidity, we must now distinguish the higher, or intelligent, stupidity. I am still summarizing Musil. The higher stupidity, he says, "presumes to accomplishments to which it has no right."[34] So here comes the element of presumptuousness, of *hybris,* of spiritual arrogance. Higher, or intelligent, stupidity is a disturbance in the equilibrium of the spirit. The spirit now becomes the adversary, not the mind. It is not a defect of the mind as with simple people, but a defect of the spirit, a revolt against the spirit, which gives rise to saying or doing things against the spirit. Therefore this condition of higher stupidity is not a spiritual sickness in the sense of psychopathology, but something quite different. We need here an expression not used by Musil but available in German analyses of the matter since Schelling. Schelling already used the expression "pneumopathology" for spiritual disturbances of this kind.[35] This means the spirit is sick, not the soul in the sense of psychopathology: so, spiritual sicknesses, sickness of the spirit,

33. Musil, "On Stupidity," 282 (translating Musil's *schlichte* as "simple" rather than "straightforward" as in Pike and Luft).

34. Ibid., 283.

35. On this attribution, see Eric Voegelin, letter to Theo Broersen, February 24, 1976 (Eric Voegelin Papers, Hoover Institution Archives, box 8, file 44), in which he recalls encountering the term during his intensive Schelling studies thirty years earlier and writes that he is now unable to locate the passage: "I refer to it only, because I do not want to be accused by some Schelling scholar of having pinched the term without acknowledging its authorship."

pneumopathic conditions as opposed to psychopathic conditions. We will use this word more often, since Schramm, for example, whom I will have to speak about later, continually tries to shift certain problems into psychopathology. This is because he has not mastered or understood that they are, not problems of psychopathology, but problems of pneumopathology, which are very well known and have been treated in detail from Plato to Schelling and up to the present by Musil and Doderer. But Schramm does not know that.

Now, to characterize this higher stupidity, a passage from Musil:

> This higher stupidity is the real disease of culture (but to forestall misunderstanding: it is a sign of nonculture, of misculture, of culture that has come about in the wrong way, of disproportion between the material and the energy of culture) [*So, all these negations of genuine education.*] and to describe it is an almost infinite task. It reaches into the highest intellectual sphere. . . . Years ago I wrote about this form of stupidity that "there is absolutely no significant idea that stupidity would not know how to apply; stupidity is active in every direction, and can dress up in all the clothes of truth. Truth, on the other hand, has for every occasion only one dress and one path, and is always at a disadvantage" [*as opposed to this intellectual stupidity, of which the ideologies are the most flagrant examples*]. The stupidity this addresses is no mental illness [*he says once again*] yet it is most lethal; a dangerous disease of the mind that endangers life itself.[36]

§11. Carl Amery on Bourgeois "Propriety" as Secondary Virtue Eclipsing Primary Virtues

So far Musil. But we need still further concretizations, so for this purpose I am choosing some passages, which, probably unintentionally, directly continue Musil's discussion. I am drawing these passages from Carl Amery's book *Die Kapitulation oder deutscher Katholizismus heute,* 1963.[37] It does not immediately deal with the problems of Catholicism, for to characterize the problems of German Catholicism one must characterize those of the German spirit. And what is now said about the milieu refers to these problems.

36. Musil, "On Stupidity," 283–84.

37. Carl Amery, *Die Kapitulation oder deutscher Katholizismus heute* (Hamburg: Rowohlt, 1963). The translation by Edward Quinn, *Capitulation: The Lesson of German Catholicism* (New York: Herder and Herder, 1967), is used here.

This milieu is a general German problem, not a German Catholic problem. Amery says:

> The key word for the lower middle class system of virtues in Germany is *Anstand.* It is untranslatable, just like "decency" or *honnêteté,* and it is (at least today) still more ambiguous and more difficult to define than these key words of foreign or past systems of virtue. What is German *Anstand*?
>
> Let us first try to say what it was: It was the sum total of virtues adequate for the urban or rural middle class way of life. It included such things as [*Now comes the enumeration, which coincides with Musil's, as you will see. It included such things as*] honesty, diligence, cleanliness, punctuality, reliability in service; mistrust of all excess and all iridescence, ambiguity, ambivalence; obedience to authority.

So the well-behaved, upright citizen, who in Musil was the simple man, partly the simple stupid man too, who is in himself a quite sympathetic figure. Amery continues here, partly coinciding with Musil:

> It is not difficult to see that this system really emphasizes none of the primary Christian virtues: neither faith nor humility, neither charity nor asceticism, are written large in this system of *Anstand.*[38]

Now Amery here is geared to the Christian perspective. You could just as well say that none of the noetic virtues are present here either, the openness to the world, the philosophic openness, the *ratio,* and so on. None of these is to be found in the "propriety" (*Anstand*) of the bourgeois. He continues:

> Let us note again the virtues implied in the notion of *Anstand:* honesty, punctuality, cleanliness, dependability of service, diligence. It is not difficult to see that the whole lot can be called "secondary virtues": virtues, therefore, which do not imply any ends in themselves [*for the setting of goals is drawn from the sphere of reason and the spirit*], but must be assigned to determined goals, in order to be positive.[39]

Because when they are not determined by such goals, they could also be very negative. And he gives examples:

> I can appear punctually for service in the priest's house or in the Gestapo cellar; I can be fastidious in writing about the "final liquidation of the Jews" or in social welfare work; I can wash my hands

38. Ibid., 29–30.
39. Ibid., 31.

> after an honest day's work in the cornfield or after my activities in the crematorium of the concentration camp. Thus Himmler [*it is a famous passage of Himmler's, which will be cited quite often*] was able to boast of his murder-commandos [*they were the murder squads sent in to wipe out the Polish civilian population*], that they remained "decent" in the midst of their difficult tasks. Himmler, of course, is not exactly a crown witness for moral or ethical affairs, but this crazy little observation throws light on one twist to the method.[40]

To further clarify the matter perhaps, may I draw your attention to the fact that all of these things are obvious at the commonsense level. It is only in this peculiar petit bourgeois sphere of "propriety" that they will never be understood. It is obvious that if a big company were looking for a director, one might recommend for it someone who is industrious, punctual, in on time every morning and remains throughout the working day, who is diligent, can be relied upon, who keeps his promises, and so on. Still, all these thoroughly agreeable qualities naturally do not qualify the man to be the director of a big company but are the qualities one would value, perhaps, in a bank messenger, and the like. The danger now is always this, that when a society is in such disorder as German society was, that the bank-messenger type, in himself a thoroughly honorable and decent type, arrives at the top and wreaks havoc as the National Socialists did, like a Himmler, for example.

So the problematic is always in the structure of the society—how a society can be so organized that these peculiar kinds of simplicity and stupidity will not become politically effective, let alone become socially dominant and determine the society.

Rebellion also belongs to the negative qualities, which Amery is particularly interested in. The citizen is against disorder. You certainly know how the Scholl siblings came to their end, since, when they threw those leaflets down, a university porter pursued and caught them, not because he was a National Socialist, but because he felt disturbed that his clean assembly hall was messed up with scraps of paper. So, the people are against disorder. Amery says that

> rebellion can take on a material or an intellectual form—both are highly suspect to the bourgeois. Intellectual revolt, he feels, is bound to lead to the mockery and unmasking of what is near and dear to him. [*That is, to the loss of the social values of his milieu; for, at this level of secondary virtues, no great achievement can be accomplished*

40. Ibid.

> *in a society. So if anywhere there is an intellectual revolt against them, he feels that he is in danger, because he will, as a result, be ridiculed.*] Material revolt, however, may lead not only to scratches on the sideboard but to the loss of the thing itself. The rebel is the enemy absolutely speaking and any measure taken against him is *eo ipso* justified. The Soviet Republic in Munich in 1919 shot about a dozen victims; the white liberators several hundreds, guilty and innocent. I have still to discover a history book for young people in which this proportion is objectively estimated. [*A very interesting problem, how the petit bourgeois reacts, if he is disturbed in his comfortableness, by an idea, for example.*] People think the same way about the French Revolution, and even about any brawl in Schwabing or elsewhere. Resentment is directed first against the idea of revolt as a voluntary initiative (an act of violence without clear orders from superiors) [*That is a very important point. In general, where initiative is taken, whether of the intellectual or active type, the petit bourgeois goes wild.*] and, secondly, against the attack on virtues which experts anyway describe as "quality."[41]

So if one says about any of these low-quality romantic oleographs that that is what it is, then he becomes very angry, for the possession of such pictures is now part of the furnishing of the home and part of the culture. So here too you have concretized the more specific German case. It is the problem of the simple man, who is a decent man as long as the society as a whole is in order but who then goes wild, without knowing what he is doing, when disorder arises somewhere and the society is no longer holding together.

Nothing is as characteristic as one of the scenes that was played out in the course of the Auschwitz trial in Frankfurt, when one of the accused there who had mass murder on his conscience said, with genuine anger and indignation, that this was surely very long ago and that it was really mean that the evening of his life should now be soured. That is the citizen *par excellence.* A proper man, father of a family, punctual official, and so on, but, if he is not kept under control, a murderous beast.

§12. Criminal Stupidity and Loss of Experience of Reality in a Disordered Society

To these concretizations of stupidity by Musil and Amery I must now add one more, which is treated by neither of them, and that is

41. Ibid., 36–37.

the consequences of stupidity when they come to the surface in a disturbed society and become socially relevant. For under these circumstances stupidity can have those disorganizing consequences that we know from National Socialism. That is the point at which stupidity—because it harms not only the one who is stupid but also other human beings (in this case millions of human beings, who through it were brought into misery and were murdered)—must in this specific social circumstance be called criminal stupidity. That is to say, stupidity is not criminal in itself, but it can become criminal through social circumstance. So whoever as a stupid man, in a place in society where he has no business to be, gives orders or tries to instruct others is criminally stupid; and because of that he becomes a criminal, even if he himself does not understand this at all.

There is now a whole series of studies of this criminal stupidity, and you should really know them in detail. Every student of political science should read them. One of the older classic studies of criminal stupidity is Shakespeare's *King Lear.* That is an excellent study. Then from the '20s there is Meyrink's *Des deutschen Spießers Wunderhorn* (*The German Bourgeois' Enchanted Horn*). In it there is a study entitled "Tschitrakarna, the Refined Camel,"[42] where the refined camel gets involved with ordered legal procedures with the gangster animals in a due process of law. Because of that it is destroyed and then torn apart; then the raven, who is one of these gangster animals, cries, "Yoohoo, silly ass!"[43] You should remember this "yoohoo, silly ass" each time you think about the upright citizens who agreed with the Enabling Law[44] for Hitler. That was Meyrink.

A more recent study is the one I already mentioned by Frisch, *Biedermann und die Brandstifter.* So we have a whole series of studies of this phenomenon of criminal stupidity, which arises from the fact that the criminally stupid man brings misfortune not only on himself but on millions of other people too. For these functional consequences of his stupidity, determined by his social position, he is obviously fully responsible. There is a sentence I will continually

42. Gustav Meyrinck, "Tschitrakarna, das vornehme Kamel," in *Des deutschen Spießers Wunderhorn* (Munich: Albert Langen, 1913), 2:26–33.

43. Ibid., 33.

44. Bill passed on March 23, 1933, by the German Reichstag that enabled the German government for the period of four years to enact law without the consent of the parliament.

draw your attention to, as I have already done in many lectures: There is no right to be stupid. It is not one of the basic rights and freedoms guaranteed by the Constitution. Especially, of course, in modern times, where the consequences could be terrible.

And now I would like to treat the matter systematically, particularly the problem of the higher stupidity. So how are we getting hold of the concepts we must employ to grasp a phenomenon like Schramm, for example? We started from the loss of reality through dehumanization. There a sector of the reality—that is, of man's relation to God, his presence under divine being—is lost and replaced, deliberately (that is always a kind of revolt) by his will.

Now here one encounters a problem, that again we just do not have in modern German—in other languages we do—the expressions to differentiate between what "will" in the classical and Christian sense is, and what "will" in revolt against God is. In the classical and Christian sense, the will, the *voluntas,* is always and only the rationally ordered will. This means that wherever the power of existence (*Existenzmacht*) joins forces with reason and spirit, there is the "will." Where power of existence separates itself from reason and spirit, we do not speak of will, in the classic Christian vocabulary, but of *concupiscentia* or of *libido.* The expression "libido" has become very popular through psychoanalysis. But it is the general expression for existence-powerful desire that is not ordered by reason or spirit. A very large part of what is called German idealistic philosophy from Fichte up to the present must always be so understood that when the author in question speaks of will, one has to put in place of the word "will" the expression "libido." When Nietzsche speaks of the will to power, then he intends the libido; he is still aware of that. "Libido" is the Pascalian expression toward which he orients himself.

That is relevant for understanding Schramm's problem when he tries to characterize Hitler as a particularly strong-willed man. There is no willpower in Hitler at all. He had absolutely no will of any recognizable kind, that is, an existence that was ordered by reason or spirit. But he did have an extraordinarily existence-intensive libido, and he maintained this up to the end. He apparently was able to do so simply because any reasonable and spiritual order was radically absent in him, and there was, so to speak, no further possibility of escape for him. So, in Hitler a radical libido, which had fully separated itself from reason and spirit. Now, that is enough on the question of libido and the loss of reality through dehumanization; but the matter goes further than this.

Man remains man in full reality, even when he loses reason and spirit as those parts of reality that help him to order his existence; he does not cease to be man. And there is no point, as is still so often done, in accusing Hitler of inhumanity; it was absolute humanity in human form, only a most remarkably disordered, diseased humanity, a pneumopathological humanity. Such a man's image of reality, therefore, although defective, has not lost the form of reality; that is, he is still a man, with the full claim to make statements of order, even when the ordering force of orientation toward divine being has got lost—even then—except that he puts a pseudo-order in place of the real order. So reality and experience of reality are replaced by a false image of reality. The man, thus, no longer lives in reality, but in a false image of reality, which claims, however, to be the genuine reality. There are then, if this pneumopathic condition has occurred, two realities: the first reality, where the normally ordered man lives, and the second reality, in which the pneumatically disturbed man now lives and which thus comes into constant conflict with the first reality.

The expressions "first reality" and "second reality" were coined and worked out by Doderer and are to be found throughout all his writings. They were already used by Musil in his *Man without Qualities,* a man who also lives in the second reality and thus comes into conflict with the first. The consequence of living in the second reality is, exactly, conflict with the first reality, which indeed is not canceled by the fact that I make for myself a false idea of it and live according to it. Now the consequences of this conflict can be classified according to the two principal categories, contemplation and practice.

In contemplation, the most important manifestation of the conflict between second and first reality is the construction of a system. Since reality has not the character of a system, a system is always false; and if it claims to portray reality, it can only be maintained with the trickery of an intellectual swindle. I have already spoken on this matter with regard to the specific cases of Marx and Nietzsche,[45] but it is found wherever there is a system. Since this

45. See Eric Voegelin, *Science, Politics, and Gnosticism* (Chicago: Regnery, 1968), 22–40. Originally published as *Wissenschaft, Politik und Gnosis* (Munich: Kösel, 1959).

intellectual swindle is inherent in the conflict between second and first reality and in system construction, the will to swindle naturally originates here. The man is indeed pneumopathic, he is sick in spirit, and the matter can now become complicated by the fact that he is aware of this swindle, as is very clear, for example, in Nietzsche, who speaks explicitly about this problem. He constantly suffered from the fact that he swindled, because he knew what reality was from Pascal's case. The constant debate between Nietzsche and Pascal is stimulated precisely by his recognition of genuine reality in Pascal and his knowledge of himself as having a false idea of reality and that he constantly lived in this tension between the image of the swindle he is pursuing and the reality he admires in Pascal.[46]

In practice, the consequence of the conflict between second and first reality is, not the intellectual swindle, but the lie. The lie becomes the indispensable method because the second reality claims to be true, and since it constantly comes into conflict with the first reality, it is necessary to lie constantly: for example, one holds that the first reality is quite a different one from what it actually is, or that the second reality is most horribly misunderstood.

The result of this conflict of the lie in the practical sphere is the phenomenon of compact honesty at an intellectually less differentiated level. While on the intellectually more highly differentiated level of contemplation Marx or Nietzsche were still aware that they were swindling, there is no longer talk about swindling at the level of the swindling petit bourgeois. Instead he simply lies, and indeed with such a good conscience that he brings about this phenomenon of compact honesty and those other phenomena we saw the last time in those passages from Karl Kraus. So compact honesty is the result that so disconcerted Kraus—when these conflicts between second and first reality occur at a relatively low intellectual level.

46. Cf. Eric Voegelin, "Nietzsche and Pascal," *Nietzsche-Studien* 25 (1996): 128–71, included in *The Collected Works of Eric Voegelin,* vol. 25, *History of Political Ideas,* vol. VII, *The New Order and Last Orientation,* edited by Jürgen Gebhardt and Thomas Hollweck (Columbia: University of Missouri Press, 1999).

3

Descent into the Academic Abyss as Manifested by Schramm's "Anatomy of a Dictator"

§13. Schramm's Conceptual and Stylistic Incomprehension of Hitler

We must now turn to the work that was one of the causes of this series of lectures in this semester, Percy Schramm's introduction to his edition of *Hitlers Tischgespräche.*[1]

In the first lecture, in anticipation, I have already described the excitement it evoked, for example, in the *Süddeutsche Zeitung* and in other German newspapers, and the angry criticisms he received. The criticisms of Schramm are for the most part unfounded. Schramm is not a National Socialist and there is nothing in the entire work that can be attributed to a National Socialist attitude. There is no trickery of any sort displayed, no intentional playing down, no falsification of sources, no intentional suppression of any of Hitler's monstrous crimes, no deliberate glossing over of any mistakes, and so on, of National Socialism.

1. Schramm's "The Anatomy of a Dictator" was published as part of the introduction to Henry Picker's *Hitlers Tischgespräche im Führerhauptquartier 1941–1942,* ed. Percy Ernst Schramm (Stuttgart: Seewald Verlag, 1963). Along with another essay, Schramm's "Anatomy of a Dictator" was published as *Hitler: The Man and the Military Leader,* trans. and ed. Donald S. Detwiler (Chicago: Quadrangle Books, 1971), and is herein referred to as Schramm ET. Minor variationsj between Detwiler's translation and the original are here silently altered. However, because the essay no longer introduced the *Table Talks,* Detwiler omitted some of Schramm's introductory remarks commented on by Voegelin. In these cases our translation is from the original introduction to the *Tischgespräche* and is referred to as Schramm.

On the contrary, we find in the book valuable material from which a portrait of Hitler can be constructed. However, the impression the critics had of Schramm and the indignation he evoked are by no means unjustified. The question is, What are the grounds that evoked such a strange phenomenon that, with good reason, arouses indignation and can give the appearance of a playing down, of a whitewash, without being one? So, a very complex phenomenon, a phenomenon of the kind Karl Kraus treated in those passages I presented last time.

How can we tackle the matter now? Let us begin with the first sentence of Schramm's portrayal. The sentence reads:

> The content of the *Table Talks* shimmers so strongly that it is not possible to exhaust it.[2]

The sentence includes a serious error in style called a mixed metaphor in English—the first thing a college undergraduate in Oxford should not do. The first part of the sentence says that the content of the *Table Talks* shimmers; that is a metaphor. When a picture shimmers, for any reason, perhaps because there is too much hot air, then one cannot make it out exactly. The second part of the sentence asserts that it is not possible to exhaust the content. To exhaust the content means that the content is so rich that it cannot be exhausted. If the content shimmers, so that one cannot make it out, then one cannot exhaust it either. So if we now use the sentence corrected in this form—first, that these table talks shimmer, and second, that there is something there that cannot be exhausted—then the task of investigating Schramm shows itself as twofold. If the picture shimmers, then of course one cannot exhaust it, but one can precisely establish the reason why it shimmers.

That is the first task. If the shimmering phenomenon cannot be exhausted, it is not, indeed, because it continually shimmers and one can grasp nothing definite. The task is to establish the reason for the shimmering through the choice of specific cases. And what is important, and is the second task, is to establish this background, which can be fixed, while the shimmering picture is precisely not fixed and also cannot be exhausted.

Now how does one do that? Let us first deal with the general construction Schramm gives to his introduction. I am comparing

2. Schramm, 28.

the introductory programmatic explanations of his intention and the concluding summary of his results. There you will see why everything shimmers. One would have to analyze each sentence thoroughly, although I will do this in only one case, that is, the first sentence, so that you see what should be done with each sentence of this hundred-page-long introduction.

So, he begins his programmatic explanation:

> Whoever sets about reading the *Table Talks* unprepared must at first experience horror regarding the undisguised manner in which Hitler openly confesses his adherence to immoral principles from the height of his power.[3]

If we now analyze this sentence, which looks so very innocent and anti–National Socialist, what more can one say? In the first place, no one approaches the reading of the *Table Talks* unprepared, for all have already heard something about Hitler. Second, there is no logical reason why only the first reaction should be horror, but not also the second, third, or nth reactions, if one continues to read about this. Further, one will perhaps not be horrified at all about immoral principles, if one is not an old prude from the supreme command of the Wehrmacht like Schramm. Perhaps one will at most be astonished, although there is no reason for being astonished, for no one will expect that a man who perpetrates these unethical deeds has ethical principles on which these deeds are based. What then should he have but immoral principles? So no one will be astonished, no one will be horrified by the reading, because he already knows that if someone who perpetrates these deeds speaks about principles, then the principles will correspond to the deeds.

Further, there is the question—to consider the next element of the sentence—about what Hitler openly declares his support for from the height of his power. Obviously, Schramm—even if he does not intend to—seems somehow to imply here that if he had openly confessed his adherence to immoral principles not from the height of his power, then we would have been far less horrified about it. And further, it is very questionable whether the principles he openly declared his support for were immoral, for Hitler naturally regarded them as moral. That they are immoral is the interpretation of Schramm or of some other reader.

3. Ibid., 29.

In this formulation regarding acknowledged immoral principles, then, you have confusedly shoved in together Hitler's admission and Schramm's interpretation, so that neither of them is clear. Thus if one were to translate this sentence into ordinary German, one would have to say that whoever reads the *Table Talks* will be astonished at Hitler's immorality. A simple, clear sentence, which perhaps is false, but at least grammatically correct, while what is written here is complete nonsense. All this adornment with flourishes from the bourgeois period, the art nouveau fringes of adverbs and qualifications that say absolutely nothing but that will be brought in because that is the clichéd style in which it is scribbled down. It continues on like this right through the whole introduction. There is not one decent sentence in it. But I cannot therefore analyze every single sentence, for then we could speak about it for a whole year. So we now see the program: one will be horrified.

> In this respect the *Talks* mean an arsenal of arguments.[4]

Please notice again the linguistic element. "The *Talks* mean an arsenal of arguments." In ordinary German that means: "The *Talks* are an arsenal of arguments,"

> not only against such as those who in the depths of their hearts have still retained something of their former veneration for the "Führer," but also against cranks inside and outside the country who believe that they must somehow continue to defend Hitler, who in the meanwhile is condemned on all sides.
>
> Aversion toward and rebellion against such an attitude dominate us still today. [*It is already so long ago, we have not yet completely forgotten it, but nevertheless.*] But in addition, the historical question forces itself on us: How was it possible? How can it be explained, that such a man became capable of such views and consequently of such deeds? [*So, it would be a historic program that we have to accomplish.*] The reader should not be worried that we are not prepared for running into the danger of excusing everything by being able to understand everything. On the contrary, grappling with this eerie man is a political requirement of the first order. [*I am stressing the adjective "eerie," because in Schramm's analysis of character, one never gets beyond adjectives like "eerie" and "terrible."*] When we realize how he came to power, exploited it and ideologically propped it up, how he misled the Germans and—having misled them—could not

4. Ibid.

> be stopped anymore, then we vaccinate ourselves against the danger that the same and similar things will happen to us and those who come after us.[5]

So, this is roughly the same program that I am developing, when I give such a course of lectures here, with only this slight difference: when he says how Hitler misled *the* Germans. He did not mislead *the* Germans, he misled certain Germans, and there was also a whole lot, perhaps half the Germans, who in no way allowed themselves to be misled. And this, however, is where we now have a social problem. For if he were not to say how Hitler misled *the* Germans, but were to say, rather, *whom* he misled, for example, Mr. Schramm, then we would of course be at the point where the matter is becoming serious. So that would be the program. He subdivides the problem into Hitler's role as Pied Piper of the Germans (the part of the lectures that I call "the Germans"), and the second, Hitler himself.

§14. Hitler's "Aura"

So, first the Pied Piper. What does he say about this in conclusion? Why were the Germans taken in by Hitler?

> A genuine historical problem, whose "mastering" we can approach without methodological difficulties, is posed by Hitler's role as a Pied Piper.[6]

He now specifies that the Germans were taken in by him and how he did it: through propaganda.

> With this . . . problem, which has still not been thoroughly discussed, we do not have to concern ourselves here. For in our discussion, we are dealing with Hitler, with Hitler only.[7]

So, on this half of the matter you will hear nothing. And now how goes it with Hitler—the second half of the matter? With a huge rhetorical question:

> What kind of a man was he that he gave rise to such monstrous deeds?[8]

5. Ibid.
6. Ibid., 112.
7. Ibid., 113.
8. Ibid., 116.

Such a thing always looks nice. And now he explains it: Hitler was enigmatic, and those who said that Hitler was enigmatic were Supreme Admiral Raeder and General Jodl, people who knew him well. I quote Schramm now:

> Everyone who concerns himself with Hitler, with his words and with his deeds, must remind himself again and again that even Alfred Jodl, who was with Hitler for hours every day for many years, and who was one of a very few who ever had the opportunity really to discuss things with him, in the end, after careful consideration, concluded that this man remained for him a book sealed with seven seals. . . .
>
> . . . Generations to come will have to reflect anew on the grim history of that frightful man who for twelve years determined the fate of Germany, and for five brought the earth to tremble. This unique event cannot be comprehended in terms of traditional conceptions and moral categories.[9]

So, about Hitler, you will hear nothing either. Neither about the Germans, nor about Hitler, nor about the contexts. But let us deal with the matter here. The sources are Admiral Raeder and General Jodl. He does not seem to know that there were people like Karl Kraus, Robert Musil, Thomas Mann, Hermann Broch, Heimito von Doderer, not to mention classic philosophers like Plato, who had very much to say about such problems of spiritual order and disorder, and who precisely in the case of the recent ones had worked through the problem of Hitler. One can't help feeling that here is the old general-staff officer who considers the persons named—those persons whom I have just now listed—to be old dimwits, about whom a refined man has no need to be troubled.

When Jodl said that the man is enigmatic, that he is a book with seven seals whom we cannot understand, then we have always to keep that before our eyes. So Jodl had experience of him and discussed things with him. I must say, I would not like to know how this Jodl discussed things with this Hitler, even if I could find out, for then I could in the end experience it and my language would become vulgar. The thing is farcical. I have spoken already of farce. A complete loss of reality, of the whole area of spirit and of reason, of every significant mind in Germany who ever said anything about Hitler, and any nitwit from the general staff—these are the sources that we are to judge Hitler by. It is a scandal. And the man is

9. Schramm ET, 131 f.

a tenured professor of history at a German university and highly regarded by his colleagues.

And now let us go into the matter in detail. That was only the general framework. So let us begin from the most peripheral things, as Schramm himself does. He begins the first section of his exposition with:

> Let us begin with the facts.[10]

Now what are the facts? I have partly already listed them for you. They were also named in Wucher's review:

> Hitler fascinated people with his "deep blue," always slightly protruding, almost "radiant" eyes. . . .
>
> Hitler had his eyes so well under control that in jest he was able to cross them. He also had keen hearing. . . . Hitler's complexion and coloring could be described as almost girl-like. . . .
>
> . . . His beard was not heavy. He did his own shaving, cutting himself only rarely.[11]

Whether he could waggle his ears, he does not say. We also find no information on whether he could stick his big toe into his mouth. So what is going on? Wucher and other reviewers are of the opinion that what is going on here is the trickery of playing things down. By no means is it playing down. Let us critically keep to the matter. What is the problem here? Obviously there is something wrong. It is the triviality of the enumerated facts established in relation to what is relevant. Schramm suffers from a serious distortion of relevance, a distortion of the contact with reality. He is not capable of recognizing what is relevant and really believes that if such facts were established exactly, a contribution would be made to the Hitler problem.

And now the second point. Let us stay with the deep blue eyes:

> Hitler fascinated people with his deep blue, slightly protruding, almost radiant eyes. Many who met him were unable to stand up to his gaze.[12]

Interpretations interfere now with the facts:

> Hitler was well aware of this effect and used to look people straight in the eye for a long time; he closed his eyelids only slowly.[13]

10. Schramm, 29.
11. Schramm ET, 17 f.
12. Ibid., 17.
13. Schramm, 29.

If we translate that now into ordinary German, one would have to say that whoever stared at people to put them off their stride was a lout. Now we get further information on this aura of the shining eyes that many were unable to bear:

> Hitler did have an amazing ability to judge people to the extent that he was able to sense immediately whether the person standing in front of him was for him, could be won over, or would be immune to his personal dynamism.[14]

Examples:

> It is almost impossible to convey to those who never experienced it the personal impact of Hitler. . . . There were nevertheless many people upon whom it had absolutely no effect. A colonel once described to me how, when he was reporting to Hitler, he felt a steadily rising aversion to the man as he watched him at close hand. [*Probably he was a decent man and was indignant at being stared at so much.*] (It is worth noting that Hitler dismissed this colonel and the others very quickly.) The reverse reaction [*please note the choice of examples always*] was provoked in a sophisticated Pomeranian propertied lady of aristocratic background and Christian convictions, who abhorred Hitler. By chance she met him on the boardwalk of a Baltic Sea resort [*where Hitler and Pomeranian propertied ladies could meet like that*], was grazed for a brief moment by his glance, and declared, as though struck by lightning, that while she still did not like him she felt that he was a great man. [*In conclusion:*] Those whom Hitler tolerated close to himself were of course more than just grazed by his glance, and they were transformed into his willing satellites.[15]

Here we have historical facts. There is no reason for doubting the testimony of the witnesses; it is a question of interpretation. Certainly Hitler had an existence-powerful (*existenzmächtige*) appearance. The power that he gained over the years derived from a center of power radiating from him. There is no doubt at all about that. And obviously, when he stared at someone, depending on the quality of whoever was stared at, some kind of reaction was unavoidable. It was either some nice girl or other, who otherwise however did not have too much in her head, or some kind of little man. And when they felt stared at by the great man, they fell under his spell. Others, like this colonel, who had some intelligence, felt disgusted. And others again, I will give an example, who had a spiritual level of the

14. Schramm ET, 34.
15. Ibid., 35.

first rank, allowed themselves to be in no way impressed by it and did not succumb to this aura. So the aura is not an objective power, but works selectively. Certain people succumb to this aura, others do not. And the selectivity of the aura again is in correspondence with the problematic that I treated the last time, the source of authority: power, reason, and revelation.

The one who reacts only to power succumbs to the aura of the existence-power that radiates from Hitler. The one who in addition is a personality of a certain spiritual rank does not succumb. That is the difference. So, little people and various other social groups succumb. At all Hitler's lectures and speeches there were a number of women in the front rows who were ecstatic fans and were always around. They were called by the SS people—people of a somewhat rougher disposition—the "varicose-vein brigade." These, then, were the kind of people who were fascinated by Hitler and succumbed to the aura of the blue eyes. Or when you read speeches of the leader of National Socialist Women's Organization, where she praises in sexually yearning ecstasy the man whom God has sent them—these are the types who succumb. The others, naturally, do not.

To those who did not easily succumb belongs the man who preceded Schramm as official diarist of the Wehrmacht Supreme Command, Helmut Greiner, a secretary to the minister, who kept this diary from 1939 to 1943[16] and often participated in and described the company at table where Hitler carried on his conversations.

The evening meal was taken among what indeed one of them called the closest circle, which never amounted to more than sixteen persons. The regular members of the circle were General Jodl, General Field Marshal Keitel, Reich press chief Dietrich, Reich Leader Bormann, General Bodenschatz, and SS Chief Squadron Leader Wolff. So, a delightful circle. And now Greiner, who sometimes was allowed to participate, describes his observations:

> [Hitler's] expositions, which always had something of a lecture about them, often had an amazing effect, because he reduced difficult problems from every area of knowledge to simple basic facts, and so, at

16. Helmut Greiner, born in 1892, became an archivist in the history department of the Reich Archive and was transferred to the Wehrmacht's Supreme Command in August 1939. He was official diarist until April 1943, working with Schramm for some weeks until Schramm replaced him. Greiner was first transferred to Italy but was dismissed because he was too critical of the regime.

> first glance, solved them in a very clear manner. For his credulous hangers-on—and his closest circle was made up only of such—that was a special sign of his genius. [*Schramm too, from time to time, has a thing about the genius. Further examination however, would show them to be*] . . . the all too primitive formulas of a doubtless highly gifted self-taught man, who had never thought the things right through to the end and gave them whatever form that he himself wished to see. . . .
>
> . . . Further, his hasty . . . judgments had such an unpleasant effect because they were expressed with the presumptuous claim to absolute validity. [*His*] arrogance . . . increased with the years, the more the conviction of his unique greatness took root in him. His religious views did not go beyond a trite rationalism and materialism . . . [*His*] attacks on the Church . . . [*had a peculiarly repellent effect, and even more*] repulsive was the obsequious and malicious agreement that these excessive attacks against the Church and Christianity found in his closest circle, who generally vied with one another on every occasion in the worst kind of bootlicking.[17]

Please note this. Generals and field marshals were there. A quite evil rabble.

> General Jodl once said to me after an evening meal, where Hitler had imitated an Upper Bavarian peasant type very accurately and comically, that the Führer, if he had not felt himself called to be a statesman and military commander, would definitely have been the greatest German actor. Less than such superlatives would never do in Hitler's closest circle.[18]

So, along with Schramm, who kept this war diary for the Wehrmacht Supreme Command, there was the man who preceded him, Greiner, who seems to have been a much more educated and cultivated man, and who had a somewhat different opinion of the aura and has now published it.[19] His opinion of Hitler is printed before Schramm's account; in this respect Schramm is completely impartial.

It is printed in a volume that brings out that this aura has its effect on certain persons, that only such persons were allowed into the circle, and that persons who did not allow themselves to be overcome by this aura could not in any way meet with Hitler. They could appear before him once, and if he noticed that the aura did not

17. Schramm, 26–27.

18. Ibid., 27.

19. Helmuth Greiner, *Die Oberste Wehrmachtführung 1939–1943* (Wiesbaden: Limes Verlag, 1951).

function, that was the end. He never saw them again. We will have to return to this point again, for it arises from the fact that only the persons who succumbed to the aura were permitted in the circle, and that this entourage had a particularly horrible composition, which did not go completely unnoticed by Hitler either. Further, the following information is to be found in the footnote that Schramm inserts:

> At the end of the war, an atmosphere developed around Hitler, which was described shortly after the catastrophe by an elder General Staff officer. He had experienced it while briefing Hitler. He wrote: "My impression—and as I determined in conversations with others, by no means mine alone—was that a person was not merely spiritually crushed by this atmosphere of servility, nervousness, and untruthfulness, but that one could even sense it as a sort of physical sickness. Nothing was genuine there, except the fear. There was fear of all shades and degrees—from being afraid of somehow provoking the displeasure of the 'Führer,' or annoying him by some ill-considered comment, to naked fear for life itself in view of the impending end of the drama. The external forms of life were still scantily preserved, but even they disappeared after the middle of April."[20]

Now, you see, Schramm is impartial in every respect. Even when he does not know what he should do with these materials, he presents them and one can evaluate them. However, his selection of materials has a restrictive effect. As you see, he takes as sources of information this colonel, who is disgusted, this general staff officer, who is disgusted, and the like.

But he never takes a man of quality, of recognized quality. Allow me, therefore, to inform you of the reaction to Hitler of a man of great quality. It can be found in the diary of Thomas Mann for the years 1933 and following, which was published in the latest edition of his works as *Leiden an Deutschland* (*Suffering from Germany*). Here Thomas Mann reports on the novelist Wasserman's account of Max Planck,

> who was making representations to Hitler regarding the anti-Semitic dismissal of professors and had to listen to a forty-five-minute response, from which he returned home completely broken. [*The aura.*] It was like the gossip of an old peasant woman about mathematics—at the level of a quarter-educated person with fixed ideas, like nothing

20. Schramm ET, 35 n. 4.

> the famous scientist had ever heard in his life. Two worlds come into contact due to the stupid, demagogic ascent to power of the one: the knowledge, great erudition, rigorous thinking listens to the haughtiness of lecturing expectorations, and bows, separating.[21]

There you have the tragedy of the German character. When this filthy rabble comes into power, the culture is finished. There one can only bow and go away.

§15. Hitler and Christianity

Let me now in conclusion, to use up a few minutes, add yet another little episode here. There was already talk of Hitler's Christianity. About this Christianity you find a flourishing nonsense from every author possible, not only from Schramm. With Schramm you find above all the information that for Christ "as Savior there was of course, no room in Hitler's world of ideas."[22] Christ has a place in no world of ideas, for he is no idea, but a reality. But, again, Schramm, who is probably a fully fledged Christian, doesn't know that and asked a Pomeranian lady of property. So we see how Hitler in fact stood in relation to religion and Christianity in his own interpretation:

> It should be one of our most important tasks to save our future generations from a similar political fate to that of the Germans of 1918–1933, and therefore to keep alive in them the consciousness of the Jewish danger.
>
> For this reason alone, the Oberammergau festival plays must definitely be maintained.
>
> For the Jewish danger in the case of the ancient Roman world-empire has scarcely ever been so vividly illustrated as in the representation of Pontius Pilate in these festival plays. He appears here as a so much superior Roman with regard to race and intelligence, that he has the effect of a rock in the midst of the Jewish vermin and mob. In his recognition of the enormous significance of these festival plays for the enlightenment of all future generations too, he [*Hitler*] was an absolute Christian.[23]

21. Thomas Mann, diary entry of December 4, 1933, *Leiden an Deutschland. Tagebuchblätter aus den Jahren 1933 und 1934,* in *Reden und Aufsätze* (Frankfurt: Fischer, 1965), 474.

22. Schramm ET, 90.

23. Voegelin cites Hitler's own remarks in the table talk quoted in Schramm, 442–43.

Now you see again how things shimmer. What exactly is going on here now, one does not know. Is Hitler in such ecstasy about the Oberammergau Passion play because he considered Pontius Pilate to be a Christian, or because he considered Christ to be a National Socialist, or because he is even prepared to become a Christian, provided someone just gave out about the Jews? That is not clear. But this unclarity remains.

These lectures are about Hitler and the Germans. This is how things look with Hitler; how does it look, now, with the Germans? I have set out here the corresponding passages of Karl Kraus from *Die Dritte Walpurgisnacht.* Listen to this one now:

> What is to become of Oberammergau . . . ? A tragic conflict had broken out there between tourism and better conviction. Those with rooms for hire who dress up as apostles, have, they say, become National Socialists and must undergo qualms of conscience because they have to represent Jewish characters. Now they had just let the long beards and sidelocks grow, which they need for the Passion play, in order to get rid of the embarrassing feeling of a disguise. What happens? Fellow countrymen come from the north, see it, and pull the genuine beard in the false belief that it is genuine. Due to this vivid participation in the portrayed Passion they had to recognize that there was no longer any, and made the suggestion to shave the beards to a minimum and in place of the suffering of Christ
>
> to portray the life of Hitler.
>
> However, this was rejected,
>
> since it was thought that this theme would attract no foreigners.
>
> Finally they agreed on the golden mean, to keep holding the play in its old form and just to freshen it up through the repeated singing of the Horst Wessel song. With regard to the actors it was ordered that "Christ was only to be a blond man with blue eyes, with a swastika on his jacket" and that his faithful apostles must be of Aryan-Germanic type, while Judas is to be shown as "a pronounced Jewish type," a reform for which the Propaganda Minister himself dedicatedly took on the responsibility.[24]

Gentlemen, these two passages from Hitler's diary about the Oberammergau affair, and this passage based on newspaper ac-

24. Karl Kraus, *Dritte Walpurgisnacht* (Frankfurt: Suhrkamp, 1989), 279. The folks from the north pull genuine beards (because the people from Oberammergau had actually grown beards) in the false belief that they were genuine (genuine Jewish beards because they falsely believed the bearded Oberammergau people to be genuine Jews). So the portrayed passion is no longer a portrayal: It has turned into a *real* passion for the actors. "To shave the beards to a minimum" refers to Hitler's tiny moustache, satirized by Kraus as a diminution of a proper Jewish full beard.

counts of the Oberammergau Passion play from the other side, tell you more about Hitler and Christ than all the other pompous talk you can read from time to time.

(Fourth Lecture)

Ladies and Gentlemen,
In the previous lecture, I first finished the analysis of the preliminary ideas—these are the ideas we need in order to be able to speak about the phenomenon of Hitler and the Germans at all. Then I began with the analysis of Schramm's "Anatomy of a Dictator," which he later published as the introduction to *Hitlers Tischgespräche.* It was a matter of establishing how the loss of contact with reality also had a linguistic effect, the phenomenon I called illiteracy.

Following that, I established through Schramm's programmatic introduction—with the complete fizzling out at the end—that he presents no characterization of Hitler and that Schramm explicitly states that we possess no moral ideas for dealing with this phenomenon. Then I referred to the problem of the enigmatic. That is the category Schramm uses, because his colleagues in the general staff too always spoke of Hitler as enigmatic. I recommend in addition that you read these parts of Schramm's introduction, for he not only simply says that Hitler was enigmatic but also gives the reasons why people like Admiral Raeder asserted that Hitler was enigmatic. This was because Hitler had occasionally said that he only told him what he had to know for his immediate task and did not tell him about other things. And behind these other things—the plans that he had and that he did not tell him about—are still further things that he himself is not too clear about. That is the reason for the assertion that Hitler is enigmatic.

Yet all of us have this kind of enigmatic nature. I too would not tell Supreme Admiral Raeder everything that I thought, but only what perhaps he needed to hear in a given context. However, the other problem behind it has obviously escaped Schramm, for this withholding of information, even from members of the general staff and the admiralty, had an institutional reason. In the last years Hitler did not have any general staff for the conduct of war but took the leadership of the army into his own hands, since he feared that if he were confronted by a group of six or seven generals and admirals, then he would in some way be put under pressure. Thus he dealt with them only individually and personally, and this merely isolated contact, where no single person knew what the whole plan was, was a deliberate tactic and an instrument for the establishment of the dictatorship. However, this finesse obviously escaped Schramm. That is what is to be said about the enigmatic, which Schramm has never got beyond. So that the enigmatic—from its being an institutionally very skillful tactic for the establishment of the dictatorship—becomes a petit bourgeois cliché about the "enigmatic man."

Then, in conclusion, I spoke further about the religious problem with Hitler. There arises a whole series of problems, where I no longer stay with Schramm, because in fact what Schramm reports completely shimmers. But here we must now pick out the essential points and through confrontation ascertain what is going on. Of no use to us are clichés such as that Hitler was or was not a deeply religious man, that he was philosophically gifted or not gifted, that he had or did not have an understanding of literature and music, of dance or theater. Instead we have to know what really is going on in the case of Hitler. And to understand his relation to religion, as the first of these examples I confronted the occasion of his remarks on Oberammergau and the reaction of the people of Oberammergau. I would now like to continue this train of thought a little further, in order to clarify the religious problem with Hitler.

§16. Hitler's Views on Religion

Hitler's ideas on religion were those of a relatively primitive monism, approximately corresponding to Haeckel's *Welträtsel* at the turn of the century. Let me quote and comment on a few passages from the later years up to 1944, contained in the English edition of Hitler's *Table Talk*[25] but not in *Hitlers Tischgespräche,* which Schramm edited. There, Hitler explained—that must then have been about 1944—that

> the dogma of Christianity gets worn away before the advances of science. . . . All that is left is to prove that in nature there is no frontier between the organic and the inorganic. [*So, final reduction to the material basis.*] When understanding of the universe [*as something caused materially*] has become widespread, when the majority of men

25. *Hitler's Table Talk, 1941–1944,* trans. Norman Cameron and R. H. Stevens (London: Weidenfeld and Nicolson, 1953), 59–61.

> know that the stars are not sources of light, but worlds, perhaps inhabited worlds like ours, then the Christian doctrine will be convicted of absurdity [*having in this case obviously treated Christian doctrine as a picture of Genesis understood in a completely fundamentalist way*]. . . . The man who lives in communion with nature necessarily finds himself in opposition to the Churches, and that's why they're heading for ruin—for science is bound to win.[26]

Bullock, who reproduces this passage, remarks about it that the vocabulary here is completely Haeckel's, in accordance with the nineteenth-century belief in science, which must take the place of religious superstition. Hitler planned a great observatory and planetarium as the center of the architectural layout in the reconstruction of Linz, which he regarded as his hometown. And he then informed us regarding this center, and how he planned it and about its meaning. Hitler:

> Thousands of excursionists will make a pilgrimage there every Sunday. They'll have access to the greatness of our universe. The pediment will bear this motto: "The heavens proclaim the glory of the everlasting." It will be our way of giving men a religious spirit, of teaching them humility—but without the priests. For Ptolemy the earth was the center of the world. That changed with Copernicus. Today we know that our solar system is merely one solar system amongst many others. What could we do better than allow the greatest possible number of people . . . to become aware of these marvels? . . . Put a small telescope in a village and you destroy a world of superstitions.[27]

That now is the same attitude as Khrushchev's, for example, who on the occasion of the Sputnik expeditions repeatedly explained what a deep metaphysical significance the achievement of the Russian astronauts had. For the Russian astronauts had flown through space and found out that up there, there is no heaven. Thus Christianity is finished off. Found out on repeated occasions. So the whole affair plays itself out at this level.

You will perhaps say, yes, but only people like Hitler, Khrushchev, and possibly Stalin act like that. But that is not so. The German university professors act like that too. So, take now, as a counterpart to these very elucidations of Hitler on the function of the planetarium as substitute for the Church, a passage from Ernst Haeckel's

26. Alan Bullock, *Hitler: A Study in Tyranny* (Harmondsworth: Penguin, 1971), 389–90.

27. Hitler, quoted ibid., 390.

Welträtsel about the monistic church and its program. Haeckel considered his monism to be a new religion—just as Comte did with his positivism—that would have to supersede Christianity. And he said:

> The religious service of the Sunday, which will continue as the ancient day of rest, of edification and relaxation that follows the six workdays of the working week, will undergo an essential improvement in the monistic church. The mystical belief in supernatural miracles will be replaced by clear knowledge of the true miracles of nature. [*It seems one is listening to Hitler speaking.*] The temples of God as places of devotion will not be adorned with images of saints and crucifixes, but with richly artistic representations from the inexhaustible realms of beauty of natural and human life. Between the high columns of the Gothic cathedrals [*which he obviously intends to take over*], which have climbing plants winding around them, slender palms and tree-ferns, graceful banana trees and bamboos, will remind us of the creative powers of the tropics. In great aquaria below the church windows, delightful jellyfish and siphonophores, brightly colored corals and starfish, will elucidate the art-forms of marine life. In place of the high altar there will be a statue of Urania, which will represent the omnipotence of the law of matter through the movements of the planets.[28]

So we are in Hitler's planetarium again, at the high altar. These sillinesses now, I must remind you again, are not a problem of National Socialism, but of the German petit bourgeois, which finds its expression in Haeckel, as in Hitler and in various phenomena of our time. Let me again fall back on Thomas Mann. In his *Leiden an Deutschland* he speaks about Hitler's presumptuousness. He refers to Hitler's speech on culture, and comments in a rather shorthand way:

> Absolutely astounding. This man, plebeian and exponent of the lower middle classes with elementary schooling, who has got caught up in philosophizing, is really a curious phenomenon—I am relying on this adjective, "curious," to be able to imply and express much laughter and loathing, much disgust, in face of an unparalleled stupid impudence.

I am afraid that Mann is mistaken there. With adjectives like "curious" you cannot make clear to a German what is going on. You

28. Ernst Haeckel, *Die Welträtsel: Gemeinverständliche Studien über Monistische Philosophie* (Bonn: Emil Strauß Verlag, 1901), 462–63. See also Daniel Gasman, *The Scientific Origins of National Socialism: Social Darwinism in Ernst Haeckel and the German Monist League* (New York: American Elsevier, 1971).

must express yourself much more crudely; otherwise he does not notice what you intend to say at all.

> There is no doubt that, unlike Göring or Röhm, the man is very seriously concerned about "German culture." The ideas, which he helplessly strings together, continually repeating himself, with strange mistakes and in pitiful German, are those of a troubled schoolboy. They could be moving, if they did not give evidence of such horrible immodesty. Never before have the powerful, the makers and shakers of the world's affairs, taken it on themselves in this manner to act as teachers of a people, indeed of mankind. Neither Napoleon nor Bismarck. They created an order, a basis, compelled by their vision, on which the higher, spiritual life, arts and sciences, might then flourish or not flourish. They publicly supported or decorated what seemed useful to them and also violently suppressed what was opposed to them. But they never prescribed a theory of culture, a program of culture for the nation by lecturing down from the podium, although their spiritual capacity would have allowed them to do so incomparably better than is the case with this poor fellow. . . . [*And he then adds:*] If one remembers with what modest deference the trade-unionist Ebert approached cultural things, then one can recognize what a horrifying direction that democracy has taken since then—the direction toward mob rule.[29]

Now, regarding the direction toward mob rule, Mann is right of course. However, Hitler cannot be understood in comparison with Napoleon and Bismarck, but from quite another context, that is, German monism, which became the creed of the bourgeois period. For example, Haeckel speaks—this will give the law students among you a laugh—about the education of law students: It should be "purely formal, not real."[30] Please notice the contrasting of "formal" and "real." Completely meaningless words.

> Our law students come to know only superficially the actual principal object of their activity, the human organism and its most important function, the soul. [*Note the same metaphysical problematic as with Hitler.*] Most law students would not dream of studying anthropology, psychology, and the history of evolution as the first preconditions for a correct judgment of the human being. . . . So they are without that basic knowledge of human nature, which can only be obtained through comparative anthropology and monistic psychology—without that knowledge of social conditions, whose organic models

29. Mann, diary entry of July 1933, *Leiden an Deutschland,* 461–62.
30. Haeckel, *Die Welträtsel,* 9.

> are made available to us by comparative zoology and the history of evolution, cytology and the study of protists.[31]

So, there you have a program for what a law student should study: cytology, protists and more of such things, biology, so that he can come to know the organism accurately, for all functions of the soul are only functions of this organism. And how could one dispense justice if one did not understand the organism that has these functions of the soul?

Regarding this, I would like to take yet another passage from Haeckel. It fits in with Thomas Mann in this context. Haeckel did not go uncontradicted in his own time; one could not contradict Hitler, and today the level of education is so low that one cannot even contradict a Schramm. An opponent of Haeckel wrote about him in his time, and indeed he must have been a devout pastor. This passage is quoted by Haeckel himself:

> Ernst Haeckel, as is well known, understands as much about Christianity as a donkey does of logarithms.[32]

Haeckel now quotes that and also responds to it. But note how he responds:

> This frequently expressed opinion [*that he understands as much about Christianity as a donkey does of logarithms*] is a factual error. [*And now he adduces the facts, in order to prove that the error in fact is factual:*] Not only did I distinguish myself at school—due to my devout education—by particular enthusiasm and diligence in religious studies, but I still, in my twenty-first year, most warmly defended the Christian faith in lively discussions against my freethinking fellow-students, although the study of human anatomy and physiology and its comparison with that of the other vertebrates had already deeply shaken my faith. I first arrived at the complete abandonment of this faith [*now comes an underlining*] *with the most grievous conflicts of soul,* through the completion of my study of medicine and through my activity as a general practitioner.[33]

He now attaches a passage about his justification for having a say in theological questions. This belongs here too:

> That as a zoologist I am justified in drawing even the opposed world-view of the theologians into the domain of my philosophical critique

31. Ibid., 9–10.
32. Ibid., 461.
33. Ibid.

> already [*again this "already" that has no meaning at all*] arises from the fact that I consider the whole of anthropology as a part of zoology and so cannot exclude psychology.[34]

Please note this last sentence! That is a key sentence of the German liberal professor, which you will find again and again in all possible contexts, including that of German historians: That anthropology is "a part of zoology" does not arise from the fact that anthropology is a part of zoology but from the fact that Haeckel regards it as such. Here you have the phenomenon of the second reality. The man lives in what he imagines, and what he imagines takes the place of reality, and from this reality that he imagines it follows that he is justified in saying stupid stuff about religious questions. So, if I imagine things that are sufficiently stupid, then I am justified for everything that follows as a result of my stupidity. That is the basic thesis of the German petit bourgeois. Regarding other things you may find here, one can only say that in some respects here in Germany it serves these churches and Christianity right:

> As a zoologist I am justified in drawing even the opposed worldview of the theologians into the domain of my philosophical critique . . .

—that serves them right for having turned Christianity into a worldview, instead of being content with faith.

§17. Hitler and Women

Now let us deal with other things. A delightful theme is Hitler and women. Schramm has a lot of things to say about this. There are plenty people who believe that Hitler cannot be explained without going into his sexual life. As a methodological principle let me say that there are indeed causations that lead from sexual life into the spiritual structures, but that man still always remains organized from the spiritual structure down and that it is much more rewarding to interpret the sexual life in terms of the spiritual structure than the reverse. So, anyway, let us hear what Hitler has to do with women, and in fact not in Schramm's account, but let Hitler speak directly:

> Man's world is large, compared with that of the woman. Man belongs to his duty, and only now and then does his thought stray toward woman.

34. Ibid., 462.

> The woman's world is the man. She thinks about other things only now and then. That is a great difference.
>
> Woman can love much more deeply than man. The intellect does not matter in a woman. Compared to educated intellectual women, my mother quite certainly was a very plain woman. She loved her husband and their children. In the company of our educated women she would indeed have had a difficult time, but she gave the German people a great son![35]

That is the reason for his immense tact in relationship to women. He says:

> It should never be that a woman should be compelled to speak about intimate matters. I have done away with that. Anyway, I cannot stand snooping about.[36]

That was too stupid even for Schramm, and underneath he has added a footnote:

> It was new [*very neutral and objective*], that for permission of marriage with foreign women whose Aryan origin was not fully clear, nude photographs were required.[37]

So he does not seem to have been all that tactful. . . . Now, what does Schramm say to these things?

> Many formulations that he produced have an absolutely homemade quality, and many could even be taken for granted by those who otherwise wanted nothing to do with him.[38]
>
> Hitler was always unfailingly gracious and correct with women. If he scorned earlier rulers who had exploited their position to indulge themselves with numbers of mistresses, he could do so in good conscience.[39]

We will have to say more about that too, but you see again where the problem is with Schramm here. He is a historian; and he once heard something about the bad influence of mistresses in previous times, today of course we have none with Hitler, so one cannot reproach him about it. It has, on the other hand, escaped Schramm that while the mistresses of the baroque period played no great role with Hitler, his relation to women extended to other matters. And once again I would like to read you a passage from Karl Kraus on how

35. Schramm, 193–94.
36. Ibid., 194.
37. Ibid., 194 n. 1.
38. Ibid., 43.
39. Schramm ET, 38.

women were treated under National Socialism. Kraus begins with—it is from *Die Dritte Walpurgisnacht* of course—the newspaper extract of a "race warden," who tells his little lambs what is right in questions of race:

> *We demand* that the Aryans *in all circumstances* should take a girl who is a virgin as a wife.

Kraus's commentary:

> But the Aryan, in these questions well-disposed to slavery, instead of giving the warden a box on the ears, accepts the additional prohibition against craving for the "Mediterranean type."
>
> > With the characteristic negro head and slim body *as well as elliptically shaped breasts.*
>
> Instead of receiving a further slap in the face for rotten German, the race warden must
>
> > *realize with surprise* that there are *still* German girls who are not ashamed to show themselves openly in the company of Jews.
>
> Therefore he must not only put them as "ladies" between ironic quotation marks, but with their names and addresses in the newspaper; there also follows "forced interrogation by the SA and SS." They should
>
> > *not be surprised*—says the race warden—if one day they get *a thrashing.*
>
> But who would still be surprised at anything? Everywhere the one who administers the beating is precisely the one who deserves it. In the satrapy of that Streicher [*who was the "Gauleiter" of Franconia*] from whose brain the thought of a more comprehensive boycott arose, a barrier was broken, and a girl with shaven head was led by six uniformed men through the bars, so that she could be spat at by the public. Someone, who on Sunday August 13 [*1933, that is*] saw it, reported it, and *The Times* also reported that a board had been hung around her neck with her plaits, which had been cut off fastened to it, and these words could be read:
>
> > I offered myself to a Jew.
>
> Storm-troopers surrounded her from time to time on the stage of the cheap music-hall and, with abuse, roared out the text into the hall. The girl, "slim, fragile and in spite of her shorn head, exceptionally pretty," was led along the block of international hotels.
>
> > She tripped a few times and then was brought to her feet again by the men, sometimes lifted up high so that the onlookers further away could see her. On this occasion she was roared at by the public, ridiculed and for a joke invited to give a speech.
>
> The children of the American consul saw it. Europe heard it. Never before was anything like it experienced in a nightmare. Some days

> later it was reported that she had gone mad. If all the revenge of a dishonored mankind was paralyzed at the sight of the specter of blood that besieged it—this act and this fate will one day kindle it into flame![40]

One case among thousands. Read these pages of the *Dritte Walpurgisnacht,* and then those incomparably obscene reports from *Der Stürmer,* which are included there. That is how the German man stands with regard to woman, and particularly Hitler. I should not be at all surprised if the people who were there then and are still alive today receive perhaps the Federal Cross of Merit. Now Hitler of course was aware of these things, and it was reported that when Goebbels told him about events of this kind, he could not stop laughing at how comic and amusing it all was.

So that is the aspect of Hitler's relation to women that Schramm discreetly says nothing about. Again this odd lack of contact with reality, that it is not a question of what stupid stuff Hitler said about women on any kind of private occasion, or that he took pleasure in a pretty girl, or more things like that—these are the things Schramm reports; but what is suppressed—again one cannot say whether deliberately or carelessly—is that precisely here a totalitarian system extending into these things was in operation. It seems as if Schramm lacks any sensitivity for this problematic, which would characterize this totalitarianism in Hitler's worldview, that is, this reaching through into the sphere of intimacy. In contrast to Karl Kraus, read Schramm now:

> He occasionally described to his circle how strongly, as a visually minded person, he reacted to beautiful women. Before the war he had found it both delightful and relaxing to chat with a lovely young woman over tea, or to fascinate elegant ladies at his receptions with his conversation.[41] When his eye led him, his resentments against nobility and bourgeoisie suddenly vanished.[42]

If you read this passage in Schramm and confront it with the one you have just heard from Karl Kraus as one of these thousands of scenes, then the contrast has the effect of an obscene joke. That is Schramm's level.

40. Kraus, *Dritte Walpurgisnacht,* 219–22.
41. Schramm ET, 38.
42. Schramm, 45.

§18. Hitler and His Entourage

Now, this relation to women is closely connected with his general relation to human beings. And so you find in Schramm too a chapter on Hitler's relation to his collaborators. I will combine that with the problem of his relation to women:

> One would like to assume that a man in Hitler's position would have done his utmost to surround himself with particularly intelligent and experienced men of character who were beyond reproach.[43]

Please notice that "one would like to assume." Of course one would not in the least like to assume such a thing, but one would first have to find out who were the people he surrounded himself with, and then find out why precisely he surrounded himself with these and not with others.

> Yet, to cite only a few examples, Hitler made Martin Bormann his closest associate, Schaub his chief adjutant, and Morell his personal physician. He tolerated people like Heinrich Hoffmann [*he was the court photographer*], Hermann Esser, and Adolf Wagner as frequent and welcome guests in his private household. All were men of a kind the German people, insofar as it knew them, would much rather not have seen in the company of their Führer.[44]

With the Führer, everything was fine; it was only with a few people around him that not everything was all right. Hasselbach, the medical doctor who for some time was Hitler's personal physician, says:

> Hitler had pointed with pride and satisfaction to the "Guard" comprised of his *Reichsleiter* and *Gauleiter,* whom in terms of personal character and extraordinary ability, he claimed to be virtually without equal in history.[45]

And now Hasselbach wonders—please, note this now, how Hasselbach constructs this. As a physician he has indeed observed rather well what was going on there:

> If we ask how such blunders and misjudgments were possible, we can hardly find a single satisfactory answer.[46]

43. Schramm ET, 32. Schramm is quoting from a memorandum of Dr. von Hasselbach.
44. Ibid.
45. Ibid., 32–33
46. Ibid., 33.

Now comes the list of reasons, which partly contradict one another but are very interesting: (1) Hitler was aware of the inadequacy of his circle. (2) Hitler was, however, very much obsessed with comradeship and loyalty. He greatly disapproved of Mussolini's changing of the guard, in which ministers were replaced. (3) He was conservative in his habits of living and broke off from people he had grown used to only with difficulty. (4) A change would have taken place, however, if Hitler had been able to see those among his men who were incompetent or with serious character deficiencies, as they really were. You see now the contradiction (we will often return to the question of the contradiction): On the one hand he was aware of the inadequacy of this circle, on the other hand he was not able to detect their incompetence, their deficiencies in character. (5) He lacked, then, precisely what he was otherwise very often praised for, knowledge of human nature. (6) "Hitler managed to suppress an entirely correct judgment which was uncongenial, in order to justify persons who seemed to him useful and devoted."[47]

With this we arrive at the crux of the matter, which will be pursued still further in the concluding consideration on Hitler. I would like to remind you of the problem of the double reality, the first and second reality. Hitler, in one reality, was aware what sort of a bunch it was that he had around him. On another level, however, he did not want to know it, and to the same extent that he successfully did not want to know it, then he also really did not know it.

But we must now draw the general conclusion: Hitler had no choice—this now is still according to Hasselbach—in the selection of his circle. There you are! And that holds also for the generals, for Jodl, Keitel, and others. And again, on the contrary, he found unbearable an intelligent, moral person of integrity. He could not stand that in his circle. And thus we return to the problem of the women. There is always a great fuss made of Hitler and his joy in beautiful women, in conversation with them, and how he fascinated and impressed them. On the other hand, to begin with, let us state that Hitler never tolerated an intelligent woman in his circle, just as he was incapable of tolerating any intelligent person who had contradicted him.

47. Ibid., 34.

There we have this curious situation I referred to the last time, that (excluding those of a few diplomatic personalities who had to see him at an official level) the immediate reports on Hitler we have are from his circle, among whom we have on the whole no reliable sources, because everything said about him is reported by inferior types. And Schramm only quotes the inferior types as witnesses, without saying that they are inferior and therefore not reliable. That holds in the same way for women as well as for men; and in general, this behavior of Hitler toward the women in his personal circle is extremely odd. He had, as far as is known, maintained personal relationships with only two women for a somewhat longer time. The first was this pitiful young creature, his niece,[48] who at the age of seventeen, I believe, became totally devoted to him and then committed suicide. Why, is not precisely known, whether she was unsatisfied with her relations with Hitler or because Hitler had stood in the way of her relations to another man. That was one case. The other, Eva Braun, was an empty-headed pretty lass. Just that: a woman in whose company Hitler could feel comfortable, because no spiritual demands were made and no doubt she never contradicted him. She too paid for her relation with Hitler with her life. These are the two cases from which one can only conclude that also in erotic relationships he was a severely disturbed person, for he was neither capable of a normal marriage nor was he capable of an *amour de passion* or any kind of normal relationship with a woman.

However, as I said, one should not now try to explain his spiritual structure in terms of the sexual sphere, for Hitler knew rather precisely what was wrong with himself, and he explained repeatedly that he could not stand such long-term relationships with women because that would affect his career, where by career he understood the unlimited expansion of power.

So he realized that he was out for power, and in this unlimited striving for power, more intimate or long-lasting bonds to a woman would disturb him. The same held naturally for relationships with men. He could not maintain any relationships with men and had no friends. He had admirers who knew that their existence depended on his success, but he had no personal friends, for every relationship of this kind would naturally have been a bond, in the sense of the

48. Geli Raubal, the daughter of Hitler's half-sister Angela Raubal.

Orphic primeval word of Goethe's *Ananke;* and he would not enter into such a bond with anyone, whether man or woman. He only wanted to get his own way; he wanted to rule or to destroy.

§19. Hitler and "The Art of Reading"

I am selecting as the next theme the relation between Hitler and his books. There is much written about it, even if it is sometimes contradictory. It is said that Hitler read enormously and had a limitless knowledge, with which he again and again surprised those he conversed with. These are the kinds of phrases that are willingly supplied, without it being asked who then were these he conversed with and who were so surprised by Hitler's limitless knowledge. Thus, no one knows exactly what the situation was. One can ascertain the following: To make Hitler popular, National Socialist propaganda always insisted that Hitler was a man who read no books. Here is a man of the practical deed, who reads only illustrated magazines, [and these reports were] accompanied by photographs of Hitler with an illustrated magazine in his hand. But he wasn't that primitive; that was probably propaganda to make him popular. He read much. The question is, What did he read? And now emerges the curious fact that it cannot be established what Hitler really had read, apart from certain things he himself reported from time to time.

He had read Karl May[49] very closely, and he could hold forth on the individual characters in his novels again and again with long explanations. On the other hand, statements from his secretaries are available that in Hitler's library there was not a single book of any kind of significance whatever, no classic that had ever occupied any rank in the history of mankind. The entire area of philosophy, from antiquity to the present, and great literature was obviously unknown to him, and in general he had never read anything of this kind. So he can only have read popular literature, of which he obviously had read rather a lot. So that was at the level of

49. Karl May (1842–1912) spent some seven years in jail, mostly for confidence trickery, before achieving fame in the 1890s as an author of adventure stories characterized by exotic coloring and imaginative ethnographical descriptions. His later novels show symbolist and pacifist tendencies. May is still one of the most popular writers of adventure stories for young people in Germany, with sales of more than 90 million copies in more than twenty-five languages.

what one saw in lending libraries as popular philosophy, popular science, Bölsche's *Kosmos*,[50] and more of that sort. Such kinds of stuff he obviously devoured in great quantities, and he could knock together for himself some kind of worldview and tie together the oddest pieces of information, which he could then show off, because he had, it seems, an excellent memory. What does Schramm say about this?

> It would certainly have been conceivable [*again this strange beginning*] for a man of such omnivorous reading habits to have invited recognized figures in German intellectual life to pick their brains or have them share their views with him. But Hitler simply did not rely on others. Rather, he remarked: "I often think about why the ancient world has perished!" It would have seemed a good idea to send for two or three experts [*for example Schramm!*] who could discuss the reasons for this course of events; for then he would not only have come to know the most recent state of research, but he would have been able to select what seemed best to him from the arguments presented. Wilhelm II, who was a listener [*as compared to Hitler, who was a "reader"*], tried in this way to enliven the monotony of his exile. But those who Hitler admitted were in some way already screened as regards their ideas.[51]

And therefore, as I already said, there were never persons of intellectual rank in Hitler's circle. Concluding:

> Hitler's knowledge, then, based on his retentive memory and assiduous reading, was remarkably extensive, but it retained a fortuitous and arbitrary character as the result of his being necessarily self-taught. [*Please always take note of Schramm's adverbs and adjectives! Why being self-taught was "of necessity" no one knows either. He could just as well have informed himself in another way.*] It never developed and matured, because the rising politician was not willing to expose himself to qualified specialists and professionals. In the end, at the height of his power, his mind became completely rigid, because he was convinced that he knew best in all matters, intellectual and otherwise.[52]

Those then are the formulae by which Schramm deals with this problem. But fortunately we now have here a primary source of the first order. In the second chapter of the first volume of *Mein Kampf* Hitler inserted a few pages on the art of reading, from which it

50. Wilhelm Bölsche (1861–1939), a German writer of popular science, was influenced by Ernst Haeckel's monism and developed a pantheist nature-mysticism.
51. Schramm, 70.
52. Schramm ET, 75.

emerges that he was by no means driven by necessity, but that he knew very precisely what he was doing and that he understood everything much better than Schramm did. Let me read out to you and comment on this passage from Hitler's *Mein Kampf.* The heading is "The Art of Reading."

> By "reading," to be sure, I mean perhaps something different than the average member of our so-called "intelligentsia."
>
> I know people who "read" enormously, book for book, letter for letter [*that is part of the fine German that Hitler writes*], yet whom I would not describe as "well-read." True, they possess a mass of "knowledge," but their brain is unable to organize and register the material they have taken in. They lack the art of sifting what is valuable for them in a book from that which is without value, of keeping the one in their head forever, and, if possible, not even seeing the rest, but in any case not dragging it around with them as useless ballast.

Please note this sentence, again very similar to Haeckel: "They lack the art of sifting what is valuable for them in a book from that which is without value." So, not what is objectively valuable or worthless; rather, the criterion is already given through the man who reads, even if he reads what is most valuable and it is not valuable for him—from a pragmatic viewpoint, as you will straightaway see. Away with it, forgotten!

> For reading is no end in itself [*note this formulation, reading as an aim in itself, that leads us again into the atmosphere of the petit bourgeois, where one goes to the lending library to read a book as an end in itself, because one has nothing cleverer to do*], but a means to an end. It should primarily be of use filling out the framework constituted in everyone by their talents and abilities. [. . . *So, talents and abilities are presupposed. The book fills out this framework; nothing will be learned.*] In addition, it should provide the tools and building materials [*so, purely instrumentally*], which the individual needs for his life's work, regardless whether this consists in a primitive bread-winning or the satisfaction of a higher calling; secondly, it should transmit a general world view. [*Please note, that is the psychology of the worldview.*] In both cases, however, it is essential that the content of what one reads at any time should not be handed over to memory to be stored away in the order of the book or in the sequence of the books, but, like the stone of a mosaic, should fit into the general world view in its proper place and thus be of use in forming this view in the reader's head.

So, the reader comes with his talents and his abilities and an already preconceived worldview. Then he uses a book to pull out relevant building blocks and further build up his worldview. That might strike you as odd, but that is the method of value-selection that has been propagated by the German neo-Kantian school of historiography: "We are not interested in reality. We have values, and we have relevant experiences that we relate to these values." There is absolutely no question of learning from reality. We have the values already.

> But whoever [*Hitler continues*] possesses the art of correct reading will, in studying any book, magazine, or pamphlet, instinctively and immediately perceive everything which in his opinion is worth permanently remembering, either because it is suited to his purpose or generally worth knowing. Once the knowledge he has achieved in this fashion is correctly coordinated within the always somehow already existing picture of this or that subject [*please note the "always somehow already existing picture"—in which nothing will be changed*] created by the imagination, it will function either as a corrective or a complement, thus enhancing either the correctness or the clarity of the picture. . . .
>
> Only this kind of reading has meaning and purpose.

Where now does this determination of meaning and purpose come from? Hitler is quite clear about that too:

> An orator, for example, who does not provide his intelligence with the necessary foundation will never be in a position cogently to defend his view in the face of opposition, though it may be a thousand times in accordance with the truth or reality. [*Again note: the truth or reality.*] In every discussion his memory will treacherously leave him in the lurch; he will find neither grounds for reinforcing his own contentions nor any for confuting those of his adversary.

That the adversary might be right and one might have to change one's own opinion and that the self-assertion might perhaps be the assertion of what is false, that again never comes into question. This is the perfect example of the liberal, arrogant imbecile, who was however produced by the German academic world at the end of the nineteenth century. You recall Haeckel, who wrote exactly the same kind of things.

> Since my earliest youth I have endeavored to read in the correct way, and in this I have been most happily supported by my memory and intelligence.

So Hitler knew exactly what he was doing. He had a worldview in general outline. He had as an orator to defend theses, these theses he underpinned with material he obtained through reading, in order then to confute his adversary in debate. Nothing is read in order to learn. This passage is very interesting:

> [I]t is essential that the content of what one reads at any time should not be . . . stored away in the order of the book.[53]

The book is, so to say, a rubbish heap, from which one pulls out relevant things. There is no understanding that a book must be read in its sequence, particularly when it is a book of any kind of significance; for in general, when it is a matter of an intellectual process, it is naturally the representation of the intellectual process, the literary outcome of a meditation, whose sequence could not be changed and which can be used for one's own formation only if one follows it in the sequence and understands it in the sequence. That means the entire area of the spiritual and rational, which is based on meditation and the reproduction of meditative experience, is systematically excluded from perception. So, what I said in earlier lectures about Hitler's curious division between pragmatic-imperious abilities, which are not to be despised, and the contemptibility of the irrational man is here confirmed by himself. He was a man without reason and spirit and had never received orientation in terms of self-development from any work whatever in the history of mankind. He is at exactly the same level as the liberal fundamentalist doctrinaire, who defends theses and then looks for arguments *pro* and *contra,* misusing world history and its literary production for his subjective purposes. That, perhaps, is the most conclusive document about Hitler that he himself has provided, and which, as far as I know, no one will ever pay attention to. Hitler's *Mein Kampf* in general is not to be so despised, for he was much cleverer than most of his interpreters—and naturally also much cleverer than Schramm, who is helpless in the face of these things.

Whence comes this remarkable inability of Schramm's to deal with such things? As I have already anticipated even in the first sentence with the shimmering, it results from a remarkable harmony between Schramm's spiritual attitude and Hitler's. I will now

53. Adolf Hitler, *Mein Kampf,* trans. Ralph Manheim (Boston: Houghton Mifflin, 1971), 35–37. Manheim's translation is used here, with a few changes. For the heading "The Art of Reading," see Adolf Hitler, *Mein Kampf* (Munich: Franz Eher, 1939), 36–39.

analyze this similarity by comparing two passages. Schramm is an impartial researcher of sources and so in this volume of the *Table Talks* he also presents Hitler's speech of May 30, 1942, given to the young officers of the German Wehrmacht. It contained nothing new. Hitler said the same on other occasions, but it is very nicely concentrated; and the speech, I believe, has not been published up to now. Let me read out the beginning of this speech, and we will then analyze in detail what is going on. I must once again deal with the analysis of language. So, Hitler addresses these young officers:

> My young comrades!
>
> A deeply serious sentence of a great military philosopher enunciates that struggle, and thereby war, is the father of all things. Whoever casts an eye on nature, as it is, will find this sentence confirmed as valid for all living things and for all events, not only on this earth, but far beyond it. [*Great perspectives are opened out.*] The entire universe seems to be ruled by just this one idea, that an eternal selection takes place in which the stronger in the end maintains life and the right to live, and the weaker falls. One will say that nature is therefore cruel and merciless, but the other will grasp that nature is thus only obeying an iron law of logic. . . .
>
> It is necessary that this fundamental insight should rule whoever is himself compelled, in the sight of the almighty creator of these worlds [*several worlds!*] to take his place at the court that will decide about the goodness or weakness of men.[54]

That is enough as text. Let us now attend to the details. The first sentence:

> A deeply serious sentence of a great military philosopher enunciates that struggle, and thereby war, is the father of all things.

You will be able to guess that the great military philosopher was Heraclitus. Note the "great" military philosopher. Perhaps it is partly due to the spirit of the place. I am happy every time I cross over Munich's Maximilian Street to the splendid figures that stand there on pedestals. One of these figures has on its pedestal the inscription "Schelling, the great philosopher." So, perhaps this is how Hitler came across the great military philosopher Heraclitus. But note what is behind it: "the great philosopher." That belongs to those persuasive adjectives with which one wishes to make clear to a man, who naturally knows nothing of the matter and has never

54. Quoted in Schramm, 493.

heard of Heraclitus, that that is a man one must pay attention to. It is moving in an uneducated milieu, just as when one says, for example, that the well-known dialect-poet has said such and such—where the well-known dialect-poet is a man about whom no one has heard anything yet, and so one must rub it in that he is well known, and woe betide you if he is not well known to you, for then you are uneducated. So, please note again this petit bourgeois atmosphere here. . . .

§20. Hitler's Social Darwinism

But that is not all. For the sentence indeed does not at all express that struggle, and thus war, is the father of all things, as Hitler confirms by all these social-Darwinist explanations. Heraclitus was no social Darwinist. May I read out to you the passage in the original, without the Hitlerian trimming. In Heraclitus, B 53, it is simply, "War is of all things the father, and of all things the king; some he makes gods and some again men; some he makes slaves and some again free-men."[55] So Heraclitus does not preach a social Darwinism but refers to a structure of the cosmos, in which there is differentiation: for example, some are gods, the others men. Then in the human sphere, there are slaves and free. Fragment 67 says how that is to be understood: "God is day-night, winter-summer, war-peace, satiety-famine. But he changes like fire which when it mingles with the smoke of incense, is named according to each man's pleasure."[56] So, it is the idea of the cosmos, which is ruled by the gods and in all its phenomena gives expression to this divine substance, in gods and men, day and night, in winter and summer. Naturally there is no talk about social Darwinism and a struggle for existence.

Hitler mixes up this Heraclitus with social Darwinism, which is enormously nonsensical. And how are things with Schramm? Schramm is filled with indignation about it:

> Thus one link was joined to the next in what seemed to Hitler to be a logical and scientifically irrefutable series. Thus was forged the horrible chain that shackled millions, threatened all Europe, and dragged Germany into the abyss.[57]

55. See Eric Voegelin, *The World of the Polis*, vol. 2 of *Order and History* (1957; available Columbia: University of Missouri Press, 1999), 233.

56. In Kathleen Freeman, *Ancilla to the Pre-Socratic Philosophers* (Oxford: Blackwell, 1971), 29.

57. Schramm ET, 87.

That is to say, the chain from Heraclitus up to social Darwinism. And then Schramm defends Darwin. I must read out this passage from Schramm in order to show the parallel with Hitler on Heraclitus. Schramm says about Darwin:

> That the judgments of such a rightly thinking man as Darwin, achieved through the exact observation of nature, should have to provide the legitimization of violent politics is no unique course of events. Discoverers and inventors have no longer control, as soon as what is new becomes known, over whether the expansion of knowledge will be used for quite other ends, and thus will be dangerous for mankind. Pseudo-Darwinian arguments have played a more or less important role in the political polemics of all civilized countries since the nineteenth century. From this viewpoint there are many intellectual forerunners and neighbors of Hitler. But no one before Hitler had actually made the consequences deduced from Darwin the basis of state policy, and no one before Hitler so consistently and ruthlessly carried those biological premises to their ultimate conclusions and then put them into practice.[58]

So [for Schramm], the man who deduces consequences is historically interesting too. But let's leave this minor matter aside. Let's go through what's written here, line by line. The first line: "That the judgments of such a rightly thinking man as Darwin." "Rightly thinking man" means nothing; it is only an empty phrase. The whole thing is wrong anyway, because there's something wrong with Schramm's interpretation of Darwin, the rightly thinking Darwin, who, through exact observation of nature, found out all sorts of things and then was misused. If you read the *Origin of Species*, published in 1859, in the second edition with the long foreword of 1860, then you will discover something quite different. For Darwin too knew what he was doing, and indeed in chapter 3 he says of the origin of species:

> I have called this principle, by which each slight variation, if useful, is preserved, by the term Natural Selection, in order to mark its relation to man's power of selection [*that is to say, the selective breeding of domestic animals*]. But the expression often used by Mr. Herbert Spencer of the Survival of the Fittest is more accurate, and is sometimes equally convenient.[59]

So the expression "survival of the fittest," which he willingly uses in place of his earlier expression "natural selection" (in contrast to

58. Ibid., 87–88.
59. Charles Darwin, *The Origin of Species* (London: John Murray, 1902), 76–77.

artificial selection by man), comes from Spencer and the context of English early liberalism. It thus contains precisely this social element that is later asserted to have been illegitimately pinned on Darwin. Darwin continues:

> Man by selection can certainly produce great results. . . . But Natural Selection . . . is a power incessantly ready for action, and is as immeasurably superior to man's feeble efforts, as the works of Nature are to those of Art.[60]

And now, how does nature carry out its selection?

> A struggle for existence inevitably follows from the high rate at which all organic beings tend to increase.[61]

That is the doctrine of Malthus, frequently applied to the animal and vegetable kingdoms; that is to say, in order to build up his theory of evolution, Darwin uses the categories of English early liberalism from the politics of Spencer and of Malthus. He hasn't observed anything at all. Indeed, after he developed his theory, he had to make yet another great restriction. In the evolutionary theories of the Darwinian type (there are also other evolutionary theories—there should be no doubt about evolution—but now we are speaking about the specifically Darwinian evolutionary theory) it is established, on the basis of observation of plant and animal breeding, that there are what later were called mutations, slight changes, producing new varieties within a species. Darwin now extrapolates from this, saying that also the species that are clearly differentiated have changed from one to the other through similar little steps, like those one observes in artificial and natural breeding within the species. But from this it would follow that between the species recognizable today—which are rather far away from each other—there must be an unlimited profusion of infinitesimal transitions, if not from one to another, then from the different species available at present back to common original species from which they have developed. And Darwin now makes this supposition too. Evolution took place through this infinitely small change of variations, from which the species then arose. But the question then arises: Why then do we have only these clearly distinguishable species, and what has happened to all these links in between?

60. Ibid., 77.
61. Ibid., 79.

And Darwin—I do not know if he was a rightly thinking man, or at any rate, a conscientious scientist—replies now to this, in chapter 10, entitled "On the Imperfection of the Geological Record." He speaks of the principal objection to his theory as

> the distinctness of specific forms, and their not being blended together by innumerable transitional links. . . . [*And then he continues:*] Geology assuredly does not reveal any such finely graduated organic chain; and this, perhaps, is the most obvious and serious objection which can be urged against the theory. The explanation [*which all these missing links, that must have been innumerable, does not produce*] lies, as I believe, in the extreme imperfection of the geological record.[62]

Now look at Schramm again: "That the judgments of a rightly thinking man like Darwin, achieved through the exact observation of nature, should have to provide the legitimization of violent politics is no unique course of events" is nonsense. Precisely this part of the theory, which for Darwin is the most decisive, has no empirical basis and has had none up to now. Rather, this part of the theory is an application to geological phenomena of the liberal politics of competition and the selection of the best in competition with each other, without a trace of an empirical observation. This is precisely what was later made out of Darwin, when this theory, strengthened by the authority of a pseudo-natural science, was used again in terms of social Darwinism as a justification for politics.

Now before I go further into this question, let me underline the parallels between Hitler and Schramm, as they are relevant to me here. Hitler understands Heraclitus just as little as Schramm understands Darwin. Schramm has read nothing, therefore brazenly talks nonsense, puts forward false assertions and scribbles them down. It's all false. This parallelism is to be found in the arrogance of men incapable of education, who cannot even read a book. Here lies the problem of the German bourgeois, which Hitler shares with Schramm and is not a thing of the past, nor is it limited to a Haeckel, nor a Hitler, but in the year of 1964 is still to be found in Schramm—exactly the same story.

And now, what about all this Darwinism? That naturally leads to all kinds of problems, one of which comes out very nicely with Hitler. If one gets involved in social Darwinism, then one gets

62. Ibid., 412–13.

into the difficulties of the dialectic of historical interpretations. I deliberately say dialectic, because dialectic, once you have got into it, is the thing that you can get away from again only by means of an intellectual swindle. Hitler says in his *Table Talks* that he is an ardent champion of the belief that in the struggle of the peoples, the better section always carries the day. In his opinion, all laws of nature would be invalidated if the inferior were to become master of the stronger. For once, let us take him at his word. The stronger (in the sense of social Darwinism), being stronger, has proven to be the better. At several periods, particularly toward the end of the war, Hitler said that the victory of the Russians and of those Slavic subhumans showed that they were still better than the Germans, who were losing the war. Sometimes he had insights of this kind. But here he says that the laws of nature would be invalidated if the inferior were to become master of the stronger. Strictly speaking, the survival of the fittest means precisely this becoming-master of the stronger as proof for his being better; but Hitler has a preconceived idea about what is better and what is inferior. For if inferior Poles and Russians win the day, then the laws of nature, according to which, indeed, the better should also be the stronger, are invalidated.

Now the absurdities a Hitler struggles with here, and which continually arise in the debate on such questions—even among very famous men—are not new. Rather it is a problem that Plato treated fully in the dialogue on the sophists, the *Gorgias,* where he also deals with the representatives of the right of the stronger. There he most painfully embarrasses this Callicles when he suggests to him that if all these inferiors, or rather those he regards as inferior, get together and kill him, that would prove they were the better. Whereupon Callicles explodes, for he knows what is better, *he* is the better, and the inferiors must be kept underneath. But the opposite does not hold; if then the inferiors, or rather those treated as inferior, in fact prove themselves to be the stronger, they are not thus shown to be the better.

So this dialectic, which one always falls into if one renounces the objective criteria of rightness and anticipates biological success, has been a sophistic problem since Plato and is still to be found at this petit bourgeois level today as a great problem we are not yet finished with.

(Fifth Lecture)

Ladies and Gentlemen,
Today we have to conclude the investigation of Schramm. It began with the problem of the shimmering content that did not allow a fixed picture to emerge. So we have the task of penetrating the shimmering in order to fix upon the reason for the shimmering itself. The lectures were constructed on this methodical principle. In the previous lecture I brought out the comparison of the kinship in thought between Hitler and Schramm, exemplified in Hitler's case through his treatment of Heraclitus, whom he turned into a social Darwinist, and Schramm's investigation of Darwin.

§21. Conclusion: Schramm's Spiritual Illiteracy Contrasted with Alan Bullock's Diagnosis of Hitler

If, as Schramm says, one has no categories of a moral, spiritual, and other intellectual kind to grasp the Hitler phenomenon, how then does one conclude an anatomy of the dictator anyway? What then can one say about him, if the most profound thing that can be said is a general-staff officer's statement that he is enigmatic, simply because he did not tell this general-staff officer all that he thought? So the conclusion of Schramm's investigation is itself our topic now. From this follows a triple division of the investigation of the conclusion.

First we must deal with the conclusion Schramm himself gives to his investigation. Then this conclusion must be critically investigated, which I shall do by references to Bullock's analyses. These are much earlier than Schramm's, but they exactly anticipate Schramm's mistakes. Then I will contrast Schramm's analysis with how one can conclude an investigation of Hitler, exemplified by the case of Bullock and his biography of Hitler. And finally I must myself conclude, which will again cast light on the relation between Schramm and Hitler and which therefore must be divided into two parts: the end of Hitler and the end of Schramm in this investigation.

Now, how does Schramm conclude his investigation? I have already read out for you the passages in which he again states near the end that we do not have the moral and other categories needed for grasping the phenomenon of Hitler. But yet, he still in conclusion—these are the final paragraphs of his investigation—gives indications for the direction in which the understanding of Hitler is to be sought; and as is proper for the German philistine in the field of education, the direction to take is that of Goethe. Schramm says that an indication of where our thoughts are to be directed is given by Goethe in *Dichtung und Wahrheit,* in the passage that deals with the nature of the demonic. That is a passage in the twentieth book, rather near the beginning, on the third or fourth page. I quote:

> They are not always the finest persons, in terms of either mind or talent, nor do they often commend themselves by goodness of heart, but they emanate a monstrous force and exercise incredible power over all creatures, and indeed even over the elements, and who can say how far such an influence may extend? All moral powers combined are impotent against them. In vain do the more enlightened among men attempt to suspect them to be deluded or deceptive—the masses are drawn to them. Seldom or never will contemporaries equal them, and they can be overcome only by the universe itself, against which they have taken up arms. And it may have been in view of this that the strange but striking proverb originated: *"Nemo contra Deum nisi Deus ipse"* [*"No one can do anything against God but God himself"*].[63]

Schramm then adds to this quotation, as the last paragraph, a further remark:

> At the end of the war, the author had his wife write out this paragraph [*the Goethe quotation*] word for word, because he remembered only its general content. As he studied it, sentence by sentence, he found that in one way it applied to Hitler, but in another it did not. [*The same happens to him again.*] Looking back over the centuries, Goethe spoke of the demonic, but he lacked the experience which would have enabled him to comprehend *how* frightful, *how* satanic, *how* infernal, it could be. We know; but there is no word in our language adequate to suggest the dimension of the demonic which took form in Adolf Hitler.[64]

The accusations that Schramm systematically plays down Hitler are, as I said, unjustified. What seems like playing down is illiteracy in the technical sense of a lack of spiritual, intellectual, literary, and philosophic education and of a linguistic deficiency. We are not

63. Schramm ET, 133.
64. Ibid.

lacking in expressions for characterizing the Hitler phenomenon, as you have already seen and will see further just now, in the case of Bullock. But you will again see how Schramm uses substitute clichés, in the second sentence from the end: frightful, satanic, infernal, demonic. Now you know something about Hitler. So, he was demonic.

But the Goethe quotation itself is very interestingly mangled; for the *Nemo contra Deum nisi Deus ipse*—as I have just translated it "No one can do anything against God but God himself"—is translated by Schramm himself for the reader who does not know Latin. He adds the following translation: "No one can do anything against God who himself is not God."[65] Now of course that is wrong in terms of Latin grammar, which is rather surprising in a historian who occupied himself particularly with the Middle Ages and presumably can read Latin sources and understand them correctly.

But it is also wrong in the context, for Goethe clearly said in the previous sentence what he thought, that the demonic types cannot be overcome except through the universe itself. That means that the sentence is to be understood in the context of the Spinozist[66] interpretation. He never meant that anyone is a God, if he fascinates people. Rather, he understood by it something completely different.

And that is Schramm's bad luck, that he obviously does not know that. But at any rate, Goethe is now quoted. For Goethe, after all, is one of the better-known authors, and even if *Dichtung und Wahrheit* is not read, what is written in some passages gets around, and the passage about the demonic is quoted very often. It was especially quoted in the Nuremberg Trial by one of the defense lawyers, with reference to Hitler.[67] And that gave rise to Bullock's dealing with this classification by Goethe of the demonic man. Similar epithets, which Schramm does not use, are, for example, that Hitler was a charismatic leader, using the Weberian category of charisma. Or Rauschning at one time said that

65. Schramm, 119. Schramm's version is: "Niemand vermag etwas gegen Gott, der nicht selbst Gott ist."

66. Cf. Eric Voegelin, "The German University and the Order of German Society: A Reconsideration of the Nazi Era," in *Published Essays, 1966–1985,* ed. Ellis Sandoz, vol. 12 of *The Collected Works of Eric Voegelin* (1990; available Columbia: University of Missouri Press, 1999), 13–14.

67. See Bullock, *Hitler,* 375.

> Dostoevsky might well have invented him, with the morbid derangement and the pseudo-creativeness of his hysteria.[68]

Bullock says of that:

> With Hitler, indeed one is uncomfortably aware of never being far from the realm of the irrational.[69]

The "irrational" is to be understood in the English sense, as the pathological. He then continues:

> For it is salutary to recall, before accepting the Hitler-Myth [*phrases like the demonic, the charismatic, and so on*] . . . that it was Hitler who invented the myth, assiduously cultivating and manipulating it for his own ends. . . .
>
> So much has been made of the charismatic nature of Hitler's leadership that it is easy to forget the astute and cynical politician in him. It is this mixture of calculation and fanaticism, with the difficulty of telling where one ends and the other begins, which is the peculiar characteristic of Hitler's personality. . . .
>
> The link between the different sides of Hitler's character was his extraordinary capacity for self-dramatization. [*Please note that we are now speaking of Hitler and that we do have the vocabulary required to speak of him, all the vocabulary that Schramm does not have.*] "This so-called *Wahnsystem,* or capacity for self-delusion," Sir Nevile Henderson, the British Ambassador, wrote, "was a regular part of his technique." [*He was thoroughly rational in pragmatic contexts and rationally prepared his decisions, but after the rational decision, based on rational consideration, was taken, then came the second phenomenon where*] . . . Hitler would whip himself into a passion, which enabled him to bear down all opposition, and provided him with the motive power to enforce his will on others.[70]

So, a characteristic performance of Hitler's.

> Hitler, in fact, was a consummate actor, with the actor's . . . facility for absorbing himself in a role and convincing himself of the truth of what he was saying at the time he said it.[71]

That is now precisely the pneumopathological phenomenon, which we have analyzed earlier, the interruption of contact with reality. That is, the contact with the first reality is absent; he is moving within a second reality. And this moving within the second reality is only possible because decisions, which are based on some kind of rational grounds, are then lifted up into the emotion of histrionic

68. Quoted ibid.
69. Ibid.
70. Ibid., 375–76.
71. Ibid., 377.

self-dramatization and the whipping up of his own passions, until one believes in what is false. So we are again at the point of how the lie becomes the truth. This phenomenon of turning the lie into truth, of changing the second reality into *the* reality, is what is meant by the phenomenon that Bullock calls the "irrational," and which is then treated in terms of clichés like the demonic or the charismatic in Hitler. So much, then, on Schramm's conclusion.

And now Bullock's conclusion, in his work on Hitler.

> To achieve what he did Hitler needed [*and possessed*] talents out of the ordinary which in sum amounted to political genius, however evil its fruits.[72]

I remind you of our earlier investigations of the fact that the power of existence and of high intelligence is completely compatible with the loss of reason and of spirit, that is to say, with the phenomenon of dehumanization.

> His mastery of the irrational factors in politics, his insight into the weaknesses of his opponents, his gift for simplification, his sense of timing, his willingness to take risks [*they are all admirable*]. An opportunist entirely without principle, he showed considerable consistency and an astonishing power of will in pursuing his aims.[73]

That is a point one must always keep in mind, that a man without Hitler's power of existence cannot have Hitler's success, even if the expression "will," as I have already explained, is not the correct expression. It is a matter of the intensity and the endurance of the libido, because what is to be understood by *voluntas* is the rationally ordered will. Again, quoting Bullock:

> The fact that his career ended in failure, and that his defeat was pre-eminently due to his own mistakes, does not by itself detract from Hitler's claim to greatness. The flaw lies deeper. For these remarkable powers were combined with an ugly and strident egotism, a moral and intellectual cretinism.[74]

Please note this vocabulary, which is at our disposal. German critics have sometimes rebelled against and criticized this vocabulary, saying that value judgments have been made here or that the expressions are vulgar. This opinion has its origin in their profound lack of philosophical education. For, if I may remind you of the earlier lectures, the concept of stupidity, of folly, the loss of reason,

72. Ibid., 804.
73. Ibid., 806.
74. Ibid., 804.

the pneumopathic condition, and so on, are not terms of abuse but technical terms for the analyses of spiritual structure. If one wished to forbid the use of these expressions because they are not used in polite society, one could never analyze a very large number of political phenomena at all. "Moral and intellectual cretinism" is the technical vocabulary for stupidity of the pneumopathological type in Schelling's sense. It is the correct and indispensable vocabulary for appropriately characterizing Hitler's spiritual structure.

Now, in detail, how does this cretinism, this spiritual pathology, express itself?

> The passions which ruled Hitler's mind were ignoble [*a concept that in German can hardly be used in the context of political analyses, because it would be taken for granted that politicians are ignoble*]: hatred, resentment, the lust to dominate, and, where he could not dominate, to destroy. [*We have a further term for that, the* pleonexia, *as in the Greek sense of "to the point of excess": What this man cannot dominate must be annihilated.*] His career did not exalt but debased the human condition, and his twelve years' dictatorship was barren of all ideas save one—the further extension of his own power. . . . Even power he understood in the crudest terms: an endless vista of military roads, S.S. garrisons and concentration camps to sustain the rule of the Aryan "master race" over the degraded subject peoples of his new empire in the east.[75]

What is astonishing, again and again leading to misunderstandings of Hitler, is that

> The great revolutions of the past . . . have been identified with the release of certain powerful ideas: individual conscience, liberty, equality, national freedom, social justice. National Socialism produced nothing. . . . [*One can find nothing in it except*] a vindictive destructiveness, Rauschning's *Revolution des Nihilismus.*
>
> It is this emptiness [*of all spiritual and rational content*], this lack of anything to justify the suffering he caused rather than his own monstrous and ungovernable will which makes Hitler both so repellent and so barren a figure.
>
> . . . But Nazism was not some terrible accident which fell upon the German people out of a blue sky. It was rooted in their history, and while it is true that a majority of the German people never voted for Hitler, it is also true that thirteen millions did. Both facts need to be remembered.[76]

75. Ibid..
76. Ibid., 804–5.

Bullock then goes beyond this immediate characterization to show that similar phenomena of decay are to be found in other countries too, even if to a far lesser extent:

> The Germans, however, were not the only people who preferred in the 1930s not to know what was happening and refused to call evil things by their true names.[77]

Note that "refused to call evil things by their true names," because here lies one of the roots of the evils of that petit bourgeois salon-culture that believes it is improper to call a murderer a murderer. Particularly in the Federal Republic we have, in consequence of the Second World War and the post-Hitler period, the tacit maxim of good taste: "In the hangman's house you don't talk about rope." Bullock continues:

> The British and the French at Munich; the Italians, Germany's partners in the Pact of Steel; the Poles, who stabbed the Czechs in the back over Teschen; the Russians, who signed the Nazi-Soviet pact to partition Poland, all thought they could buy Hitler off, or use him to their own selfish advantage. They did not succeed, any more than the German Right or the German army. [*Or the German churches. We will have to speak about them right away.*] In the bitterness of war and occupation they were forced to learn the truth of the words of John Donne [*the seventeenth-century English poet and cleric*], which Ernest Hemingway set at the beginning of his novel of the Spanish Civil War [*I would ask you to learn this quotation by heart. We will come across it again.*]:
>
> "No man is an Iland, intire of it selfe; every man is a peece of the Continent, a part of the maine; If a clod bee washed away by the Sea, Europe is the lesse, as well as if a Promontorie were, as well as if a Mannor of thy friends or of thine owne were; Any man's death diminishes me, because I am involved in Mankinde; And therefore never send to know for whom the bell tolls; It tolls for thee."[78]

This elementary humanity—that what concerns my neighbor concerns me too—this was lacking. In a wider sense, it was lacking in the whole Western world, and, in what became a quite specific and criminal sense, in Germany, and especially in the churches, which used their theological position to renounce humanity. That is the end of Bullock, with the quotation from Donne. This is where the problem is (we have again arrived at the problem we began with) of dehumanization and the retreat to individual interests.

77. Ibid., 806.
78. Ibid.

And now the third conclusion, my own, where I have to deal with Hitler and with Schramm. How did Hitler come to an end? By suicide in the Führer's bunker in Berlin, after he had allowed the whole of Germany up to a hundred meters from the Führer's bunker to be destroyed. The end of the career of the libido without reason or spirit was reached. What he could not dominate he destroyed, and at the very end, he destroyed himself. However, that is not all. That would be the first reality, in which the drama—by no means the tragedy—the drama of the libido played itself out. But behind this first reality is the second reality. Hitler left a testament. And Bullock now analyzes this testament. He says:

> Characteristically, Hitler's last message to the German people contained at least one striking lie [*for the second reality is indeed built up on the lie; it is always in conflict with the first reality*]. His death was anything but a hero's end; by committing suicide he deliberately abandoned his responsibilities and took a way out which in earlier years he had strongly condemned as a coward's. The words in the Testament are carefully chosen to conceal this; he speaks of his "unity with our soldiers unto death," and again of fulfilling his duty unto death. It is worth noting that when General Weidling, the Commandant of Berlin, discovered that Hitler had committed suicide shortly after refusing the garrison permission to fight its way out of the city, he was so disgusted that he at once released his soldiers from their oaths. [*So there was still then a first reality that at least did not let itself be completely stupefied by the second reality.*] None the less, the fiction [*of Hitler's being united in death with his soldiers*] was maintained in the public announcement, and his short-term successor Dönitz, in his broadcast of May 1 [*Hitler had committed suicide on April 30*] declared that the Führer had died fighting at the head of his troops.[79]

The post-Hitler period begins with this lie. So here we have the first and second reality for the end of Hitler. We have the counterpart to Hitler's second reality, the parallel to Hitler's ending with a lie, in the case of Schramm, who has been made chancellor of the Order *Pour le Mérite.*[80] One can rely on our Federal Republic. That is the Schramm case. With this we have mastered a piece of the present.

79. Ibid., 797.

80. Membership in the Order *Pour le Mérite* was originally awarded by the kings of Prussia for outstanding military achievement; since the introduction of a "peace class" in 1842, membership has also been awarded for excellence in the fields of science and art. Beginning in 1922 it was conferred by the existing members of the order, which was revived in 1952 as a "Free Union of outstanding scholars and artists." Schramm was elected to the order in 1958 and became the chancellor in 1963.

4

Descent into the Ecclesiastical Abyss

The Evangelical Church

§22. Lack of a Theoretical Articulation of "Church"

I can now go on to the no less unappetizing object of the churches. I remind you that the lectures are called "Hitler and the Germans." Nothing can be explained with the cliché of National Socialism. It is a matter of a pneumopathological phenomenon of social corruption. One must be conscious of this above all in the case of the churches. The problem of the churches, however, is not easy to deal with, and with regard to this lecture I find myself in the grotesque situation of having to develop something like a philosophy of the church because—you will hardly believe it, but it is so—there is no theory of the church available. The churches are spoken about, but no one has yet really concerned himself with the question of the church. Just take a look at the theological dictionaries, under the heading "church."

So, let us begin where we all are, at the commonsense level, in order to differentiate the many meanings of the word "church." In the first and nearest meaning, which is the meaning we have primarily to deal with, "church" means the Evangelical and Catholic Churches of Germany as social institutions. In addition, we speak of the churches in other countries, Evangelical and Catholic, so of churches in the plural. Then, there is the supranational institution of the Catholic Church with its organizational center in the Roman Curia, which again is something else. Then there are the other Christian churches and sects, for example, the Greek Orthodox Church, which do not fall under any of these first terms. Then there is Christ's church, as a collective term for all ecclesial institutions that confess themselves as Christian. Sixth and last in this series there is the *corpus mysticum Christi,* a theological term, which according to the theology of Thomas includes all men, from the beginning of the world to its end, therefore far exceeding what falls under ecclesial institutions. The problem of the churches exists at all these levels.

Now we have above all to deal with the German Catholic and Evangelical Churches, and what I say about churches, if I do not further qualify it, refers to these, and not, for example, to the Catholic Church as a supranational organization, nor to the *corpus mysticum Christi,* nor to the Evangelical and Catholic Churches in other countries, and so on.

But if we now speak of the Evangelical and Catholic Churches, and their role in relation to National Socialism, we must first explain one point that is readily forgotten, and which then leads to the strangest misinterpretations, criticisms, and anticriticisms in public debate. The German people—not understood in a *völkisch* sense but, let us say, German society within the 1937 borders of the Reich—was at the time essentially a church people (*Kirchenvolk*). There was only a small percentage belonging to no Christian confession and 1 percent who were Jewish. So church people and German people are more or less identical. Now this identity will be obscured by the persistence of the clichés of institutions when we speak of church and state, because we thus obscure the human and political fact that the church represents the spiritual order of man toward God.

That is to say, the German people in politics and the German people in the church are the same; as human beings it belongs to their constitution to be transcendentally oriented. The churches are nothing other than the representation of the spiritual transcendence of man. They are not anything else. However, if we speak in clichés of church and state, it then looks as if two different societies are opposed to one another here, and we forget that the personnel of these societies is indeed identical, that they are thus the same societies, only with different representations, temporal and spiritual.

If, therefore, a society—not now the state or the church—is in spiritual and intellectual disorder, then this is not only the case in the sphere of temporal politics and order, but holds just as much in the sphere of spiritual order to be maintained by the church. So there arises Jaspers' proposition, which he then wrote in his *Die geistige*

Situation der Zeit,[1] that the formation of élites for the salvation of the order of a people is impossible in a corrupt society. So, the church is not an élite within a people that is generally corrupt, but it participates in the corruption. This proposition of Jaspers, incidentally, was developed by Plato and Aristotle. In contrast to this fact, that church and state are identical in their social personnel, there is now the role that has fallen to the churches, that they should represent spiritual order as separate institutions, even if they do not do this.

Moral corruption, in the sense of intellectual and spiritual corruption—which expressed itself in various ideologies and in membership in the National Socialist party—made democracy, in the form of the Weimar republic, impossible. This was to the extent that toward the end of the Weimar republic we had a blocking majority—that is, the radical ideologists of left and right, Communists and National Socialists, had the majority in the Reichstag; between them the democratic center was helpless. The political helplessness and lack of judgment of the democrats is itself a component in the general state of corruption that expressed itself in the ideological left and right wings and in their party power struggles.

This disintegration in the temporal sphere of social order then led to the disintegration of all parties after Hitler's accession to government. That is, in the political-temporal sphere there were no further representatives who could express themselves publicly in order to take a position against National Socialism. Since a political representation of opposition to the regime no longer existed after the regime had come to power, the church was left as the representation of the spiritual order of man. It was a remnant of representation of the human over against National Socialism, and from this strange situation there fell to it the role of defending and maintaining the interests and dignity of man.

§23. Intellectual and Spiritual Decline in the German Churches

However, the church could not satisfy these demands. The churches were unable to defend the dignity of man—not only to defend it successfully, but to defend it at all—because they themselves, laity

1. Translated by Eden and Cedar Paul as *Man in the Modern Age* (London: Routledge and Kegan Paul, 1966). See pp. 104, 117.

and clergy, were participants in that corruption, too, even if to a lesser degree than the National Socialists themselves. The church was unable to cope with the situation of a dehumanized society because the loss of reality had already taken place within the church itself. The contact with the reality of man in his individuality as *theo-morphes,* and thus his real human nature, had got lost. This state of loss of reality in the churches can now be differentiated in various directions. How did it come about? I am speaking now only of the churches in German society; in other societies it appears somewhat differently.

First, through isolation from philosophy. It would of course have been possible to obtain an image of man from Platonic-Aristotelian philosophy, from classical ethics. But this picture of man in classical philosophy was never available in Germany because of the parallel decline of university philosophy. This then is linked on the church's side—since it did not interest itself in man—with its restriction to institutional, cultural-political interests, that is to say, to specific interests of the church, while it was indifferent to the interests of man. Further, penetrating still deeper into the structure of the church, interest in man had also become excluded from the theological sphere of interests (we shall speak about this again in particular instances), with the result that from the theological side, too, there existed no possibility of mastering the situation intellectually.

Therefore it is characteristic that the ecclesiastical resistance, Evangelical and Catholic, only begins when the institutional interests of the church are endangered by National Socialism. A church isn't in the least interested as long as only a few concentration camps are set up in which people are ill-treated or where Jews are beaten. So elementary humanity of a temporal kind had disappeared from the German churches.

A further element in this picture is the radical ignorance, particularly in Germany, of the nature of a modern political movement. In the Western world, since the Middle Ages—but only outside Germany—we can see the formation of society and the image of man, through the Renaissance, through humanism, through the natural law of the seventeenth and eighteenth centuries, through the Enlightenment. Wherever a society is characterized by the image of man of a temporal kind, however philosophically dubious it may be from another perspective, movements of the National

Socialist type cannot emerge with the radicality and social impact they had in Germany. It was characteristic for Germany that contact with the temporal reality of politics was not established by humanism, Renaissance, natural law, and Enlightenment, but through German Romanticism and irresponsible chatter about *Volkstum* since Friedrich Ludwig Jahn,[2] the "father of gymnastics," so that the churches in Germany were tied in a very specific way to the *Volkstum*. We will later have to speak of this *Volkstum* and the admission of this concept into theology. As a consequence, humanity was replaced within the churches and theological circles by Romantic *Volkstum*-ideology. Further, there was radical ignorance regarding the character of modern gnostic movements of the Communist or National Socialist type, an ignorance that still exists today.

And this, again, is a sub-phenomenon of intellectual decadence and hostility to science, which the church has had for several centuries. However, this decadence not only is related to the temporal sphere and the questions of national order in politics but also affects the most internal area of the church's theological formation and theological knowledge. Parallel to this, as a further phenomenon within the general intellectual decadence, we must establish the quite fantastic decadence of theological knowledge among clerics and theologians. And I will again give you the evidence from the source materials.

This condition of decadence is not a phenomenon limited to the National Socialist period, but it can be seen most painfully throughout the nineteenth century in relation to the new social questions posed by the industrial society. And it has lasted up to the present time, 1964. Not only has this condition persisted—that might perhaps be still excusable, for one cannot bring centuries-long decadence back into order overnight—but the resistance to the overcoming of this decadence is intense; and it is not only a passive resistance, but an active opposition. It expresses itself on

2. Friedrich Jahn (1778–1852) was a scholar of the German language who tried to purify it of all non-Germanic words. In his *German Folkdom* (1810) he coined and developed the term *Volkstum* as "that which the *Volk* has in common, its inner existence, its movement, its ability to propagate." Inspired by the romantic concept of *Volkstum* and the political aim of one unified and democratic-egalitarian German nation, Jahn founded the gymnastic movement (*Turnbewegung*) and hence was named the "father of gymnastics" (*Turnvater* Jahn). In 1848 he became a member of the German National Convention.

the clerical side by the systematic keeping secret and hushing up of the events of the National Socialist period.

On the question of this systematic suppression of reality, may I read out two passages relating to the Munich auxiliary bishop Neuhäusler,[3] from the new book by Guenter Lewy, *The Catholic Church and Nazi Germany,* which came out a few weeks ago.[4] Neuhäusler has already published a book, *Kreuz und Hakenkreuz,* in 1946, I believe, where the role of the Catholic Church's great resistance under National Socialism is glorified.[5] On closer investigation, it turns out that the whole story is not true; and not only that, but Neuhäusler systematically distorted sources through omissions and often by verbal changes, too. On the occasion of one such omission from the declaration of the Bishops' Conference of March 28, 1933, Lewy notes now:

> This short but important paragraph also represented an addition to [*Cardinal*] Bertram's draft.[6] It is symptomatic of the boldness with which some Catholic writers after 1945 have falsified important documents from the Nazi period that this passage is omitted by Auxiliary Bishop Neuhäusler, without the customary indication of an ellipsis.[7]

The paragraph omitted by Bishop Neuhäusler is the following, from the nonfalsified text of this declaration of the Fulda Bishops' Conference:

> Catholic Christians, to whom the voice of their Church is sacred, do not require at this time a special admonition to be loyal to the lawful authorities and to fulfil conscientiously their civic duties while rejecting on principle all illegal or subversive conduct.[8]

That is what the bishops said to the German Catholics on March 18, 1933: Obey the lawful authorities. We will have to speak about

3. Johann Neuhäusler (1888–1973) was, from 1933, a consultant and spokesman for church policy to the diocese of Munich-Freising. He was jailed and later held in Sachsenhausen and Dachau concentration camps from 1941 to 1945, and was appointed auxiliary bishop of Munich-Freising in 1947.

4. Guenter Lewy, *The Catholic Church and Nazi Germany* (New York: McGraw-Hill, 1964).

5. Johann Neuhäusler, *Kreuz und Hakenkreuz: Der Kampf des Nationalsozialismus gegen die katholische Kirche und der kirchliche Widerstand* (Munich: Verlag Katholische Kirche Bayerns, 1946).

6. Adolf Bertram (1859–1945) became bishop of Hildesheim in 1906 and of Breslau in 1914; was created cardinal in 1916; and was president of the German Bishops' Conference, 1919–45.

7. Lewy, *The Catholic Church and Nazi Germany,* 353 n. 47.

8. Ibid., 40.

the question of authority immediately after this. And in a second passage, where again such omissions come, Lewy says:

> Neuhäusler, who edits the joint pastoral letter in a way that completely changes its meaning, leaves out the words "On the other hand" and does so, again, without the customary use of the ellipsis. This hides the existence of the preceding part of that section, which he omits. Hans Müller (in a review article "Zur Behandlung des Kirchenkampfes in der Nachkriegsliteratur," *Politische Studien*, XII [1961], 474–81), has counted twenty-one cuts in Neuhäusler's reproduction of the text of this pastoral letter: ten of these passages very clearly are omitted because they do not fit the thesis of Neuhäusler's book [*on the Catholic resistance*]; nine times omissions in the text are not indicated; in five instances the wording is actually altered.[9]

So that is how things look. Therefore we have a very powerful resistance legend (if I now speak just of Catholic cases, have no fear of prejudice—you will in a moment hear what is to be said about the Protestants), about which the following is to be said. I quote one of Lewy's concluding paragraphs:

> There is no reason, of course, to single out for criticism the Catholic Church. The German Catholics were part and parcel of a milieu that, with few notable exceptions, lacked a sufficient leavening of political sophistication and moral backbone to see through the patriotic shibboleths of the Hitler regime. But there has spread a legend [*what I have just now been discussing*] of resistance on the part of the Church . . . that badly needs historical corrective. The fact is, as the Catholic historian Friedrich Heer has aptly put it, "that Christian resistance to Hitler during the Third Reich from the beginning had the character of the unique, . . . the undesirable. . . . In 1945 the situation was so critical that only a gigantic attempt at concealment was regarded as able to save and restore the face of official Christianity in Germany."[10]

So, the systematic suppression of the position of the churches faced with the Hitler regime—and not only suppression, but occasionally also systematic falsifying of texts—is the instrument by which active opposition to a mastery of the past is carried out and by which, consequently, in the present nothing is mastered either. Therefore, we are in a remarkable situation regarding sources. What these churches did during the National Socialist period has become known only in the last few years. If you look at the dates, for example, Goldschmidt and Kraus's edition of *Der ungekündigte*

9. Ibid., 363 n. 7.
10. Ibid., 320–21.

Bund (*The Unbroken Covenant*), which publishes the Evangelical documents, appeared in 1962,[11] and Hans Müller's work *Katholische Kirche und Nationalsozialismus,* which publishes the most important Catholic documents, appeared in 1963.[12] A dispute by the Evangelical bishop Otto Dibelius about the brazen nonsense that was carried on with Romans 13, maintaining that one had to obey the authorities, appeared in 1963, and we now finally have, at least for the Catholic side, Lewy's *Catholic Church and Nazi Germany,* which appeared a few weeks ago, so, in 1964.

Thus, we are not now about to liquidate the past, but we are at the beginning of what will require decades of investigation into the corruption of German society, more specifically, into the corruption in the church. That is only now beginning. And now to the churches themselves.

§24. Evangelical Church's Participation in Nationalistic-*Völkisch* Ideology

First, the Evangelical Church, not only because it is numerically stronger in Germany but also because it offers certain advantages for the investigation over the less useful Catholic materials. That is because of the church's structure. In the Evangelical Church there exists no disciplined dogma that the clergy must observe; rather, theological interpretation of the Scripture is free. As a result, there is possible a range from radical perversion of the Bible to relatively decent—I say *relatively* decent, there is no good—theology, which shows the entire breadth of the phenomenon of decline.

There are the same phenomena within the Catholic Church, but they are disguised by the iron discipline of the organization. You must remember that great differences existed in the Catholic episcopate of the Hitler period, and if a Preysing in Berlin,[13] a Galen in Westphalia, did not found something like a Catholic Confessing Church over against the very much more degenerate among their

11. Dietrich Goldschmidt and Hans-Joachim Kraus, eds., *Der ungekündigte Bund: Neue Begegnungen von Juden und christlicher Gemeinde* (Stuttgart: Kreuz Verlag, 1962).

12. Hans Müller, *Katholische Kirche und Nationalsozialismus: Dokumente, 1930–1935* (Munich: Nymphenburger Verlagshandlung, 1963).

13. Konrad, Graf von Preysing (1880–1950) became bishop of Eichstatt in 1932 and of Berlin in 1935, and was created cardinal in 1946.

colleagues, the only reason they did not was not to break the unity of the episcopate. In the Evangelical Church, on the other hand, the different directions, radical and more respectable, fell apart into clearly discernible groupings, with their own manifestos. So, the problem can be grasped more clearly in the Evangelical Church, because the phenomenon of decline, along with the opposition to it, was publicly given a thorough debate. Within the Evangelical sector of the church there is a large number of very different kinds of people who were active as writers and provided Christian manifestos ranging from the neopaganism of the Ludendorff type, for example, to the more moderate Christianity of the German Reich Church, the German Christians in the Reich Church under Reich Bishop Müller.

Let us now make classifications; I will give examples. The furthest in the zone of decline, close to the pagan believers in Germanness, is a *Confessio Germanica*, 1933, by a Mr. Ernst Bergmann,[14] whom I cannot further identify. His *Confessio* consists of three propositions:

> I believe in the God of the Germano-religion, who works in nature, in the high spirit of man, and in the power of my people.
>
> And in the Reliever Krist [*with a "K" so it looks more German*], who fights for the nobleness of the human soul.
>
> And in Germany, the land where a new humanity is being forged.[15]

That is what you find, at the extreme wing, so to say, of the dehumanization and decline in the Evangelical Church. Somewhere in the middle was the religious movement of the "German Christians," represented by Joachim Hossenfelder, who exemplified the more radical wing. He was a pastor in Berlin and later bishop of Brandenburg. He made use of the National Socialist vocabulary, as it is to be found in the party program. So, he was not as crazy as Bergmann was; that was too stupid even for the National Socialists.

> We stand on the ground of positive Christianity. [*That's in the party program.*] We confess an affirmative, race-conformed (*artgemäßen*) belief in Christ, as he is in accordance with the German spirit of Luther and heroic piety. . . . We see in race, *Volkstum,* and nation what God has bestowed upon us and the orders of life entrusted to us, to care for

14. Ernst Bergmann, professor of philosophy at the University of Leipzig. His *Confessio* is to be found in his book, *Die deutsche Nationalkirche* (Breslau: Ferdinand Hirt, 1933), 266–67.

15. Goldschmidt and Kraus, *Der ungekündigte Bund,* 192.

> whose preservation is God's law for us. Hence the mixing of races is to be opposed. . . .
>
> . . . We reject the Jewish mission in Germany, as long as the Jews possess the right of citizenship and thus the danger of race-concealment and bastardization continues.[16]

So that is the German Christians' left wing. Then there is the German Christians' moderate wing, represented by Reich Bishop Müller, which again was supported by the National Socialist party. A theological declaration was produced by a Friedrich Gebhardt. All this is in 1933. He explains, in lapidary sentences, that

> Belief in Christ is race-conformed in form, Christ-conformed in content.
>
> . . . The New Testament in itself is Gospel, the Old Testament does not become Gospel even through the New Testament. [*So, out with the Old Testament.*]
>
> Israel was the chosen people (*Volk*), but God rejected it, and gave the Gospel to a "people" ("*Volk*") who would bear his fruit. [*That is to say, to the Germans.*] No nation may claim the Gospel for itself alone, but God even today can still espouse or reject peoples, as he once did.[17]

So he can espouse the German people. The editors of the book, *Der ungekündigte Bund,* say of these sentences of this Gebhardt, that

> this moderate direction within the religious movement had many points of contact with the prevailing average theology [*Please note this. That, then, was the average level—total intellectual, spiritual, theological, decadence.*] because here too—as a by-product of the Luther-renaissance—there had come about a theological high regard for one's own *Volkstum* as the cradle of the Reformation, and the transfiguration of German history almost into the history of salvation.[18]

—as an incorporation of Luther-propaganda in the context of Romantic *Volkstum*-ideology. Note the continuous return of the word *Volkstum,* from the "father of gymnastics" Jahn, who is a father of the church for all German churches. That was this first phase. These were, so to say, gymnastics in theological thinking.

The matter became critical when the National Socialist government threw out a few scraps that one now had to chew on. The Law for the Restoration of the Civil Service was issued on April 7, 1933,

16. Ibid., 192–93. This is an extract from "Guidelines of the 'German Christian' Faith-Movement," May 26, 1932.

17. Goldschmidt and Kraus, *Der ungekündigte Bund,* 194.

18. Ibid., 191.

and contained the famous Aryan paragraph, according to which the Jews had to be eliminated from the civil service. In the summer of 1933 the Evangelical Church was presented with a law on the relationship of clergymen and church officials to the Reich, which also applied this Aryan paragraph to the church. They now had to discuss this, and these discussions are of the greatest interest. Let us first take what the editors of the documents say. That is, how,

> while the defamation of their Jewish fellow-citizens in public through the boycott of their businesses on April 1, 1933, and the suspension of various government offices by means of the application of the Aryan paragraph was accepted with an astonishing matter-of-factness (Dietrich Bonhoeffer was one of the few who spontaneously declared themselves to be in solidarity with the victims of the new social order), resistance flared up as soon as the church itself was affected by the new legislation in the form of its office-holders.[19]

So here you have this pattern of social behavior: As long as the neighbor gets it in the neck, we all happily join in, but as soon as our own turn comes, then there is resistance. But by that time it is a bit too late, and naturally the basic rules of humanity were not available when the other was being massacred.

§25. Theological Opinions Regarding Race Laws

What now do the various church assemblies make of this law? In the Prussian General Synod the discussions about it took place on September 4 and 5, 1933.[20] On that occasion there was the split, as I have already mentioned, which did not occur in the Catholic Church because of its inner discipline. During this discussion, the "Gospel and Church" group, which had been formed on July 23 and which was to become the kernel of the later Confessing Church, left the hall. The law, with its Aryan paragraph, was accepted. Other remarks were made by a fellow named Coch, who was the *Land* bishop of Saxony:

> The legal basis of the new law for state officials lies in membership of the Aryan race. This membership of the Aryan race must consequently also be incorporated into the church's law for its officials.[21]

19. Ibid., 194–95.
20. Cf. ibid., 195.
21. Ibid., 195.

So the ecclesiastical officials, that is to say, the pastors, are state officials; the church, so to say, is a component of the operations of the state, which were carried out by the National Socialist party. That view however was not generally shared. For example, the presbytery of the Evangelical Church of Lower Barmen was of another opinion. This presbytery "rejected the law as unbiblical and unevangelical, and therefore as unecclesiastical"[22]—in itself a decent attitude, which was only somewhat marred by the fact that when the Jews got it in the neck, the presbyterium of the Evangelical community of Lower Barmen twiddled their thumbs too.

In the autumn of 1933, the Pastors' Emergency League was founded by Martin Niemöller.[23] And on this occasion it was announced

> that the application of the Aryan paragraph in the space of the Church of Christ would create an injury to the Confessing position.[24]

So, again, the narrowest restriction to the Church of Christ, "in the space"—ghastly German—"of the Church of Christ." All the rest are of no concern to him. The whole situation becomes clear through the list of decisions in which, finally, the civil service law with the Aryan paragraph came into effect for the Evangelical Church. Look at the dates. On September 6, the law for church government was passed with the Aryan paragraph. On November 16, 1933, the law was canceled by the church government. On January 4, 1934, the cancellation was further canceled. On April 12, 1934, the cancellation of the cancellation was again canceled, and on the same date, in paragraph 4, it was decided that the cancellation of the cancellation remained in force. That is what the Church of Christ looks like. Thus for the Confessing Church and for those who wanted to offer resistance, the first round "was lost."[25] Again, this is a remark of the editors, who know the situation of the Evangelical Church better than I do. The church was not prepared for

22. Ibid.

23. Martin Niemöller (1892–1984), a famous U-boat commander in the First World War, supported the Nazi party from the mid-1920s. Having studied theology, he was appointed pastor of the parish of Berlin-Dahlem in 1931. Soon after Hitler's accession to power, Pastor Niemöller was a key figure in what became the Confessing Church's opposition to Nazi interference in the church and was imprisoned in concentration camps from 1938 to 1945. After the war he played an important role in the repentance and renewal of the Evangelical Church.

24. Goldschmidt and Kraus, *Der ungekündigte Bund,* 195.

25. Ibid., 196.

such problems.[26] Therefore they issued appeals to the Evangelical faculties, requesting an opinion.

We now come to the theological faculties. Such opinions were in fact delivered by the requested faculties. And indeed an opinion from the Marburg faculty was delivered by Dean von Soden on September 19, 1933. Six days later an Erlangen opinion was delivered by Professors Althaus and Elert, on September 25, 1933.[27] Let us now take a look at these opinions. I will in fact concentrate on the Erlangen opinion, because it is clearer than the Marburg one in its linguistic structure, that is to say, it is even viler. But it has the advantage, too, that a theologian of higher rank like Rudolf Bultmann[28] launched an extremely energetic criticism against this lousy opinion, which I will show you too, so that you get the extreme positions and can see approximately the distance between them. So from the Erlangen opinion:[29]

> The external order of the Christian Church, according to Reformed teaching, as distinct from the Roman Catholic, must correspond not only to the universality of the Gospel but also to the historic-*völkisch* structure of Christian men. [*Please note the "historic-völkisch structure"!*] . . . For the Lutheran confessions, being one in Christ is not a question of external organization but of faith.
>
> In accordance with these principles, the churchdoms (*Kirchentümer*) that emerged from the Wittenberg Reformation adapted to the borders of the different peoples, and in their ecclesiastical language in worship and constitution they not only preserved the national particularities but contributed considerably to their cultivation and conservation.[30]

Note the expression "churchdom" (*Kirchentum*), an analogous formation to the *Volkstum* of Jahn, the father of gymnastics. Thus Jahn intrudes into theological language—when the theologian is speaking of the church—since now we don't have "church," but a "churchdom" of a *völkisch* type. Now,

> If the *völkisch* diversity of the external church orders is a necessary consequence (which is both fateful and must be ethically affirmed) of

26. Ibid., 203.
27. Ibid.
28. Rudolf Bultmann (1884–1976) was professor of theology in Breslau, 1916–20; in Giessen, 1920–21; and in Marburg, 1921–51.
29. Its full title is "Theological Opinion on the Admission of Christians of Jewish Origin to the Ministries of the German Evangelical Church (Erlangen Opinion)." See Goldschmidt and Kraus, *Der ungekündigte Bund,* 205.
30. Ibid., 205–6.

> the *völkisch* structure in general, then it is indeed to be taken into account in the admission to church offices. . . . The bearer of spiritual office shall be so bound to his community in its earthly existence that the bonds arising from that earthly existence are also his own too. Part of this is the bond to the same *Volkstum*.[31]

So you now have the correspondence between *Kirchentum* and *Volkstum*. And on this basis the Jewish question is decided:

> Whether, and to what extent, this principle is to be applied to the Christians of Jewish origin living among us requires special discussion. In the first place the question arises whether the Jews resident in Germany belong to the German *Volk* in the full sense, or have a *Volkstum* of their own, and thus are a guest people (*Gastvolk*).[32]

You can see, now even the Jews have received a *Volkstum*. Not only the Germans, not only the churchdoms, but also the Jews have a *Volkstum*.

> The church as such cannot decide . . . whether Jewry (*Judentum*) living among us belong to the German people in the full sense or constitute a foreign, a guest people. . . . The question regarding the *völkisch* relationship between Germandom and Jewry [*Please note the vocabulary, at the most vulgar level, as you find it in Schramm and in Ernst Haeckel and in Hitler.*] is of a biological-historical kind [*now you have biology in it too*]. It can only be answered by our people, as is the case with every other people, in view of its particular biological-historical situation.
>
> The German people today experience the Jews among them more than ever as a foreign *Volkstum*. It has recognized the threat to its independent existence by emancipated Jewry and defends itself against this danger with special legal regulations. [*It has not yet recognized the threat to its own way of life by Protestant and Catholic theologians and has not defended itself against that with special regulations.*] . . . The church must acknowledge the fundamental right of the state to take such legislative measures. [*Why, no one knows. But it must, the church. Please note that we will later have opposing views.*] It knows that in the contemporary situation it is itself called to a new awareness of its task of being the people's church (*Volkskirche*) of the Germans. This entails that it deliberately asserts its principle of the *völkisch* responsibility of office-holders, and applies it against the Christians of Jewish origin. . . . In belonging to Christ there is, before God, no difference between Jews and non-Jews. But the common adoption of all Christians as children of God does not abolish the biological

31. Ibid., 206.
32. Ibid.

> and social differences but binds everyone to the class to which he was called. (1 Cor. 7:20).[33] The biological bond to a particular people [*Please note the "biological bond": The most vulgar race-rubbish is brought forward here by theologians, professors of a theological faculty.*], fatefully inescapable for us, is to be acknowledged by Christians with conviction and action.[34]

So it is plainly made the duty of Christians to conduct themselves inhumanly and unchristianly. Note the word "fatefully."

Ambrose Bierce's *Devil's Dictionary* defines fate or destiny as "a tyrant's authority for crime and a fool's excuse for failure."[35] So we should always be careful whenever someone says something about fate; something already stinks then. That then is the Erlangen theologians' opinion. Still it was a bit too much for somewhat more intelligent theologians. And so Rudolf Bultmann energetically opposed this Erlangen opinion:

> Does not the Erlangen opinion say that all Christians have a common adoption as children of God, which does not abolish the biological and social differences? Rather, is not every Christian bound to the position in which he is called? Yes, with complete justification. [*Now comes this passage, 1 Cor. 7:20.*] I am surprised at the rashness of the appeal to 1 Cor. 7:20. For there is nothing to be read here saying that those differences also hold for the space of the church and have significance. [*Please note, again, "the space of the church," a wishy-washy expression of Bultmann's too.*] On the contrary! Paul says that the distinctions that are meaningless for the church maintain their validity in the world. He opposes 1 Cor. 7:17–24 against such fools, who wish to make the principles of the ecclesiastical community into the laws of the world, against the desires for the emancipation of slaves and women. [*Hence, egalitarian politics, since all men are the same as children of God. Bultmann's reference to this passage is correct.*] And shall we now perpetrate the opposite folly, and make the laws of the world into laws of the church?[36]

Bultmann has constrained himself and (he is otherwise a fine man too) therefore speaks only of a rash usage—"I am surprised at the rashness of the appeal to 1 Cor." I do not consider this kind of linguistic pussyfooting appropriate. Let us be clear about it! The

33. 1 Cor. 7:20–21 RSV: "Every one should remain in the state in which he was called. Were you a slave when called? Never mind."

34. Goldschmidt and Kraus, *Der ungekündigte Bund,* 206–8.

35. Ambrose Bierce, *The Devil's Dictionary* (1911; reprint, Ware: Wordsworth, 1996), 63.

36. Goldschmidt and Kraus, *Der ungekündigte Bund,* 210.

opinion of these Erlangen theologians is a matter of pronounced intellectual mischief, the falsification and misuse of the text of Scripture for National Socialist ends. However, Bultmann does not essentially go beyond this theological criticism. On the political side also, nothing comes of it. May I read out another passage here?

> So the state may decide whether the Jews resident in Germany may belong to the German people in the full sense or are a visiting people. The church as such cannot decide, so the Erlangen opinion correctly says.[37]

So, here too, refusal of the whole of human ethics, of the whole of classic philosophy, of the whole of classic ethics. It does not interest even a man like Bultmann. It is only inconsistent for the church to take on the decision made by the state. The church knows Jews only in the sense of their denomination: Jewish Christians are for the church simply Christians, and the National Socialist State can do what it likes to whoever is not a Jewish Christian, but only an ordinary Jew. . . .

(Sixth Lecture)

Ladies and Gentlemen,
Today I will finish with the problem of the Evangelical Church. The next time I will pass to the Catholic, since at twelve o'clock I must give the Max Weber lecture.[38] This Max Weber lecture really belongs to these lectures as the first lecture on those Germans who with great success offered resistance to this decline, but it should come after the analysis of the problem of decline. However, I have to insert it here now.

In the previous lecture, I presented some documents to you. The last was the biological opinion of the Erlangen faculty with its remarkable theological vocabulary of *Volkstum* and, constructed on analogy with that, *Kirchentum*—that is to say, with a conceptual language coined by Jahn, the father of gymnastics, which, strictly speaking, is empty of meaning. There are no *Volkstümer;* they belong to the second reality of the Romantic linguistic exhilaration, about which I will have to speak later. And then, Bultmann's answer to this Erlangen opinion, where he especially demonstrated the rash

37. Ibid., 211–12.
38. See the concluding chapter.

misuse of biblical passages with the intention of incorporating them into the propaganda for the Aryan paragraphs in the church.

§26. Anti-Semitic Tendencies in *Land* Bishop Wurm and Pastor Niemöller

I now have two biographical matters to present as the next documents. How did people behave and where lies the deeper reason for this remarkable weakness and of this belated resistance? I will illustrate that by two examples, that of the Evangelical *Land* Bishop Wurm[39] and the case of the famous Pastor Niemöller, who today is the Evangelical Church president. As late as the year 1938—that is to say, after five years of rich experiences with concentration camps, National Socialist politics, anti-Jewish legislation, Aryan paragraphs, attitude toward the church, and so on—*Land* Bishop Wurm had written in a letter submitted to Reich Justice Minister Gürtner:

> I do not with a single word dispute the state's right to combat Jewry as a dangerous element. From my youth, I have regarded the judgment of men like Heinrich von Treitschke and Adolf Stöcker on the subversive effect of Jewry in the religious, ethical, literary, economic, and political sphere to be appropriate.[40]

So the man is a pronounced anti-Semite, and he speaks about subversion in the religious, ethical, and other spheres. . . . By 1943 he was a bit sick of it. A letter from Wurm to the German government was submitted in December 1943, a wonderful document. The bishop writes:

> Out of religious and ethical feeling, must I declare, in agreement with the judgment of all positive-Christian people's circles in Germany [*Note the "positive-Christian." That is still the National Socialist party program.*], that we as Christians feel this politics of extermination against Jewry to be a heavy, and for the German people, disastrous injustice. Killing without necessity of war and without sentence contradicts God's commands, even if it is ordered by the authorities [*Now, all of a sudden; up to 1938 it did not contradict them!*], and like every conscious transgression of God's commands [*now comes the core of the matter*], the penalty for this is paid sooner

39. Theophil Wurm (1868–1953) was *Land* bishop of Württemberg, 1933–45, and president of the Council of the Evangelical Church in Germany, 1945–49.

40. Goldschmidt and Kraus, *Der ungekündigte Bund*, 242.

> or later. Our people feel in many ways the suffering that it must undergo from enemy air-raids as retaliation for what is done to the Jews. [*So, when the bombs are flying over his head, then he notices that something is not in order.*] The burning of houses and churches, the splintering and crashing during the nights of bombing, the flight from destroyed houses with few possessions, the helplessness in seeking a place of refuge, remind the population in the most painful way of what the Jews had to endure on previous occasions. It is indeed also here as clear as daylight, that all the earlier measures against the non-Aryans have had an extremely strong influence on the war politics of the enemies, and still influences them.

So, he has also noticed, that one does not like to see people murdered just because they are Jews. But now the very interesting conclusion:

> Whoever among the German people serves God can only pray that no further injustice will be committed against those of mixed race and those Aryans married to Jewesses.[41]

Thus one can if necessary turn a blind eye to ordinary Jews, even in this situation, where one suddenly realizes that the dear God sends a bomb onto one's head if one kills Jews. That was *Land* Bishop Wurm.

Now we will have a look at the famous Niemöller. A very interesting report on Niemöller has been presented.[42] Reich leader Rosenberg had an observer sit in on the Niemöller trial, and the notes of the observer and his report to Rosenberg have been preserved. What does this National Socialist representative of Rosenberg now write about Niemöller and his conduct during the trial?

> He [*Niemöller*] is not concerned about minor details [*he reports on what Niemöller says in his defense*], but about Christianity according to Scripture and creed. As a National Socialist he had a good conscience about it. Niemöller read out two pages from *Mein Kampf*, then a chapter from the New Testament, finally a sermon from the year 1932 on the question of the Führer. He stated that he was anything but an unrealistic pastor. However he did not wish to interfere in any way in the politics of the day. He had done that only once, which was in 1933, when the Führer withdrew Germany from the League of Nations and Niemöller was informed that very night by a friend in the Wilhelmstraße. As a result he immediately sent Hitler a congratulatory telegram, probably the first that the Führer received

41. Ibid., 247–48.
42. Hans Buchheim, "Ein NS-Funktionär zum Niemöller-Prozess," *Vierteljahreshefte zur Zeitgeschichte* 4 (1956): 307–15.

> for this measure. Otherwise, he [*Niemöller*] concerned himself only with the Gospel. In this context, he expressed himself in detail on the Aryan question in the church. The Jews were distasteful and foreign to him. That one could indeed believe of him, the scion of an old Westphalian family of farmers and theologians, the former imperial naval officer. But Scripture would not allow baptism to be substituted for by the family tree. We are not permitted to form God according to our image, the Aryan image, but must take him as he is: revealed in the Jew, Jesus of Nazareth. This very painful and serious vexation must be accepted for the sake of the Gospel.[43]

So, have a look at that. Here is this noble old Westphalian of farming stock and a fine naval officer, who voted for Hitler since 1924, and it is terribly painful for him that God had the bad taste to incarnate himself in a Jew and not in Pastor Niemöller. But now one just has to accept it; Westphalians would have been better suited for this purpose, but one cannot do a thing about it.

§27. Anti-Semitic Residues in Present-day Evangelical Church

We have again to deal with the phenomenon of dehumanization. Brutal ignorance, petit bourgeois stagnation, intellectual slovenliness and sloppiness—as others said already at that time—no possibility of resistance when injustice is done to man, intervention only when it is their own skin that is in danger. This happens in the case of Bishop Wurm, when he notices that his church is next and when the bombs are flying. In Niemöller's case, too, resistance occurs when, as with the Aryan paragraph, the church organization as a social institution is at stake. As long as only human beings are murdered by the authorities, contrary to the commandment "Thou shalt not kill," everything is perfectly all right. That now is a general characteristic of the German resistance, with several exceptions, who I will now indicate. Wherever resistance occurred in the churches—and it did occur there—in the Evangelical and Catholic Churches, it was only after it was too late.

43. Ibid., 313. Voegelin gave a more detailed diagnosis of Niemöller's homiletic procedure in his lecture "The German University and the Order of German Society: A Reconsideration of the Nazi Era," in *Published Essays 1966–1985*, ed. Ellis Sandoz, vol. 12 of *The Collected Works of Eric Voegelin* (1990; available Columbia: University of Columbia Press, 1999), 11–12.

Once the regime was established, it was naturally very difficult to do something. It was like this with the military, who went along with this foul behavior until there was the danger that the war would be lost through Hitler's strategic mistakes. Then, all of a sudden, they were the great resistance fighters and then there was July 20. Personalities who really understood what Hitler meant and were ready to resist were extremely rare: among the military, perhaps General Beck; on the Protestant side, younger people like Dietrich Bonhoeffer in Berlin; on the Catholic side, the young Jesuit father Alfred Delp. I will have something further to say about him later, in the Catholic section. He really offered resistance in the spiritual sense, but that was the younger generation. When Bonhoeffer and Delp were murdered, they were only thirty-seven or thirty-eight years old. They also got caught up in this matter only when everything had already been ruined by the older generation, which had the possibilities for decision. So here there are some genuine victims of resistance; but what is usually called resistance is a resistance apropos of the threat to people's own social, material, or institutional interests, and otherwise nothing, as emerges from these documents.

The reprehensibility and ethical decadence, clearly expressed by the documents of the delayed resistance, is incontestable. This is why, again from the ecclesiastical side, Hitler was able to come to power: because the very ones the people relied on for their spiritual guidance told them to vote for Hitler and obediently voted for Hitler themselves. And because they had no spiritual organ for perceiving the problem posed by National Socialism, they didn't foresee what would happen then. Again you can see that we can get no further with National Socialists alone. We have to establish the general problematic of bourgeois decadence in the churches too. This situation of decadence, predating Hitler and National Socialism, has not essentially changed since Hitler. I will present some relevant documents to you from the Evangelical *Kirchentag* of 1960.

At that time there was great excitement, because—I don't know if you remember these circumstances—in 1959 the synagogue in Cologne was daubed with swastikas, and that was the prelude to widespread anti-Semitic excesses in Germany. Then an Evangelical countermanifestation was held and an attempt was made to pass a resolution at the synod of the Evangelical Church in Germany on

February 26, 1960. There Professor Gollwitzer, a theologian who knew what was at stake, proposed the radical-Christian motion, that the synod should adopt the resolution that "whoever strikes our Jewish fellow-citizens, strikes us!"[44] In the synod, this resolution was dropped, for forty-seven members of the synod were for it and exactly the same number, forty-seven, were against. There was no majority. Thus, at the level of the synod, that is to say, the governing body of the church, an even division. So almost the same situation as at the beginning, 44 percent for Hitler and the conservative right, which was also Evangelical, for him.[45] Almost the same situation as 1933: Half is for, the other half is against. That is to say, on the whole, nothing can be done, the presence of the same decadence. For Gollwitzer now, that was a bit too stupid. After this ballot, he said:

> If we must say that our communities do not yet understand clearer, sharper, formulations [*these were obviously the arguments that were brought against such a formulation*], then we have thus just declared that the great brakes, the great obstacles of our people, are to be found in our Christian communities.[46]

Now just think about what I said when introducing this question of the churches, that it is not a situation where first there are churches and second a political people: rather, the people are the same in both cases. So when it is established here that the brakes, the retardations, are to be found in our people, in our Christian communities, that means simply that they are to be found in the people. The people are still exactly in the same situation as before, and as you will later see, the same thing holds for the Catholic communities. So we have still the same situation of decadence of the people as a whole, the incapacity to give themselves representatives of spiritual rank, as we had in the twenties and in 1933. Gollwitzer said more on this matter:

> [O]ur words regarding this resolution have not yet expressed the shock. This recognition of ours, not a confessional and professional recognition of guilt that is now quite normal among Christians, but a concrete recognition, that because we have treated them, the Jews,

44. Goldschmidt and Kraus, *Der ungekündigte Bund,* 260.

45. Voegelin is referring to the results of the Reichstag elections of March 5, 1933, where the Nazi party won 43.9 percent and the German National People's Party 8 percent of the votes.

46. Goldschmidt and Kraus, *Der ungekündigte Bund,* 263.

> in this way, we can hardly look them in the eye again, and the word Jewish Mission, etc., sticks in our throat, and we hardly know any more how we can really witness to them the Gospel of their own Lord and Savior, Jesus, the Jew Jesus, the Messiah of Israel, since we have made ourselves so incompetent in this matter. Yet our words should express our shock still more; but as I said, it was held that our communities are not yet so advanced, that means, they are still too little shocked with regard to the Jews. They do not recognize that the Jewish question is in reality a Christian question. To contribute to this recognition should be our common task, when we now go out and realize that what we did here as synod was a very poor thing.[47]

And up to today this poor declaration was all that there was.

What this situation among the people looks like, in these communities, can be seen from the Bergneustadt Conference in June 1960. This was a conference on the depiction of Judaism in teacher training and in schoolteaching. Up to now I hadn't known about it, until I found it in this book on *The Unbroken Covenant.* So, what are the problems, what must one teach the people in school? Amazing! One must make clear to them that the same God speaks in the Old and in the New Testament, and not two different ones. And that one cannot chuck out the God of the Old Testament and treat with the God of the New Testament. One must teach them what the people obviously do not know, that the commandment of love comes from the Old Testament. That seems to be directed against the widespread opinion that the God of the Old Testament is a God of revenge and of anger, and such things. One must teach them that the Jews have no collective guilt for the death of Christ, that the Jewish people has not been rejected by God, as the theologians like to assert. That's written nowhere, except by theologians. That the choice and suffering of the chosen are inseparably bound together, and that Jewish sufferings are not to be reckoned up according to the vulgar conception of guilt and punishment, whereby the sufferings of the Jews are to be understood as punishment for having murdered Christ, or similar things.[48]

Please note that the problematic is to be found at this grotesque, vulgar level, of which one has hardly a clue (at least I didn't have), that is, what one must first narrate to the people. That one, for

47. Ibid., 263–64.
48. Ibid., 266–67.

example, should depict and explain the Pharisees in terms of knowledge of the internal Jewish history of faith and not assert that the Jewish Pharisees were evil and bad fellows, who killed Christ and more things like that.[49]

All that, however, is not to be found in the real substance of this conference. But to protect themselves for putting forward such propositions against the generally widespread opinions, they deliberately invoked a French cardinal, Achille Liénart, who had unequivocally emphasized in a pastoral letter in 1960—so, only a short time ago—that our sins were the deepest reason for the Lord's death on the cross. Ours, here and now. And equally clearly he declared that the Jews were not murderers of God, not even those who in Jerusalem demanded the crucifixion from Pilate, because they were not aware of the divinity of Christ.[50]

Now, on the one hand, that shows that obviously in Lille a Catholic cardinal has his own problem with his little sheep and must say such things to them. But at least he does say it to them. In Germany it would never be said, and if someone dared to open his mouth, as at this Bergneustadt Conference, then one must first invoke the cardinal of Lille, who, however, was not stating anything new but what was the most ancient knowledge of this problematic.

I would like to read you out a couple of verses from John Donne's seventeenth-century *Holy Sonnets* that concern the relationship between Christians and Jews, where everything is said; again, nothing new, but just as common knowledge to be remembered and to be kept alive. So Donne writes:

> Spit in my face you Jewes, and pierce my side,
> Buffet, and scoffe, scourge, and crucifie mee . . .
> They kill'd once an inglorious man, but I
> Crucifie him daily, being more glorified.[51]

That is the Christian attitude, and no bishop, either in the Evangelical or the Catholic Church, has been felt to show any sign of it, or to show it even today, at least in public pronouncement to the communities. Nothing!

49. Ibid., 267.
50. Ibid., 269.
51. John Donne, *The Divine Poems*, ed. Helen Gardner (Oxford: Clarendon Press, 1978), 9.

§28. Theoretical Inquiry into Romans 13

And now, in concluding this investigation on the Evangelical side, a theoretical inquiry into Romans 13 for the Evangelical part, and then for the Catholic part an inquiry into the theological idea of the *corpus mysticum Christi,* so that the decadence I have repeatedly spoken of will come to light.

In all the documents, Evangelical and Catholic, with which those belonging to the communities were enjoined to obey Hitler, there are two texts from the Bible invoked by the clergy in order to command obedience to the authorities. Among the two, on the Catholic side, in the documents I will present to you next time, the fourth commandment is preferred. That commandment is "Honor your father and your mother." This father and mother is now interpretatively expanded as "Honor the state, carry out its laws, obey the authorities!" Please note that. Not a word of all that is in the fourth commandment—for the good historical reason that precisely in the covenant of Sinai, within which the Decalogue was announced, the people existed under God and not under authorities. There was no occasion for speaking about having to obey any kind of authorities at all. So it is unhistoric and anachronistic, and if such an alteration of an interpretative kind were made to a text in a secular context by a scholar, one would say: Absolutely barefaced falsification of the text! When theologians do it, then it is the church.

The same is now done with Romans 13, and here indeed the link is Luther, who in this regard is fully adopted by the Catholic Church, that is to say, that "everyone should be subject to authority." That is the first sentence of the thirteenth chapter in the letter to the Romans in the Luther translation. Of this assertion, that "everyone should be subject to the authorities," there is not an iota in Romans 13. I will now therefore undertake an investigation of Romans 13—which is always gladly referred to, especially this first verse—as a whole. I have for this purpose translated the text. The whole text of chapter 13 in the letter to the Romans falls into three parts: the first part, verses 1–7, the second part, verses 8–10, the third part, verses 11–14, and I will read out and comment on each of them. The first part, verses 1–7, reads, in literal translation:

> Every soul must submit to the higher authorities, for there are no authorities except those under or by means of God. And the existing authorities are ordered by him. Therefore, whoever rebels against the

> order of the authorities, resists a divine order. And those who offer resistance will bring judgment [*krima*] down upon themselves. For rulers are not terrors for the good but only for the evil. If you do not want to fear the authorities, do what is good, and you will have their approval, for they are God's assistants, in order to do good to you. However, if you do evil, then fear them, for they do not bear the sword without reason. They are God's servants, who cause his anger to be felt by him who does evil. Therefore you should submit yourself to them, not only from fear of anger, but for conscience's sake. Therefore also bear these burdens, for they are the servants [*the leiturgoi*] of God, who dedicate themselves to this service. Fulfill all your duties, tax where tax, tolls where tolls, fear where fear, honor where honor, is due.

So that is the first part, of which only the first verse is ever quoted. The language Paul speaks here, in order to clarify the relation to the authorities, as he calls them, is conventional, taken from the Stoic philosophy of politics. The idea is that of a hierarchy of authorities in the cosmos, where God is in the highest place, in the lower places are the authorities in society, in the lowest place is man himself. That is the hierarchy of being in its order. So, whoever fits into this order must submit to the law of the world, which for whatever reasons has provided that there are also orders in society and representatives with the power of punishment, who must take care that men obey the moral law and that its violations are punished.

The presupposition of this entire instruction is naturally that one lives in the Roman Empire at the time when the Stoa had established the ethics of worldly order. That means that the imperial government, its officials and their administration, in fact obey and sanction the moral law in the Stoic sense. That is the presupposition. There isn't a word there that one should be subject to any authorities whatsoever, let alone, as we shall then see from the documents the next time, that one should have to be subject to the authorities even when they do evil. Let alone what Kant, for example, following Luther, read into obedience to authorities, that the authorities are holy or anything of the sort. Nothing of this. The passage is quite obviously directed toward persons in the Christian community who misunderstand the freedom of the Christian under God as meaning that one no longer has to obey the ethical order of society, that is to say, it is directed toward those who violate this ethical order. These are admonished that in this *aion* we find ourselves in, there is also a moral law, the one that will be sanctioned by these higher authorities. The kingdom of God, that comes only in the future. So, on the whole, it is not very different from Aristotelian politics, which also presuppose ethical behavior through orientation of the spirit and the continuous practice of the virtues.

It then presupposes the corrective—since people are inclined not to be virtuous—for violations of this order. The correctives in this case are the power of public order, the higher powers, the municipal authorities, the *archontes* of the polis, whose responsibility it is for restraining these violations or, if they still take place, for punishing them.

So it is classic politics, a bit Hellenistically changed in terms of vocabulary, but that is all. And always presupposed is the moral order as what these higher authorities make effective in this world. What now these men should really do is by no means merely to obey the authorities; rather that comes now in verses 8–10. There it says:

> Owe no one anything, except love for the other, for whoever loves his fellow man has fulfilled the law. For the commandments "you shall not commit adultery, you shall not kill, you shall not steal, you shall not covet," along with all the other commandments, can be summed up in this one rule, "Love your neighbor as yourself." Love cannot do evil to the neighbor; the fullness of the law, therefore, is love.

If now we translate the language of Paul into the philosophical language of Aristotle, we would have to say this: All the different virtues from which the concrete commands follow are subordinated to what I call the existential virtues, in Aristotle, justice, *philia,* love, which is the fundamental ethic of the political community, as the *philia politike* in the spirit, the *homonoia,* the noetic virtue, that is positive order. Subordination is required under the existing *authorities,* whose precise goal it is to reestablish order, only if this positive order, which is enjoined here, is not kept.

Now the Christian element in this matter is something different. It is that all these negative worldly admonishments—subordinate yourself to the authorities or the powers!—should be existentially characterized by their positive accomplishment through love, which has then become one of the theological cardinal virtues. All of this becomes more urgent because the end of the world, spoken of in verses 11–14, is imminent:

> And above all, you should be aware of the critical time [*of the kairos*] and the hour for you to awaken from sleep. [*Demands formulated like this go back to Heraclitus.*] For salvation is closer to us today than when we first believed. [*That means, the time from now to salvation is shorter than from that point in time when we began to believe up to the present. So, in a short time, in our lifetime, the end of the world is coming.*] The night is almost over and the day is near. Let us therefore cast aside the works of darkness and put on the armor of light. Let us live decently as in the day, not with feasting and drinking, with lust and fornication, with quarreling and jealousy. Put on the Lord Jesus Christ [*as the armor of light*], and do not turn your thoughts toward the desires of the flesh.

So, a carefully thought-out literary context aimed at those who are inclined to misunderstand the Gospel and the arrival of the *aion* as implying that one may now be licentious, that everything is permitted. But nothing of the kind. In this *aion* the higher powers, to which one must subordinate oneself, continue, and behavior toward the neighbor is positively characterized by love as the existential, spiritual virtue. And above all one should bear in mind that the end of the world and the second coming of Christ is close, very close indeed, closer than the time from the beginning of our faith, which has already run out, and that in this situation of the critical time one should therefore behave according to the *kairos.*

All of this has nothing, absolutely nothing, to do with one having to be subject to any kind of authorities—above all, naturally, nothing to do with having to comply with the Hitler laws, as the bishops commanded, in their pastoral letters, by invoking the fourth commandment and, here, Romans 13. This scandalous misuse of a literary text for subjugation—and, indeed, for unconditional subjugation—under the authorities in the sense of power politics, if it happened on the secular side, would also be considered a barefaced falsification. But again, in the theological sphere one may say such things about the relations of church and state, with which the New Testament has nothing to do.

However, of late, there has been a certain relaxation of these misinterpretations. In 1963 the Berlin bishop Otto Dibelius—I am now still speaking of the Evangelicals—published a study on the authorities.[52] And already from the layout of the book, in the first

52. Otto Dibelius, *Obrigkeit* (Stuttgart: Kreuz Verlag, 1963). Dibelius (1880–1967) was general superintendent of Kurmark from 1925 until deposed in 1933. Deeply

part on Romans 13, you can see an interpretation not very different from what I have given you here. In the second part, he discusses Luther and the authorities, the bowdlerizing of this text through Luther's notion of authority. Further, he treats of the objections, that Romans 13 also held good for the totalitarian state, and finally considers the freedom of a Christian. These would then be the problems of the second and third parts of the letter to the Romans. There we see that already something has been relaxed. But all of this relaxation takes place under a very ominous indication. I will read out this passage to you:

> But when we speak of Romans 13, it is a question, firstly and above all, *of a theological matter within the church.*[53]

And a page later:

> Once again: it is a question within the church how an important passage of the Bible is to be interpreted. But certainly it is a question that must be considered by the Christian throughout the whole world.[54]

That is a masterpiece of barefacedness. Christ has come among men, but what he has said may only be interpreted by the theologians. It is only a matter within the church. And if the theologians within the church interpret the passage of Romans 13 in such a way that their fellow citizens are slaughtered, not even then is it a public matter having to do with men and victims. Oh no, it remains even now a pure theological matter within the church. Here again you have this problem of the complete lack of human awareness among Christians. Christ is a private possession of the socially institutionalized organizations one pays church tax to. Even the lay people within the church have no say here and may not say, "Look, but that isn't in the Letter to the Romans 13 at all." And naturally whoever does not belong to the church, for example, Jews, who will be slaughtered, have no say, because these theologians have interpreted the letter to the Romans in this way.

So, there is this complete perversion in the treatment of Scripture, this complete failure to be a member of human society, this complete failure in the duty of being a citizen as well as a human being,

---

involved in the Confessing Church, he was bishop of Berlin, 1945–66; president of the Council of the Evangelical Church in Germany, 1949–61; and a president of the World Council of Churches in 1954.

53. Ibid., 72 (emphasis in the text).

54. Ibid., 73.

this arrogance in treating Christianity and the words of Christ as a private matter for theologians, which then can cause horrible murderous wrong. That is still the attitude of Bishop Dibelius in the year 1963. That's how things are!

5

Descent into the Ecclesiastical Abyss

The Catholic Church

§29. Layout of the "Hitler and the Germans" Lectures

(Seventh Lecture)

Ladies and Gentlemen,

May I briefly remind you of the layout of the lectures. They consist of two parts. First, the investigation of Hitler and the Germans from the viewpoint of what type of Germans, and what peculiar attitude of spirit, brought Hitler to power. That is the question of the German petit bourgeoisie, the educated philistines, the intellectual decadence of the elites, and so on. Second, naturally, is the question of those Germans who did not join in but grasped the problem with very precise analyses, and who develop that analysis further today. It was from this second part that I had to anticipate last time the lecture on Max Weber, or at least a large part of it, because of these academic duties. And I would like to add that the rest of the investigation of Max Weber will then be prefixed to the lecture on Thomas Mann. There will follow the lecture on first and second realities, beginning with Rabelais and Cervantes and its continuation with Musil and with Doderer. In conclusion we will have another lecture on Goethe and Novalis, in order to explain further the internal German problematic. Unfortunately this enjoyable part of the lectures, where we have to deal with men and works of spiritual rank, still lies in the future. For the time being, we must now descend into the depths and continue the investigation of the churches.

§30. Difference between Catholic and Evangelical Attitudes toward Nazism

I dealt with the Evangelical Church the previous time. Now we must concern ourselves with the Catholic Church. I put the Evangelical Church first, not only because it is numerically the larger but because there was a methodological reason. The methodological reason is that under the Evangelical Church's conditions of freedom of speech and free interpretation of Scripture, and so on, the debate on basic questions is much more differentiated, and a wide spectrum of attitudes, from the spiritually most decadent to the spiritually highest, becomes public. As a result, the inner tensions that exist in German Christianity, and which probably exist just as much in the Catholic Church too, are much more clearly expressed in the Evangelical than under the conditions of the Catholic Church, which, by virtue of its inner discipline, does not allow these tensions to become publicized as much.

I have already drawn your attention to the fact that in the episcopate during the Third Reich there were very considerable tensions between personalities of higher rank, such as Preysing and Galen,[1] on the one hand, and the rest of the episcopate on the other. However, these tensions were never openly expressed, because the inner discipline prevented such a break between the bishops becoming public.

But there are still other very remarkable differences between the two churches. Because of the freedom of interpretation in the Evangelical Church, there is a very free theology, in the sense of not being bound to a tradition of dogmatic doctrines. This very high degree of freedom in practice expresses itself in the fact that the investigations into sacred scripture can be scientifically treated much further, and that a freer scientific atmosphere in the secular sense exists. To this freer scientific atmosphere in the secular sense, however, there was not a corresponding theoretic-philosophic penetration of the material at the same level. The theoretic-philosophic penetration in the Catholic literature is very much higher because of the patristic and scholastic tradition that has entered into the

1. Clemens August, Graf von Galen (1878–1946), was bishop of Münster in 1933 and created cardinal in 1946. He delivered outspoken sermons in July and August 1941 criticizing the Nazi euthanasia murders.

formulation of doctrinal pronouncements. So, on the Catholic side, we have a higher philosophic level; on the Evangelical side, a higher level of secular science. That then has its further consequences for the forms in which the clerical dignitaries of the Evangelical and the Catholic Church express an opinion regarding these questions.

In the expressions of the Catholic episcopate we cannot find these individual nuances we found in the Evangelical bishops and theologians. Rather, here the analysis must focus more on the pragmatic attitude, because whatever the real attitude of the men who spoke was, it remains opaque behind a cliché language that comes from tradition and yet has a relatively high philosophical level. So, in the Catholic Church we can observe, for example, the following curiosities. While in the Evangelical Church there was a whole series of figures who later played an important role, and who already in the Weimar republic cheerfully voted for Hitler (for example, the famous Pastor Niemöller), such a phenomenon did not occur in the Catholic Church. Before Hitler's seizure of power we have documents firmly condemning National Socialism as an ideology incompatible with the Christian attitude. Condemnations of such a radical kind do not exist on the Evangelical side. It is all the more remarkable that these Catholic condemnations of a radical kind before 1933 clearly had no spiritual or intellectual depth. For immediately after the seizure of power, in March 1933, there begins the great political turnaround, when the Catholic Church, speaking through the episcopate, expressed its support for Hitler and enjoined all Catholic Christians to be fine, true, and obedient citizens under him and to be at his disposal in every way. However, that is also only a phase, which was influenced by the conclusion of the concordat.

I will not deal further with the history of the concordat. It is not yet fully clarified in every point. Who the people involved were is still a rather doubtful matter. Again, only in the last few days the *Osservatore Romano* has published a whole series of documents concerning the attitude of the pope to the German question, where it is affirmed that those really to blame for the catastrophe were the German bishops and that the Vatican only complied and accorded with their suggestions and advice. Thus that discussion will continue for a long time, until all the details are clear. So let us leave it aside.

But closely connected with the negotiations for the concordat was this sudden compliance and the willingness to cooperate. This attitude, however, experienced its first setback immediately after the conclusion of the concordat, when the National Socialists' systematic struggle against all Catholic organizations began, not indeed as a breach of the concordat, but by exploiting the particular provisions that had obviously not been read properly by the episcopate's jurists before the concordat was concluded. For it was provided in the concordat that the church's position would be protected in every way, but always with the proviso "within the framework of the law." And then laws were passed that simply abolished all that had been expected to be guaranteed. Then there was a longer period for seeking compensation and for resistance in particular cases. Parallel to this period, however, is another, which takes up again what had already caused opposition against National Socialism before 1932, that is, the continued existence of the ideology represented particularly by Rosenberg's *Mythus des 20. Jahrhunderts.*

With regard to this ideology, the episcopate presented the view that neopaganism, as this phenomenon was called, was not identical with the regime. The regime was delighted to encourage this misunderstanding—if it was a misunderstanding—in order to divert the opposition to figures like Rosenberg, who allegedly had nothing to do with National Socialism as a form of government, and to distinguish him from the Hitler regime itself as the government of the German Reich. So, under the pretext that the church was against neopaganism but had really no objection to an authoritarian regime, the matter dragged on for some time.

We can then distinguish a further phase, where the entry of the church into the language and ideology of National Socialism became so deep that the Gestapo got angry. We have Gestapo reports from the time of the mid- and later 1930s, where the Reich government is warned that the Catholic Church now sought what it had already sought in other cultures, to adapt itself to the outer forms and thus to use camouflage to work its way in. It is specifically mentioned that the clergy had now gone on to speak of Jesus as the Führer, and that "Heil Bishop" had been introduced as a form of greeting, and that that was perhaps going a bit too far and one had to pay attention to it.[2]

2. See Guenter Lewy, *The Catholic Church and Nazi Germany* (New York: McGraw-Hill, 1964), 165 f.

And we have then from this period, 1937, studies of Austrian Catholicism, which at that time had still greater freedom, and the formula had come about from the Catholic side that it "could with justice display the sign, 'We carry all the items that are sold by the competition [*that is: National Socialism*], only in better quality.' "[3]

That was the judgment of the Austrian Catholic paper, the *Christliche Ständestaat,* in 1937. Then the matter became serious. We have to observe again the same phenomenon we also find in the Evangelical Church and with the generals, the same as in all the various other so-called resisters. First, everyone joins in. Then when it affects their own affairs, they become angry. So when it came to the immediate interests of the church as an organization, such as the question of sterilization, the question of euthanasia, the question of baptized Jews, and the like, then the clergy began to offer resistance, even if not in a very intense form. And that not very intense form of resistance dragged on until the end of the war.

§31. Dehumanized Response of Catholic Church to State Authority and to Persecution of Those outside the Church

Such an overall survey is however completely inadequate for the actual situation. We must now return to the basic question of these lectures, the problem of dehumanization. In the case of the churches as well as of other organizations we have already discussed, it is the problem that man becomes completely insignificant in comparison to his membership in an interest group. That is to say, as long as those in the interest group, whether Czechs or Poles, German Evangelicals or Catholics, are not themselves immediately affected in their interests, they do not have a word to say about it if their fellow citizens are killed, taken to concentration camps, mistreated there, or finally, if they are gassed in Auschwitz—not a word against all these crimes against humanity. Please note that, and that nothing was done at certain critical, decisive points!

Another such critical point, about which a public expression would have been desired, was the events of June 30, 1934. In response to these, again there was complete silence in public. It was

3. Ibid., 166.

only behind the scenes that complaints were made, even though a whole series of Catholic figures was involved, like Klausener, the head of Catholic Action in Berlin; the Catholic youth leader Adalbert Pröbst; a Dr. Fritz Gehrlich, the former editor of *Der Gerade Weg;* and others, who were murdered. A whole series of Catholic figures was murdered, and the clergy, represented by the episcopate, did not say a word. Naturally that aroused enormous surprise, especially among Catholics abroad, and this surprise was further increased by the behavior with regard to the question of the concentration camps, about which nothing was said either.[4]

For the peculiar attitude of the Catholic Church toward the race question, I will read out a few sources, since they are indeed not known in Germany because of systematic suppression and the methodical falsification of the sources. I quote from the article "Race," in the manual edited by Archbishop Gröber.[5] The attitude to race is formulated in the following manner:

> Every people bears itself the responsibility for its successful existence, and the intake of entirely foreign blood will always represent a risk for a nationality that has proven its historic worth. Hence no people may be denied the right to maintain undisturbed its previous racial stock and to enact safeguards for this purpose. The Christian religion merely demands that the means used do not offend against the moral law and natural justice.[6]

The saving clause always comes at the end; you will notice that also in other, similar documents, which I still have to read out. For the German citizens of the Catholic confession—the same holds, of course, for the Evangelicals—who read that, this is naturally the *carte blanche* for mass anti-Semitism.

> In his celebrated Advent sermons of 1933 Cardinal Faulhaber observed that the Church did not have "any objection to the endeavor to keep the national characteristics of a people as far as possible pure and unadulterated, and to foster their national spirit by emphasis upon the common ties of blood which unite them."[7]

That was 1933, at the time Karl Kraus wrote *Die Dritte Walpurgisnacht.* Cardinal Faulhaber's remarkable behavior in 1933 and 1934, his Advent sermons and the events that followed them, belongs

4. Ibid., 169–71.
5. Konrad Gröber (1872–1948) was bishop of Meißen in 1931, archbishop of Freiburg, 1932–48.
6. Lewy, *The Catholic Church and Nazi Germany,* 275.
7. Ibid., 275.

to this context of the question of the Jews.[8] Let me just give the facts. Faulhaber's Advent sermons of 1933 have become famous especially because of their defense of the sacred character of the Old Testament. But he went beyond that to make it clear to those listening that when he defended the Old Testament, he did not defend his Jewish contemporaries:

> We must distinguish, he told the faithful, between the people of Israel before the death of Christ, who were vehicles of divine revelation, and the Jews after the death of Christ, who have become restless wanderers over the earth. But even the Jewish people of ancient times could not justly claim credit for the wisdom of the Old Testament. So unique were these laws that one was bound to say: "People of Israel, this did not grow in your own garden of your own planting. This condemnation of usurious land-grabbing, this war against the oppression of the farmer by debt, this prohibition of usury, is not the product of your spirit." [*Lewy adds:*] It, therefore, is little short of falsification of history when Faulhaber's sermons in 1933 are hailed by one recent Catholic writer as a "condemnation of the persecution of the Jews."[9]

That relates to the writing bearing the title *Die Katholische Kirche und die Rassenfrage* (*The Catholic Church and the Race Question*), published at Recklinghausen in 1961, by a man called Congar, who is a priest belonging to a religious order.[10] So, still the systematic falsification. If his position seemed still in any way ambiguous, Cardinal Faulhaber endeavored to dispel this ambiguity. And now comes the following rather amusing episode:

> In the summer of 1934 a Social-Democratic newspaper in Prague published a sermon against race-hatred which Faulhaber had allegedly preached. The Basel *National-Zeitung* . . . reprinted excerpts from this sermon, and the World Jewish Congress at a meeting in Geneva praised the Cardinal's courageous stand. But the sermon turned out to be a fabrication, and Faulhaber had his secretary write a widely-publicized letter to the Jewish organization protesting against "the use of his name by a conference that demands the commercial boycott of Germany, that is, economic war." The Cardinal, the letter continued, "in his Advent sermons of the previous year has defended the Old

8. Michael von Faulhaber (1869–1952) was professor of theology in Strasbourg in 1903; bishop of Speyer, 1911; archbishop of Munich-Freising, 1917; and created cardinal, 1921.

9. Lewy, *The Catholic Church and Nazi Germany,* 276.

10. Ibid., 395 n. 30.

> Testament of the Children of Israel, but not taken a position with regard to the Jewish question of today."[11]

Now that is all ambiguous and could possibly also be just the expression of a wise reserve, but these manifestations have consequences. Just as in the case of Archbishop Gröber,

> lesser Church dignitaries quite naturally took the cue from their Archbishop. An article written by a canon of the cathedral chapter of Regensburg, and published in *Klerusblatt,* the organ of the Bavarian Priests' Association, advised Catholic teachers to point out to pupils that the sacred books of the Old Testament were not only beyond the Jewish mentality, but in direct conflict with it. "The greatest miracle of the Bible is that the true religion could hold its own and maintain itself against the voice of the Semitic blood."[12]

I would like you again to note that it needs American scholars to bring all this out. No German moves a finger to bring something like this to light. It was painful for the Catholic clergy, just as for the Protestant clergy of Niemöller's type, that Jesus was a Jew. How does one deal with this inconvenience?

> The embarrassing fact that Jesus had been a Jew was handled in a similar manner. In a pastoral letter of 1939 Archbishop Gröber conceded [*1939—please note the date!*] that Jesus Christ could not be made into an Aryan, but the Son of God had been fundamentally different from the Jews of his time—so much so that they had hated him and demanded his crucifixion, and "their murderous hatred has continued in later centuries." Jesus had been a Jew, admitted Bishop Hilfrich of Limburg in his pastoral letter for Lent 1939 [*again as late as this*] but "the Christian religion has not grown out of the nature of this people, that is, is not influenced by their racial characteristics." . . . Christianity . . . was therefore not to be regarded as a product of the Jews; it was not a foreign doctrine or un-German. "Once accepted by our ancestors, it finds itself in the most intimate union with the Germanic spirit."[13]

I ask you to read the whole book. It's a treasure trove of this material. I am only picking out a few short passages. Another interesting problem that confronted the Catholic just as much as

11. Ibid., 276.

12. Ibid., 276–77. Voegelin notes in his lecture that "the man is called Scherm, and the article is entitled 'Der alt-testamentliche Bibelunterricht, Planungen und Wegweisungen' ['The Old Testament Bible Lesson: Planning and Direction'], *Klerusblatt* 20 (1939): 225." (See Lewy, *The Catholic Church and Nazi Germany,* 395 n. 3.)

13. Lewy, *The Catholic Church and Nazi Germany,* 277.

the Protestant Church was the problem of research into ancestry, which was decreed to establish who was of Jewish origin. Now in the period before the introduction of a state register, the registers of births were kept by the churches. One could have expected that—since the establishment of Jewish origin had the aim of inflicting harm on those German citizens concerned, of delivering them to concentration camps, of mistreating them, of massacring them, and, finally, of gassing them—that perhaps the episcopate of both churches would have refused to make the ecclesiastical records available for picking out who the Jews were. In fact, neither of the churches refused to cooperate in the establishment of who was of Jewish origin so that they could later be killed.

Another similar critical point was the so-called *Kristallnacht* of 1938. Nothing, no official statement. Only isolated statements.

> Cardinal Faulhaber is said to have provided a truck for the Chief Rabbi of Munich so that he could save some of the religious objects from his synagogue before it was completely demolished. [*So, private, individual actions. That is Faulhaber.*] Provost Lichtenberg[14] in Berlin prayed for the persecuted non-Aryan Christians and Jews on the morning after the pogrom, and added: "What took place yesterday, we know; what will be tomorrow, we do not know; but what happens today that we have witnessed; outside [*it was exactly opposite the church*] the synagogue is burning, and that also is a house of God." Lichtenberg's protest remained a solitary act of witness. His bishops remained silent in the face of the burning temples and the first round-up of the Jews [*for annihilation. Not a word!*].[15]

Further, there is the interesting question of conscientious objection. On this there is Zahn's investigation, which established that in the whole of Germany there were only seven Catholics who refused military service.[16] That should not be seen as a prejudice against Catholics in favor of Protestants. I do not know how it was with them; there are still no investigations of that. It is just by chance that the matter has been investigated from the side of the Catholic Church—probably it would look even worse on the Protestant side. Seven refused war service. Six of those who refused were executed;

14. Bernhard Lichtenberg (1875–1943), provost of Saint Hedwig's Cathedral, Berlin, and collaborator with Bishop Preysing of Berlin, was held in custody, 1941–43, and died en route to Dachau concentration camp, 1943. He was beatified in 1996.

15. Lewy, *The Catholic Church and Nazi Germany,* 284.

16. Gordon C. Zahn, *German Catholics and Hitler's Wars: A Study in Social Control* (London: Sheed and Ward, 1963), 80 n.

the seventh survived because he was declared to be insane. In almost all of these cases, the church brought its pressure to bear on these conscientious objectors to bring them into conformity with the official line. After his arrest, the Pallotine priest Franz Reinisch had to suffer being denied communion by the Catholic prison chaplain, because by his refusal he had failed in his Christian duty to take the military oath of loyalty to Hitler.[17] Josef Fleischer, a layman, remembered that in prison he was visited by a high church dignitary who tried to persuade him to give up his refusal of war service and who, when he did not go along with that, left him with an outburst of anger and declared that people like Fleischer deserved to be made shorter by a head.[18] The name of this man, who has the rank of bishop, cannot be given, because he is still a bishop and disputes that this is what happened. That, then, was the problem of the refusal of war service.

On principle, regarding the question of revolt, could one rebel against the Nazi regime? Lewy, summarizing the question of revolt and its treatment by the church, remarks:

> Catholics who actively fought against the Hitler regime were rebels not only against the state, but against their ecclesiastical authorities as well.[19]

An example from the year 1936:

> When a Swiss Catholic in June 1936 was reported to have asked children to pray for Hitler's death, and the German press thereupon accused all Catholics of being in sympathy with sedition, Cardinal Faulhaber declared in a sermon:
>
>> A lunatic abroad has had an attack of madness—does this justify wholesale suspicion of the German Catholics? You all are witnesses for the fact that on all Sundays and holidays at the main service we pray in all churches for the Führer as we have promised in the concordat. And now one can read in big headlines of the papers at the street corners, "They pray for Hitler's death!" We feel offended on account of this questioning of our loyalty to the state. We will today give an answer, a Christian answer [*he is speaking to the Christians in the church*]: Catholic men, we will now pray together a paternoster for the life of the Führer. This is our answer.[20]

17. Ibid., 24 n.
18. Ibid., 219 n.
19. Lewy, *The Catholic Church and Nazi Germany,* 309.
20. Ibid., 310.

Very much later, in 1941, Bishop Galen:

> We Christians make no revolution. We will continue to do our duty in obedience to God, out of love for *Volk* and fatherland. Our soldiers will fight and die for Germany, but not for those who . . . disgrace the German name before God and man. [*So, he was already somewhat more courageous.*] . . . [A]gainst the enemy in our midst [*this can only refer to National Socialism*] who tortures and beats us, we cannot fight with arms and there remains only one weapon: strong tenacious, obstinate perseverance.[21]

Now, please note that Galen here was one of the most qualified spiritual figures of the German episcopate. He had dared at least to distinguish between the external enemy and the internal enemy and knew who the internal enemy was; but if we come again to the political, human level: Offer resistance? Not at any price! We Christians make no revolution.

From this enumeration of critical situations, in terms of which the behavior of the church can be examined, I previously omitted the question of the concentration camps, saying only that there are no official statements of the church about them and the shameful events occurring there. But there is one, which I will now report on.

> In June 1936, Bishop Berning of Osnabrück,[22] member of the Prussian State Council [*appointed by Göring*], visited a number of concentration camps in his diocese. The *Kölnische Volkszeitung* reported that the Bishop had commended the furnishings of the camps visited. Addressing the inmates in the camp Aschendorfer Moor, Berning reminded them of the duty of obedience and fidelity towards *Volk* and state that was demanded by their religious faith. In a talk to the guards the Bishop was reported to have praised their work in the camp, and to have ended with three *Sieg Heil* for Führer and fatherland.[23]

That is the only statement of the Catholic Church at the episcopal level on the concentration camps. It evoked horror throughout the world.

§32. Karl Kraus on Concentration Camp Life

You are young and no longer know what the concentration camps were in reality. Therefore I will read out a few selected passages

21. Ibid., 311.
22. Wilhelm Berning (1877–1955) was bishop of Osnabrück in 1914 and was named titular archbishop in 1949.
23. Lewy, *The Catholic Church and Nazi Germany,* 172–73.

for you from the description of concentration camps in *Die Dritte Walpurgisnacht.* It is much more comprehensive. You know that I have repeatedly brought your attention to the fact that reading Karl Kraus's *Die Dritte Walpurgisnacht* is the duty of every German student who wants to have something to say in politics. Whoever does not know that must keep his mouth shut. This is again the method of confronting the second reality of Bishop Berning and of the German episcopate in general. Now the first reality, what was really going on:

> The press . . . chooses the simple definition, that a concentration camp is
>
> > a *temporary curtailment of liberty with an educational aim.* But in many cases *one may also* speak of a *spiritual rehabilitation.*
>
> Oh, one practically must. In Dachau it was even noticed that
>
> > the Communists, *who came to the camp in a grim mood,* after some time *learned to like good, patriotic songs again. "I once had a comrade"*[24] is particularly popular.
>
> In short, patriotic memories
>
> > are gaining the *upper hand*
>
> provided this upper hand does not happen to be busy elsewhere, and today the Communists are
>
> > *quite different people* from what they were when *brought* here.
>
> While the
>
> > *fresh arrivals* are morose, *obdurate,* and care-worn.
>
> Of course, this does not mean that they are still fresh when brought in and become morose later, but the other way around.
>
> > After an *educational cure* of a few weeks, they too will be different persons.
>
> Sometimes one day is said to be enough. These people, obviously, cannot testify to this themselves—for one thing because they are not allowed to, and for another because the psychic transformation which often occurs at a stroke not infrequently results in unconsciousness or at least an impaired memory, and because astonishment at unaccustomed things may result in speech disorders. But we shall content ourselves with the statement of the representative of the press that they received the distinct impression
>
> > that *Germany has nothing to hide in this area either* and that the prisoners *have nothing to complain about.*
>
> Everything goes like clockwork, sometimes dead on time.

Another similar description of an episode:

24. An early nineteenth-century folksong of a soldier killed in battle.

Hygiene leaves nothing to be desired. Work, exercise, curfew at nine o'clock, fill the day. The educational cure and the other slaps take place in between; the civic instruction comes from *Mein Kampf*. Here there is still order; out there in freedom things are all upside down; there everyone is both *Führer* and being led, and does off his own bat what he can batter himself. There a man faces the irrational; here he only faces the guards. Here the weak are to be "toughened up to make them useful members of human society again"; there the scum of society predominates. . . .

. . . What goes on there frequently seems to be connected with the fields of music or lecturing. The hangman leans against the doorpost and sings "*Dawn's red sky, dawn's red sky, Shine on me about to die.*" Fire on a person's soles causes the Horst Wessel song to be struck up. In addition to patriotic songs, hit tunes are practiced, accompanied by instruments. There is a number called "playing the zither" or "playing the phonograph" in which a number lying on a plank-bed is the phonograph. Of course things are not always as lively as they were in the beginning, when Count Helldorf came to the Brown House at Annaberg to watch two hundred men with bandaged heads standing to attention and singing a variation on a popular song:

Where did I get those nice black eyes?
From the SA. They're all great guys.[25]

§33. Catholic Resistance to Dehumanization: Alfred Delp

. . . From these depths of moral degeneration, which we have had to deal with, some personalities stand out on the Evangelical as well as on the Catholic side. The last time, I referred to Evangelical personalities like Bonhoeffer, and now I would like to speak of Father Delp. Delp was embroiled in 1944 in the resistance affair of July 20, but he had not participated in it, was not a part of the conspiracy. He was also not consulted about it. It was more an accidental matter, because some of the members of this circle of conspirators, including Count Helmuth von Moltke, had requested the Jesuit order to place a sociological expert at their disposal. This was to advise them what should be set up after the collapse, which already could be foreseen at that time. And in this capacity Father Delp spoke with members of the circle from time to time. In the

25. Karl Kraus, *Dritte Walpurgisnacht* (Frankfurt: Suhrkamp, 1989), 210–14. These pages of *Dritte Walpurgisnacht* have been translated in Harry Zohn, ed., *In These Great Times: A Karl Kraus Reader* (Manchester: Carcanet, 1984), 110–12, and Zohn's translation is used here with some changes.

trial before the People's Court, presided over by Roland Freisler, he was then sentenced on the specific ground, not of participating in the conspiracy, but of, in general, entertaining and expressing the thought that the war could be lost. That is the high treason for which he was executed. He was hanged on February 2, 1945. On the third of February, a bomb fell on the People's Court in Berlin, and Freisler was buried under its rubble. April 30 of the same year was Hitler's end. Delp was a young man. When he was executed he was in his thirtieth year. And so there are young people [who resisted], and it is one of the frightful catastrophes of Germany that people like that were murdered. To preserve the order of a people one doesn't need all that many.

Now, he has something to say about this church problematic that sounds different from what we hear from the episcopate. I will read out to you some passages from Delp's work, so that you see where the problems are. He says:

> That is indeed one of our great difficulties, the silence of the creative powers, which, in possession and power of the whole, grasp the situation spiritually and religiously. And because we have no great theology and no great leading ideas, the minor "theologies," the solutions stemming from a limited but totalized approach, spring up like mushrooms. . . .
>
> We are somehow lacking the great courage that comes, not from hot blood and youthfulness nor unbroken vitality, but from the possession of the Spirit and the consciousness of the blessing we have received. And so we are anxious and go on the run. We flee to Christian antiquity, we flee to other periods of the Christian past—as if we could ever expect an answer and an instruction from the past, and as if we were not given a mission up to the end of the day and thus possess a genuine promise for each day. These "continuous renaissances" are signs more of weakness than of life. A similar manifestation of an anxiety of life and of responsibility is indicated by the ever repeated and recurring restriction to religious and "essentially ecclesiastical" concerns. And thus is overlooked that what is at stake here is the fundamental—and even for the continued existence of religion more important—reality of man in general.[26]

This is one of the few cases in the Catholic literature, and equally in the Evangelical literature by the way, that the word "man" occurs, and not "member of a church."

26. Alfred Delp, *Zwischen Welt und Gott,* ed. Paul Bolkovac (Frankfurt: Verlag Josef Knecht, 1957), 96.

> [H]as the church forgotten man and his fundamental rights? How will the church save the Christian, if it leaves the creature who should become Christian, in the lurch? [*A question that no bishop ever asked, at least not officially.*] That . . . these questions . . . will be asked must make us thoughtful. Thoughtful, not for the sake of the approving word of men, but before the sovereign God, who has entrusted to us his creatures.[27]

A very rare evidence that a man of spiritual rank in the church is conscious of why he is there. Another quotation:

> With man dies the Christian. . . . [T]he struggle for the freedom and spirituality of man, the struggle for a genuine, decent culture, are not only possible concerns of the church, but fundamental rights and duties. Not only of the people in the church, but also of the church institutions.[28]

That is from the decline of the spirit in the church. Then there is also a volume of notes from the prison cell shortly before the execution, from which I would also like to read a few.[29]

> Modern man is sick. . . . Modern man has become an expert in many departments of life—his range of power is enormous. . . . [T]hat worldly wise person who thinks he knows all the answers, is extremely sensitive to any form of presumption, real or imagined. And the precision which the scientific age imposes on many people makes them highly critical of the slovenliness and sloppiness with which we churchmen often perform our duty in the widest sense of the word.[30]

Later, I will give you, in the example of the idea of the church, which I still have to develop, instances of this slovenliness and sloppiness.

> Most men of the ordained in the official Church must realize for themselves that at present the Church is a misunderstood—and incomprehensible—reality to contemporary man and must be aware how disturbing, threatening and dangerous a state of affairs this is [*which burdens their life*]. . . . Nowadays, personal regeneration and revitalization is far more important than even the most comprehensive, factual knowledge. [*So, the matter isn't ended with theological exactness and reading Denzinger;*[31] *one must also be a decent man.*]

27. Ibid., 97.
28. Ibid., 101.
29. Alfred Delp, *Im Angesicht des Todes: Geschrieben zwischen Verhaftung und Hinrichtung, 1944–1945* (Frankfurt: Verlag Josef Knecht, 1963). Translated as *The Prison Meditations of Father Alfred Delp* (New York: Herder and Herder, 1963).
30. Delp, *Prison Meditations,* 115, slightly modifying the translation.
31. Denzinger's *Enchiridion Symbolorum* is the standard collection of official Catholic Church documents on matters of faith and morals.

> In sober honesty we must face the fact that the Church today is no longer one of the controlling powers in human affairs [*that is required*].[32]

Delp there has pointed to a big historical problem that holds for both churches, that is to say, their loss of contact with the intellectual developments and secular science that have occurred since the Renaissance. Insofar as philosophy in general is done in the church, it is clinging to a fading echo of scholastic or patristic philosophy.

There is no revival of philosophizing in the church. When one attempts to modernize, in order to adapt to the time, there always arises the evil situation of compromising where one should not compromise. That means that this or that well-intentioned cleric or religious is taken in by positivistic sociology or psychoanalysis or existentialism. The church cannot be brought into intellectual order again in this way. Now, we want to remember this Father Delp, especially in view of July 20, which will soon come again, and you should think about it if you hear the profiteers of the resistance make their speeches on this occasion, making a mockery of the sacrifice of a man like Delp.

§34. "Guidelines" for German Clerics and Theologians

In concluding this matter it seems to me necessary to draw up some guidelines for German clerics and theologians in order to teach them the elements of Christianity. Naturally, that would be an enormous task, so to keep the matter in check, I will limit myself to the traditional ten points.

Point 1: As first guideline, a sentence from Father Delp, which is to be considered as the guiding principle for everything here: "Arrogance anywhere near the Church is objectionable—and never more so when it occurs in the name of the Church, or worse, actually as part of the Church herself."[33]

Point 2: This is not from Delp, it is from me: By the grace of the word man will be elevated above his nature. The word of revelation has not gone forth to give clerics and theologians the opportunity of debasing man below his nature.

32. Delp, *Prison Meditations,* 117.
33. Ibid.

Point 3: Christ is the head of the *corpus mysticum*, which includes all men from the beginning of the world to its end. He is not the president of a special-interest club.

Point 4: To be a Christian does not relieve one of the duty of being a human being.

Point 5: It would be good to read the whole of chapter 13 of the Letter to the Romans and to think it over carefully. Whoever subjects himself to this discipline will lose the desire to quote the first verse on its own and, with that, to get up to political mischief.

Point 6: It would be good to read the fourth commandment, "Honor your father and your mother," before asserting—as can be read in the pastoral letters of the German episcopate—that it commands reverence of state authorities and obedience to their laws. Clerics and theologians, even when the Spirit blows in the direction exactly opposite to theirs, should at least not falsify the words of the texts entrusted to them.

Point 7: This is related to the Erlangen opinion: Father of gymnastics Jahn is not a church father.

Point 8: In the Sermon on the Mount, Matthew 5, verse 3, it says, "Blessed are the poor in spirit"; it does not say, "Blessed are the weak in the head."

Point 9: Regarding the relationship between Christians and Jews, that verse of John Donne I read out to you in another lecture is to be learned by heart. I quote it once again—it cannot be quoted often enough:

> Spit in my face you Jewes, and pierce my side,
> Buffet, and scoffe, scourge, and crucifie mee . . .
> They kill'd once an inglorious man, but I
> Crucifie him daily, being more glorified.

Point 10: And as tenth point, to learn off by heart the prophet Ezekiel, chapter 33, verses 7–9 [RSV]. I am reading it out to you. God is speaking to the prophet, to Ezekiel:

> So you, son of man, I have made a watchman for the house of Israel; whenever you hear a word from my mouth, you shall give them warning from me. If I say to the wicked, O wicked man, you shall surely die, and you do not speak to warn the wicked to turn from his way, that wicked man shall die in his iniquity, but his blood I will require at your hand. But if you warn the wicked to turn from his way, and he does not turn from his way; he shall die in his iniquity, but you will have saved your life.

Instructions for use of these guidelines: Lower clergy, copy it out daily ten times; bishops and theologians, daily a hundred times; theologians who have received a Cross of Merit from the Federal Republic, daily two hundred times, until they have got it.

Now there are extremely unpleasant phenomena, but there are also gratifying ones. There are always isolated figures like Father Delp, who, after the statements I have read out to you, seems to have been really a man of high spiritual rank. However, they are isolated. It's not always a dead loss; when one sees these things, one doesn't simply have to throw in the towel. But one must do what one can to support those who try to change these horrible conditions. In the previous lecture, at the end of the investigation into the Evangelical Church, I referred to the 1960 *Kirchentag* and the appearance of Gollwitzer. We have similar phenomena today. The church's behavior with regard to the question of humanity, of mankind, and especially of the Jews as part of mankind has naturally led to a reaction, and precisely the German cardinals, like Cardinal Bea and Cardinal Frings, are very deeply concerned to remove certain liturgical remnants of a stigmatizing of the Jews.

§35. Tension between the Church as Social Institution and as Community of Universal Humanity under Christ

One of the most interesting theoretical problems, however, which indeed is at the basis of all this incredible behavior—the intellectual slovenliness and sloppiness, as Delp called it—is the fact that there is no worked-out idea of the nature of the church, neither in the Evangelical nor in the Catholic Churches, and that the relationship of the church members to their humanity is not the object of theoretical investigations. That was not always so. And so I will now present to you a text from which you will see how one spoke about such things in better times, when spiritual heads were still dominant in the church. For this purpose I will read out to you Thomas Aquinas's section on the *corpus mysticum* in the *Summa theologiae,* third part, chapter 8, article 3. It is headed "Utrum Christus sit caput omnium hominum," "whether Christ is the head of all men." In the corpus of the article can be read (I am translating it now):

> The difference between the natural body of a man and the mystical body of the church [*the ecclesia*] is that the members of a natural body all exist together, whereas members of the mystical body do not. They are not together in their natural existence [*esse naturae*], because the body of the church is made up of people from the beginning to the end of the world. Nor are they all together in grace [*esse gratiae*], because at any given moment there are people who do not have grace then but may have it later on; and there are others who already have it. So people can be classed as members of the mystical body because of their potentiality, and not merely when they are actually in it. Some members have a potentiality that will never be actuated. Others are eventually actuated, and this in three degrees: the first is by faith, the second by charity on earth, the third by the enjoyment of heaven.[34]

Therefore, it is generally to be taken that for the entire time of the world, Christ is the head of all men, but at different degrees. So there now follows the distinctions of degree and the question of the manner in which the heathen and the Jews, particularly the patriarchs of the Old Testament, belong to the *corpus mysticum* of Christ. The text passages that support the investigation are, first, the [First] Letter to Timothy, chapter 4, verse 10, he is the *salvator omnium hominum et maxime fidelium,* "the Savior of all men, especially of those who believe"; and the First Letter of John, [chapter 2], verse 2, *ipse est propitiatio pro peccatis nostris,* "he is the expiation for our sins, and not for ours only but also for the sins of the whole world."

Please note now this definition of what the *corpus mysticum* means in comparison with later interpretations. Let us first be clear what is proposed here: Christ is the head of all men, not only of the members of the church. Humanity is not disavowed by a thinker like Thomas. What happens to the nonmember of the church happens to a member of the *corpus mysticum* of Christ, just as much as what happens to a church member.

There is a big theoretical problem behind that, which I can only briefly indicate here. I am afraid I will have to explain this still further the next time: What is the significance of the appearance of Christ and of his incarnation as a historical event? It means that, in the sense of Thomas, the presence under God, and the presence of God in the world, which up to then was available to

34. Thomas Aquinas, *Summa theologiae,* vol. 49, *The Grace of Christ (3a, 7–15),* trans. Liam G. Walsh (New York: McGraw-Hill, 1974), 61–62.

men only in a profoundly ineffable form, was differentiated through the incarnation and became historically clear. Thus the whole of mankind can become retrospectively included in the incarnation as a historic event, and all of mankind is a member of the *corpus mysticum* in the sense of inclusion in God, as he realizes himself in history. And this holds similarly for the entire future.

As opposed to the philosophic heights of the understanding of the problematic, there always arise the concrete practical problems. For the churches are organizations in the world—in relation to the appearance of Christ in historical reality—and therefore tend to set themselves up as interest groups and legal persons, which is quite all right. It is not all right, however, that the Catholic Church and other churches that have branched off from it, through schism and separations of other kinds, then set themselves up as the one and only *corpus mysticum,* as if the rest of mankind did not belong to it. So, since the Middle Ages, we have in theology a strange tension running parallel to the development of the nation states, where, in the idea of the *corpus mysticum,* the church understood as a social and legal institution predominates over the universal conception of the *corpus mysticum* as formulated from a philosophical height by Thomas.

From this tension arise the peculiarities of the churches in the contemporary situation, which in Germany are much more dangerous than in other countries. Because in other countries the church people and the clergy belong to a people's society, or rather, to a national society, that, moreover, is civilized through the Renaissance, Enlightenment, and so on. These civilizational factors are missing in German society. Hence the particular danger that membership in the church, which, theologically, we need not further speak about here, is somehow misunderstood as a special position opposed to the rest of mankind, as if the rest of mankind did not belong to mankind, and as if that belonging to mankind were a privilege of church membership. . . .

So, because of the tension I have just characterized, there is this ghettoizing tendency that exists between the church as institution and the church in Thomas's sense, the *ecclesia* as *corpus mysticum,* which comprises the whole of mankind from the beginning to the end. For Germany this is a particularly dangerous tension on account of the miserable intellectual and philosophical level that prevails in this country.

(Eighth Lecture)

Ladies and Gentlemen,

In the previous lecture I began to discuss the problem of the *corpus mysticum,* because it underlies the peculiar behavior of the clergy and theologians and must be clarified. I have first referred to the passage in Thomas where it is said that Christ is the head of all men from the beginning of the world to its end. And this community of all men under Christ is the *ecclesia.* From this comprehensive idea of the church are to be distinguished the ideas of churches as social institutions in specific historic situations.

§36. Advances and Regressions in Differentiation of Knowledge of the Presence under God

Regarding the question of this tension between the broad Thomasic definition of the *corpus mysticum* and the very narrow ideas of churches as made up of persons who through the sacrament are received into a community, and which do not extend beyond this circle of persons, there is the general problem that mankind in history is not egalitarian, but has a history. And that means that men, insofar as their history is known at all, are always under God and express this knowledge of their existence under God through corresponding organizational and ritual institutions. But in the insight into the nature of man's existence under God there are developments from relatively compact conceptions of this order of existence of individual men and of society under God to the highly differentiated ones. And the unfolding of this problem of existence under God as the central problem of order, that is history. Please note this definition; it is very carefully considered. The problem of history lies here, not anywhere else. So there is history insofar as the presence under God and the knowledge of such presence under God runs through phases of compactness and differentiation.

In this historical process of increasing transparency for the central problem of order, Christianity takes a special place, insofar as in it, through the symbolism of the incarnation, the presence of God in man in society and in history is thoroughly formulated. That happened nowhere else. Only in terms of this problematic of incarnation, which then had as a consequence the whole problematic of the Trinity and the dogma of the Trinity, is it unequivocally said what man is. That is to say, man is man insofar as he is *imago Dei*, and insofar as he is *imago Dei* are all men equal as participating in the reality of God and thus united with God, who historically has become flesh in the process of history. This is precisely what is characteristic of Christianity, its unique achievement. Every attempt to withdraw from this achievement is a regression in differentiation and an attempt to reintroduce more compact ideas of the existence of man and of his order. To such regressions, however, also belongs, now in a sociological sense, the attempt within the church at restricting Christianity or the membership of Christ to members of a historical church.

The second point to notice is the following. These advances in differentiation do not occur in the sense that suddenly, through a kind of biological mutation all over the world, all men pass on from a more compact to a more differentiated insight into their order. Rather, these insights occur in determinate men, who, again, are in determinate societies, and very often they do not immediately penetrate beyond the bounds of the given society. Very often they are ineffective even within the bounds of this society, for the one who is immediately understanding is always only one individual human being, and whether he is a prophet or a philosopher makes no difference. And so we have a remarkable structuration of history insofar as the insights that are representative because they more sharply differentiate and make clearer the nature of man are bound to determinate historical points and are only gradually able to spread out from such centers.

From this structure of history, that insights are found to be representative for the whole of humanity, there now arises a whole series of encumbrances upon this insight. Think for the moment about the problems of philosophy. It is in Greek philosophy that an insight into the nature of man was attained, one which indeed was representative for all men, insofar as there, too, all men were recognized as being under God and recognized as being in an order that is to be determined in terms of its transcendent type of openness. But these ideas—think for example of classic politics in Plato and Aristotle—were at the same time bound up with the order of the society in which they were found, so that politics, in its first formulation, for example, in Aristotelian politics, then become the politics of a determinate type of society, that is to say, of the polis. The ideas of the order of man and of society were not expanded beyond the polis and, within the paradigm of the polis as sketched in the seventh and eighth books of the Aristotelian *Politics*,[35] remain as the pattern of order of a society that naturally cannot be used anymore today, because we do not have a polis anymore.

Exactly the same problem occurs in the pneumatic sphere, if it is to be distinguished as such from the noetic sphere of philosophy. The insights into the presence under God, as they were found in Israel, especially by Moses, are immediately connected with the idea of the chosen people, that is, of the people in which this insight was found through one of its members, Moses, and then crystallized in the covenant of Sinai. Now, these orders under God are primary, and that applies above all to the pneumatic sphere. They are primarily clarifications of the relation of man to God, and secondarily of man to man. The Decalogue, which contains the essence of the Sinaitic covenant, thus contains rules for the behavior of man to God and to his fellowman. It does not contain any determinations of any kind as to how a society should be organized, not even that of the chosen people. This is because the internal social organization according to clans or families is presupposed and will be questioned by no one. There now arise, therefore, remarkable problems. The clan society as such, which is not put in question, exists under God. That is the situation that Martin Buber denoted by the expression "theopolity."[36]

The same problematic repeated itself in early Christian times. What is in question is the further clarification of the relationship of the existence of men under God through Christ, and again the emphasis is on the problematic of right order in relationship to God and to the fellowman. But once again, there are no statements regarding the organization of a society for duration in the world. Now, in one passage in the sacred scripture, these problems do become explicit. When the tribal constitution (Israel in its old form), under the pressure of external political events in the wars of the Philistines, is compelled to transform itself into an organization under a king like the other nations, then there arises the problem

35. See Voegelin, *Plato and Aristotle,* vol. 3 of *Order and History* (1957; available Columbia: University of Missouri Press, 1999), 281, 295–96, 299, 350–55.

36. See Martin Buber, *Moses: The Revelation and the Covenant* (New York: Harper and Row, 1958), under index references to "Theopolitical Idea," and Voegelin, *Israel and Revelation,* vol. 1 of *Order and History* (1956; available Columbia: University of Missouri Press, 1999), under index references to "Theopolity."

of the king, who emerges now as ruler in competition with the ruler who up to then was the ruler of the chosen people, namely, God.

This problem reaches into the modern era: There is always the question that the order of man to God and to his fellowmen has been laid down through the covenant with God. Now if the ruler, who has the instruments of power at his disposal, violates this order by setting up a temple for other gods, or violates the duties of the Decalogue regarding his fellowmen by building up the military or at least some kind of bureaucratic organization where certain levels of society, of employers and merchants, emerge who no longer display the right behavior in the decalogical sense toward their fellowmen, then there arises the question of the control of the ruler in the social as well as political sense, through representatives of the idea of the covenant, of the covenant with God. That means that the prophet will now be the critic of the political and social organization. This is a new phenomenon. So, the prophet is first and foremost a social critic, because he must keep the political organization under control, in accord with the standards of the covenant. The question now is, Who in each individual case has the calling to be the interpreter of the covenant and its determination?

As I have said, these problems continue into the modern era, where the prophets are no longer a social institution, but where new prophets must emerge in order to carry out the social criticism. In the discussions of the sixteenth and seventeenth centuries, particularly in the English revolution, we therefore have two opposed viewpoints. One holds that the king is the legitimate interpreter of God's covenant, which is the opinion represented above all by James I. The other holds that the people is the legitimate authority for the interpretation of God's covenant, represented in particular by Puritan preachers. That would play a great role in the Puritan revolution. So we have to detect in the seventeenth century the emergence of a new wave, which now, in order to distinguish it from the Christian and old Israelite problems, may be called that of "Hebraism" in the sense of the problematic of the king and of the prophets, approximately as in the books of Samuel.

Within Christianity itself there is no such development with regard to social organization and social criticism, for the early Christian idea of the relationship to God and to fellowmen is apocalyptically determined, that is to say, it is dominated by the expectation of the approaching end of the world. So, unlike in the ancient Israel of the kingdom, there is not developed a Christian organization and a Christian organizational criticism. When the Christian communities come into contact, positively or negatively, with political organizations, the church—now transformed into an organization in the world—must, in order to clarify conduct within its organization and to explain the relationship between it and the permanent secular community, consult as sources above all the classic philosophers and the post-classic Stoic natural law.

As a result, the early church fathers, above all Lactantius, inserted the natural law, particularly in its Ciceronian form, into the Christian idea of order in the world, thus making that order viable in the world.

Thus we have two great sources for world organization in the Western world: the Hebrew tradition and the Stoic–natural law tradition, one introduced to ancient Israel, the other to early Christianity. Consequently further problems arise.

Representative for order, therefore, are not only the covenant or the Sermon on the Mount or the formulations of the New Testament—handed on in apocalyptic expectation—but also the philosophic insight into the nature of man and the ideas of human and social order arising from it, as they were taken over from the pre-Christian philosophic complex.

From this rather complicated situation there now arises a whole series of problems for the relationship of the church to the temporal community. Because the church took over the worldly idea of order from classic and Stoic philosophy, this became a component of Christian theology, as for example in the *Summa theologiae* of Thomas. This had disastrous consequences for the later development of natural law, for, first of all, it became, as it were, Christian natural law and the church took on the role of guardian of natural law. However, it is nowhere written that in the various historical situations church personnel are particularly suitable guardians of the natural law. For all the propositions of the natural law derive from the noetic experience, whereas within the church the noetic experience is not the primary source of experience and truth for clerics and theologians, but is replaced by the pneumatic experience of revelation. Thus there is a very considerable stock of knowledge of order coming from philosophy that is denatured and deformed in the theological field, because it had to be inserted into a complex of pneumatic symbols of revelation not intended to establish the order of temporal society.

Therefore we have the odd situation today that the Social Democrats, for example, who want to get out of revolutionary ideology and again recognize that there is something like natural law—which indeed also held for Marx, before the aspect of natural law was completely lost in the revolutionary phase—turn to the churches for information on natural law. They flirt with Christian natural law, apparently in complete ignorance of the fact that it is a pre-Christian, philosophically pagan phenomenon concerning existence in the world, with absolutely nothing to do with the church as such. So it would be much better for such rather open-minded Social Democrats to begin to interest themselves in the pre-Christian natural law instead of allowing themselves to be instructed by the church about what natural law is.

§37. The Church's Representation of Universal Humanity: Its Duty and Its Failure

Now let us return to the problem of representation. The church exists in relation to the world and thus must also define its behavior with regard to the temporal aspect of its existence in the world. On both sides, the spiritual side from revelation and the noetic side from philosophy, the representative function—being human—in history has traditionally been encumbered by the fact that the insight became part of the respective dogma.

This means, that on the one side, the temporal side, there is the insight that the order of society has to be at the level of humanity—in the sense that the nature of man achieves fulfillment in the order of society and has to determine its order. But this insight is restricted, because the order only occurs within a limited community, so that the interests of the limited community in history enter into an amalgam with the general problematic of order at the level of humanity. And the particular interests of a society can thus appear in the cloak of more universal formulations of humanity—and thereby again denature and deform humanity in general.

In the church, the matter is even more critical, because here we have the problem that there is not one particular church but several concrete churches, Evangelical, Catholic, Greek-Orthodox

Churches, and so on, each one claiming for itself the specific purity of representation of man under God, which only they can preach. Moreover, this specific historical form again amalgamates with the claim of generality, so that this church with the claim of generality, since it must indeed exist in the world and in specific societies, somehow balances its interests with those of the temporal aspect of the society.

We come again then to the grotesque situations that when a war breaks out anywhere, the priests on both sides willingly explain that the society is engaged in a just war, that the others are really bad types, and that God is always on their side. Always the same God. That can, in the extreme case, as we have seen in Germany in the National Socialist period, lead to the fact, first, that from the purely ecclesiastical problematic no one is seen as human who does not belong to the church—he lies outside the interests of humanity. And second, when it's a matter of coming to terms with the temporal aspect of the society, the respective church in the specific society will always side with those who are the strongest at the time. And if those who are strongest, as for example the National Socialists, exclude from humanity everyone who is not a National Socialist, then arises the terrible consequence of mass murder, where the church does not intervene.

You must remember, for example, that the *Einsatz* commandos—who, to make *Lebensraum* for Germans, perpetrated mass murder on the civilian population in Poland in order to exterminate Poles—were 22 percent Catholic. Yet no representative of the German Catholic Church, and even less any representative of the German Evangelical Church, told any of these members of the SS (if they themselves did not know that already), who very happily still remained members of the church, that one was not allowed to shoot people dead. So, a complete decline, because the historically concrete actions were encumbered with the National Socialist idea that they were representative of the whole of humanity, with the result that the general humanity gets lost.

Against this tendency there are now a few passages to be noted. I am speaking only of the German situation; in general, of course, people know that everywhere. But within the German churches it is not so well known. I refer you to a very interesting treatment by Karl Rahner, "Membership of the Church according to the teaching of

Pius XII's Encyclical, *Mystici Corporis Christi.*"[37] This encyclical, which first appeared in 1943, makes the most severe contraction of the membership of the church that it had ever received, insofar as here the community of the *corpus mysticum* is limited very strictly to members of the Catholic Church who have received the sacrament. Whoever does not have this sacramental character is not a member of the church, and since "church" is now identified with *corpus mysticum,* he is, so to say, not a member of the *corpus mysticum.* In this situation, a theologian like Rahner has to first establish that these very restrictive formulations of the encyclical make only positive statements about this narrower membership, define only membership of the church, but—since they draw no conclusions—that they have nothing to say about the wider problem of the *corpus mysticum.* So, the theologian is free to go beyond the encyclical and make a series of reflections that then lead to where Thomas began in the High Middle Ages, that is to say, that Christ is the head of all men from the beginning of the world to its end.

However, a theologian like Rahner, certainly in the framework of the formulated Christian doctrinal pronouncements, as, for example, in this encyclical, has to behave himself. He must now erect all sorts of interesting constructions to make these doctrinal pronouncements compatible with his intended thesis, that Christ is the head of all men. The worst offense is naturally the problem of the sacrament. For if, according to an explicit doctrinal pronouncement, church membership and membership of the *corpus mysticum* is limited to persons who have received a sacrament, how then can persons who have not received a sacrament still be members of the *corpus mysticum*? And arising from that, something remarkable is now achieved. From this lack of proper terms (which is precisely that of the theologian—we are not bound by such a problematic of having to start with the sacrament), he established that being a follower of Christ outside the church is not only an individual problem of personal acceptance of the word, or something like that, but, as he discreetly expresses himself, has a "quasi-sacramental" character. So if we drop the expression

37. Karl Rahner, *Theological Investigations* (Baltimore: Helicon Press, 1963), 2:1–88.

"quasi-sacramental," which is caused by the lack of theological terminology, we can say what every anthropologist, every archeologist, everyone who is involved with the science of religions, and so on, knows in the secular sphere: that is, that obviously all men who are historically known to us and who have existed in historic societies have always had sacraments to express their presence under God. So there is absolutely no reason to restrict to the church, or to any specific church, the idea of sacrament, whose general and constitutive idea holds for every community. Every primitive tribe has sacraments of divine worship, of rituals for initiation into the community, all of which always represent the presence in terms of very compact ideas of attachment to the world of the divine, in space-time reality. From the point of view of comparative religious studies and of history in general, there is absolutely no problem. There have always been sacraments, and there are only specifically Christian sacraments that have something to do with the higher degree of differentiation, of the incarnation and of the insight into the presence of all men under God. So the problematic, which Rahner tried to formulate very carefully, resolves itself in the insight that all men exist under God, and that, however, this insight into the existence under God passes through a historical process from compactness to differentiation. Therefore, the results of modern science are absolutely compatible with, for example, the Thomasic theology of Christ as the head of all men. For, indeed, nothing else is expressed in the symbolism of Christ than the differentiated insight that all men always exist under God and under grace and salvation. And all men in all communities have always known that and symbolize it through the institution of sacraments. So we have here, from the theological side, an attempt to develop ideas that are again compatible with the contemporary level of secular science. However, one must say that secular science, since it is not bound by this balancing act between theological doctrinal pronouncements, has proceeded much further along in the understanding of what the community of mankind is.

6

Descent into the Legal Abyss

§38. The *Rechtsstaat* as a Specifically German Concept

. . . We now come to the next theme, the *Rechtsstaat.* These problems of the *Rechtsstaat* were there before Hitler, remained during the Third Reich, and are still here today. They are at their clearest and most acute at present in the famous Auschwitz and other trials, the euthanasia trials, and the remarkable verdicts pronounced on such occasions. These verdicts are so remarkable because there are phenomena involved that cannot be contained within the context of the *Rechtsstaat* but belong to the political sphere. In Germany, the political sphere is taboo; and not only taboo, but generally there are also no adequate personnel for dealing with it. I will first of all provide evidence for that.

I have had members of the Institute make an inquiry into the question of whether, in monographs or longer published essays, German legal professors have taken a position on the trials of National Socialist crimes. Is there any literature on the question? The result of the inquiry is this: Professors of the philosophy of law and of public law have not expressed themselves in monographs on the trials of the *Einsatzgruppen,* that is to say, these mass murders. Regarding monographs, this is what it looks like in detail: With the aid of the list of professors and part-time professors in untenured positions of legal science, it is established that the author catalog of the law seminar reference library, along with the Bavarian State Library, contain no monographs. There are none in the other libraries either. Further, no monograph on the National Socialist crimes could be detected in the author catalog of the reference library of the law seminars, in the Bavarian State Library, or in the regular book reviews from 1958 to 1963 of the *Neue Juristische Wochenschrift* (from 1958 to April 9, 1964), the *Juristenzeitung* (from 1958 to 1962), or the *Zeitschrift für die gesamte Strafrechtswissenschaft* (from 1958 to 1962) either. Not one monograph could be found under the headings *Rechtsstaat,* National Socialism, National Socialist crimes, war crimes, crimes against mankind, crimes against humanity, *Einsatzgruppen* trials, in the library of the law seminars and in the Bavarian State Library. There is none there. . . . [1]

So, on the whole, nothing. No one who is legally competent in these matters, with the exceptions indicated, says anything at all about them. The political scientists too, keep a deep silence, and so, in the literature, one can come across nothing on this whole problematic of the *Rechtsstaat.* The subject is taboo. Now, why is it taboo? Not only because the people are anxious, or have a bad conscience, but also because intellectually all kinds of things are not all right.

I will open this question of the *Rechtsstaat* with some sentences from Herbert Krüger's *Allgemeine Staatslehre,* published this year, in 1964:

> Today, hardly any state does not claim to be a "*Rechtsstaat,*" to proceed "according to the principles of a *Rechtsstaat,*" and so on. It is exactly the widespread use of this ideal that necessitates an exact understanding of it, so that it does not degenerate into a commonplace.[2]

Now, just note what we have here. The typical attitude of an author who just jots anything down. For to say that today hardly any state does not claim to be a *Rechtsstaat,* and so on, is false, of course, because *Rechtsstaat* is a German word and has a meaning only within the German study of institutions since the beginning of the nineteenth century. Outside Germany no one knows whether he is in a *Rechtsstaat* or not. It is an internal German problem,

1. In the lecture, Voegelin referred to his assistants' search, in the law seminar library of the University of Munich and in the Bavarian State Library, for legal monographs and journal articles on the trials of those involved in Nazi crimes against humanity, including the *Einsatzgruppen* murders. Neither the standard recent survey of the subject, Langbein's *Im Namen des deutschen Volkes: Zwischenbilanz der Prozesse wegen nationalsozialistischer Verbrechen* (Vienna: Europa Verlag, 1963), nor monographs referred to by Langbein were available. Nor were there any extended essays on the topics to be found in the journals. The list of references actually discovered is quoted in the typescript of "Hitler und die Deutschen," 238–39, on the basis of the assistants' report contained in Eric Voegelin Papers, Hoover Institution Archives, box 86, file 13.

2. Herbert Krüger, *Allgemeine Staatslehre* (Stuttgart: Kohlhammer, 1964), 776.

where the concept of *Rechtsstaat* has never been clarified and has been given all possible, indeed the most remarkable, meanings. . . . We are floating in the second reality of word exhilaration, with words like *Rechtsstaat,* where one talks in circles without knowing exactly what is meant.

The best introduction to the development of the term is *Die neuere Entwicklung des Rechtsstaates in Deutschland* by Ulrich Scheuner, published in 1960. That gives a survey of the problematic. But it is also written from within the problematic. He accepts the expression and does not critically confront it.

Now we will deal with the expression *Rechtsstaat* somewhat more critically. If we wish to do so and get beyond accepting it as a political topos, we must attend to the occasions where it is most profusely spoken of. These occasions are definite models, that is to say, models of the idea of what a legal order might look like.

§39. Conflict between Hierarchical Legal Systems and Separation of Powers, as in the German Basic Law (*Grundgesetz*)

The first model to which expressions like *Rechtsstaat* were attached is the model of the hierarchy of legal propositions in the legal order, as it was first systematically developed by Bodin in the sixteenth century. This was the idea of a closed legal system, which had its origin in the leadership of the monarch, who is the highest lawgiver of the society concerned. I will not now go into Bodin's theory—the structures have changed somewhat in the meantime—and I will use the modern model. If one uses the model of a hierarchy of legal propositions, then, internal to the state there are legal propositions at different levels. At the highest level are the legal propositions of the constitution, under which are the legal propositions of the legislator; under these are the administrative orders, the individual administrative acts, the judicial application to concrete cases, and so on. So that is a hierarchy, where on principle every lower legal proposition is procedurally legitimated by the next higher legal proposition. This simple model, of a sequence of legal propositions in a so-called context of delegation, however, is complicated by all sorts of further questions.

One can imagine, for example, a further model—which is also historically concrete—where the legislation applies to certain areas in which administrative orders and administrative acts are issued. These administrative orders, however, not only concretize what is to be found in the laws; there are also administrative orders *praeter legem,* ordinances outside the context of law. They are not *contra legem,* they are not allowed to conflict with the law, but they regulate social relationships that are not regulated by laws.

Concretely, for example, that is the administrative model still very often applied at the end of the eighteenth century. And one of the legal-political processes that occupied the nineteenth century was the successful attempt at not permitting any more administrations *praeter legem* but placing all administrations under the law. That is to say, if an administrative organ is not positively empowered by a law to issue ordinances and administrative acts in relation to a specific area, then it is not empowered to deal with this area at all. So, in this further model then, there are no ordinances *praeter legem.*

This tendency, which makes itself felt here, from the first model of ordinances *praeter legem* to the second model where there are no ordinances *praeter legem,* shows you that the direction of the rationalization of the legal order goes toward bringing the whole process of legislation under the control of a central authority. As a result, there are no enclaves of legal norms that cannot be derived from the highest legal propositions within the legal system.

Now, to this idea of the hierarchical order of propositions, ideas of the *Rechtsstaat* can be added on. One can say, then, that a *Rechtsstaat* exists if all laws in the society are derived from a norm acknowledged as the highest legitimate norm, that is, from the constitutional norms. That would be approximately the idea of a thoroughly rationalized legal system as it has been developed in legal theory.

However, one runs into difficulties with these ideas, as you will best see if again you take concrete cases. Let us take article 20 from the Basic Law.[3] That says:

> (1) The Federal Republic of Germany is a democratic and social federal state.

3. The Basic Law is the constitution of the Federal Republic of Germany.

(2) All state authority emanates from the people. It shall be exercised by the people through elections and voting and by specific legislative, executive, and judicial organs.

(3) Legislation is subject to the constitutional order; the executive and the judiciary are bound by law and justice.[4]

I must now comment on that. We can leave aside the first section: "The Federal Republic of Germany is a democratic and social federal state." We will later come to what that means. But now the second part: "All state authority emanates from the people. It shall be exercised by the people through elections and voting and by specific legislative, executive and judicial organs." So here you see legitimized three powers, which are placed side by side—apart from the people itself and the introduction of the idea of popular sovereignty and its voting rights. It is, so to speak, a principle of the separation of powers. That means that this power will be exercised by three powers placed side by side.

However, that is now contradicted by the third section of article 20: "Legislation is subject to the constitutional order; the executive and the judiciary are bound by law and justice." That means that the layers of constitutional norms as such are isolated, and legislation is now subject to the constitutional norms, on the model of the simple hierarchy of legal propositions, which is subject to the constitutional order.

But how is it now with the government and with an organ such as the Federal Constitutional Court? These are not subject to the constitutional norms, for according to the hierarchical model, the right of the law is subject to the legal propositions of the constitution. And the other organs, now, the executive power and the judiciary, are subject to law. So here you have a model that is not in agreement with reality and absolutely not with the reality as it is precisely formulated in article 20, section 2, namely, of coordinated powers that divide the highest power among themselves.

So, here: I am not a legal historian and have not checked out the matter historically; I can only express a conjecture that the persons who formulated this article as legislators have indeed once heard a rumor about the principle of the separation of powers. And since

4. Translation in David P. Currie, *The Constitution of the Federal Republic of Germany* (Chicago: University of Chicago Press, 1994), 351.

they had to have a decent constitution, they therefore incorporated it into section 2 of article 20. However, they also live as good, fine jurists in the dutiful model of this hierarchy of the norm of law, and there at the top is the constitution, under that is the legislature, and under that the executive and judiciary. It did not dawn on them that that does not go together with the principle of the separation of powers, which, by coordinating the government, the legislature, and the Federal Constitutional Court, is subject to the constitution and cannot be garnished with the model of a hierarchy of legal propositions.

Now this is not a matter of indifference. For in the first place, this conflict among the models, where two models are introduced to describe legal concepts incompatible with one another, shows that there are very serious problems with the political and legal methodological education of the authors of this constitution. In an absolutely fundamental point they have not correctly given it technical legal formulation.

However, on the other hand, even if the misfortune is now over, the most terrible things pass into practice. For according to the principle of the separation of powers as expressed in article 20, section 2, the Federal Constitutional Court is in fact an organ immediately under the constitution, coordinated with the legislature and the government. But since there is no basis available for this assertion—rather, one must appeal to article 20, section 3, which operates according to the hierarchical model—there is now a big debate about whether the Federal Constitutional Court is a constitutional organ or not. And amazing constructions are invented to help, just like the theologian Rahner has to invent them if he wants to bring mankind back into the *corpus mysticum*. These are invented, despite the opposed provisions of this article, in order to make the Federal Constitutional Court into a constitutional organ that, with regard to the separation of powers, is on the same level as both other organs. This article is one of the most interesting documents we have from the legal texts of the Basic Law itself for showing where the problems are to be found here.

I have already read out the remarkable passage from Krüger's work, showing that there too in the formation of jurists something was not all right. There is quite obviously a lack in their formation, insofar as such elementary problems as the separation of powers—and how I can make a separation of powers visible in the constitution, how I can organize my legal norms so that a separation of powers comes across—come into conflict with the hierarchical problems. In this conflict the petty official or the lower judge is subject to the laws that are decreed by the monarch and would never claim to be, as would a Federal Constitutional judge, beside the government and have to slap it across the fingers if it is in conflict with the constitution. So, the dutiful psychology of little people: That is the problem of article 20.

Similar problems run through the whole constitution in the *Rechtsstaat.* You see now what comes from a *Rechtsstaat.*

§40. Legal Positivism, Judge-made Law, and Authoritarian Rule

So, one could now, of course, understand by *Rechtsstaat*—and it has now and then been so understood—a state in which there is a separation of powers. But the primary problem is the hierarchical model of legal propositions, to which the ideas of and debates about the *Rechtsstaat* are connected. Let us advance from the situation of the little people, of the subordinate administrative officials, and of judges who are subject to the law that is issued by the princes, to the sphere of the constitution. Then you see what has most deeply penetrated legal theory at the end of the nineteenth century under the influence of the authoritarian state and under the label of "positivism": It is the idea of "positive law."

At the end of the nineteenth century, positive law was understood as the content of the enacted law, seen as enacted and applied by jurists, that is, by administrative officials, and by judges, by the professor of the law faculty, who had to pass it on to his students, by the students, who had to learn it and who in their turn would become administrative officials and judges.

That these legal propositions, which one learns so well and which one has to follow, must also be enacted by someone—this problem does not lie within the horizon of the legal world of ideas in Germany. Here now is the political problem. For if they have once agreed, emotionally and psychologically, to live in a *Rechtsstaat* and are obliged as obedient citizens of the *Rechtsstaat* to do what the laws command, and if the question about who makes the law is eliminated, then you again have the situation of rabble-like demoralization, which takes no interest in the questions: Where do we find order? What are the contents of the law and what do they command? Where are the criteria of justice? How far may one allow the calculation of error to go? So from the positivistic situation of the jurist applying the law, who has not himself participated in the creation of law and submits unconditionally to the authorities who create and promulgate law, it is psychologically impossible to rebel, if the content of the positive law, that is to say, of the laws, is criminal.

Now that is a specifically German institution. In the Anglo-Saxon countries we have a completely different problematic of law, insofar as the law is traditionally judge-made law: that is, the judge and, as far as administrations exist, to a very high degree the administrative organs create law. Thus they themselves are responsible for the content of the law that is being applied in the concrete case. This kind of legal system is found at its highest in the institution, as in America, of a Supreme Court where the judges, in a very independent manner and on the basis of not very differentiated ideas about what justice requires, control the laws and further develop the constitution in a legally creative way by restricting or amplifying the precedents, interpreting the laws as invalid or valid, and so on.

All this freedom of legal creativity obviously lies beyond the readiness for responsibility and the emotional capacity of the German legal profession. That is the real crux of the matter. The law is set before them and then it is applied. It is an attitude that still plays a big part today. Since the Basic Law has made a whole series of fundamental rights immediately open to legal procedures, the question of fundamental rights in legal cases has come to be discussed by German jurists. One can very clearly distinguish two camps: those who are prepared to apply fundamental rights with judicial immediacy, in order to decide what is right, and those who say that this introduction of general principles, which are to be immediately applied in the creation of law, denatures the whole essence of the administration of justice and opens the way to arbitrariness. In this, these more radical positivists—like Forsthoff, for example—are not completely wrong, because the way to arbitrariness is indeed opened if one applies such general fundamental rights at will, but only if those doing so are dubious types. But if they are people who have more or less precise ideas about what justice is, then it functions excellently.

So you can see how, at this highest place in the hierarchy of legal norms, the problem of the content of the norm is interfered with by the problem of the personalities of those who have to decide about this content of the norm and apply it.

There is no law that is mysteriously enacted somewhere and that can be applied by some fine jurist who otherwise would have absolutely nothing else to rack his brains about. Rather, there only exists the law, which is made by concrete men—again the problem of man; and if the men are corrupt and not capable of law and justice, or if they proffer some kind of ideology under justice, then, of course, one cannot have any legal order.

That leads again to other variants of the problem of the *Rechtsstaat.* People speak today of a kind of restoration of thinking in terms of the *Rechtsstaat* and are very quick in disqualifying the Third Reich as a state of injustice (*Unrechtsstaat*) without paying attention to why it really became an *Unrechtsstaat.* Here now there are difficulties similar to those that arose with the church problematic. You will remember that representatives of the church, particularly in a specific phase of the Catholic Church's resistance or nonresistance, were not clear that there is a difference between an authoritarian state and a totalitarian worldview. This occurred because they were orienting themselves to the model of fascism in Italy, which was not a totalitarian worldview but in fact an authoritarian regime, or to the authoritarian regime in Austria. Orienting themselves to these models, it was not seen that, apart from the authoritarian structure of power and, possibly, of the creation of law, there was the problem of what is written in the law and what is effected by means of the authoritarian organization.

So, in certain circumstances, it is possible not to have too many objections to an authoritarian organization. For when an undeveloped people is not ready to function democratically, it would be better if an energetic master should rule in an authoritarian way. There is nothing wrong with this: Under the circumstances, it is a necessity for the functioning of society in primitive cultural conditions. What is quite different is if the authoritarian master is at the same time an ideologue and kills masses of people if they offer resistance to whatever fantastic projects he has. That is something quite different. Therefore, one could not, from the standpoint of justice, immediately object if there was under certain circumstances something like an authoritarian leading authority even in Germany. The presupposition, however, is that the authoritarian leading authority does not consist of National Socialists or Communists or other ideologues but of persons who live in a classic-Christian idea of what justice is.

Then, in certain circumstances, even an authoritarian form of organization can be better than a democratic form—if, for example, the majority consists of blocking-majorities of Communists and National Socialists. So, there are authoritarian regimes, as in the Weimar republic through the system of emergency decrees, of which we cannot automatically say that they should in some way be adapted to the standards of justice. For in this social situation there was no other possibility of enacting law except through emergency decrees, that is, in the authoritarian way. But these distinctions are not made, and then the further development of the problematic of the *Rechtsstaat* runs aground.

(Ninth Lecture)

Ladies and Gentlemen,
The last time I began to analyze the problem of the *Rechtsstaat,* and I had to go into somewhat complicated explanations. For we are always faced with this problem of political science—especially under German conditions, with the philosophizing background—that we have strayed very far from the commonsense sphere, and so we must first work through the different topoi toward reality. The so-called concept of the *Rechtsstaat* is a topos that in itself means absolutely nothing, and to get an idea of what it really means we must first break through to reality again.

If you now ask why we bother to do that at all—let us simply ignore the whole thing—then one has to reply that, unfortunately, that won't do. For this topos has entered into the German history of legal thought and is also a legal concept in the Basic Law, in article 20. So we must be clear about what this *Rechtsstaat* is all about. But I must once again draw your attention to the fact that it exists only in Germany, nowhere else.

Now, to break through to reality, I have developed a few models, that is to say, the models immediately following article 20 of the Basic Law. First, there is a hierarchy of legal norms, a conception that goes back to Bodin; I will speak in a minute about the political reasons for it. And then there is another conception—incompatible with this hierarchy of legal norms—where the powers are separated horizontally. That is to say, if the judiciary, the executive, and the legislature are coordinated with each other, then these three cannot be brought into a hierarchy any more. And if the separation of powers is turned into the political principle of a constitution, one can no longer operate according to the hierarchical model. It is typical of article 20 that it tries to do both, because obviously the authors of this article were incapable of grasping the problem. This is as far as I had gone the previous time.

§41. Historical Background to Closed Legal Systems

And now we will discuss the reasons why, in general, such constructions, such models, are employed. What is the purpose of the hierarchical model? I said that it went back to Bodin, and having started there one could distinguish a series of political purposes for the hierarchical model. If the legal system is constructed downward from a highest authority—which meant in the constitution as it was understood in Bodin's time that the legislation is in the hand of the prince—then it is, first of all, a political fact that the highest positive legal propositions are enacted by the prince. All competing positive legal propositions from other sides are thus excluded.

This meant that in the political situation at that time neither the pope nor the emperor could interfere in any way with France's legislation. It was a warding off of outer authorities who claimed or tried to usurp the higher powers of legal enaction against those powers of the national state represented by the royal authority.

The second reason for setting up such a closed hierarchy is again a political one, namely, to exclude all legal enclaves within the state, within this national state. When I say "state" now, I mean national state, for the national state is to be defined precisely as this idea of a closed legal system. This means that within this state no enclaves of independent legal enaction may appear, but that all legal enactions at a lower level must be legitimized through delegation from legal enactions at a higher level. Thus neither from outside nor from inside can the hierarchic sequence, which goes from the king down to its execution by the judiciary and by the administration, be disturbed by anyone. That was the original reason for the closing of the legal system: that the national community, which has arisen through dynastic achievements, is subject to the authority of the king and may not be disturbed either from within or from without.

A new phase in this problematic of hierarchy is then reached in the German authoritarian states of the eighteenth century, and thus the career of the German expression *Rechtsstaat* really begins.

In the first place, the administration, which indeed from the prince's viewpoint is princely administration, corresponding completely to the Bodinian principle of subordination to the prince, shall be brought under the control of laws. Here now, a new political factor arises, for who demands that the administration—which indeed, seen from the prince's viewpoint, is completely all right, princely hierarchically, as it is—must be brought under the control of the laws? Why should the laws alone authorize what the administration does, so that the administration has no authority outside the laws? These are consequences in the context of the new popular sovereignty. So, a liberal citizenry expects that the laws are binding and that the administration has no scope outside the laws, rather within the laws, with the usual room for discretion that one also finds within the law.

However, that is not enough, for even if there is thus achieved a safeguard—seen from the civic standpoint—against arbitrary administrative procedures, the content of the laws is not yet decided. And the next political problem of the *Rechtsstaat* is therefore to bring the legislation itself under the control of a representation chosen by the people. That, then, is the parliamentary principle of legislation, that only representatives of the people shall be allowed to make laws and that the content of the laws no longer remains at the discretion of the prince. That would be the second phase.

A third phase then arises, which, however, became really pressing in Germany only in the Weimar republic and in the aftermath of the Hitler regime. In this phase, legislation could no longer be entrusted to the legislature, but the principle of the separation of powers had to enter; for whoever makes the laws is a man, and men are fallible. Thus it is better if several powers—three, in this case—are balanced against each other so that none is allowed to make laws without the others. It aims at some kind of right of the executive to propose legislation, which in this context would be the government and not the administration. The government now stands beside the legislature as initiator of legislation and possibly also as the body that approves legislation, insofar as laws that the parliament has passed still require a signature of the executive, for example, that of a president. Finally, in addition to the legislature and the executive, the judiciary also participates in it, by testing the content of the laws in terms of its constitutionality. However, that is only possible if there is a constitution according to which one can judge the legality of the content of the laws. Bare legality, in the sense that the law was passed according to correct procedure by resolution of the legislature with the approval of the government and of the president, is not enough. That would indeed leave the content of the laws, so to speak, free. The most terrible things could be written in there. All of that is now thrown into a big drawer marked *Rechtsstaat* and thus totally obscured.

But it is a matter of completely different things: the elimination of all independent legal enclaves within the state; then the control of the administration by a legislature, which again is chosen by a parliament on the basis of the principle of popular sovereignty; and finally the principle of the separation of powers. We have expressions for all these things, and there is absolutely no reason to call any part of them or all of them together a *Rechtsstaat.* In science, we can dispense with the expression "*Rechtsstaat.*" It only conceals the problem we are concerned with here: the functioning of a legal order as a legal order.

§42. "Positive Law" and "Natural Law": Primacy of the Moral Substance of Society

I mentioned the last time that toward the end of the nineteenth century the idea became accepted in jurisprudence that the law was identical with positive law and that what goes beyond positive law is not the business of the jurist. This then falls under the general title of natural law, which again is a jumble of things that does not explain anything. But at any rate, the situation where the jurist is only bound by positive law as the basis of the order of a society functions only as long as this society is socially and morally intact. If it is not morally intact, then parliament, as we have seen under the National Socialists, can make things law that indeed are formally right in terms of positive law but run counter to all principles of justice.

So if you think about matters of criminal law, we are coming to a new problem. Crime is primarily what is indicated as crime by the law and assigned a penalty. However, the presupposition of a legal order where a criminal law is in operation is naturally that the crimes that are committed are recognized as such and assigned a penalty. But what a crime is can never be inferred from the legal order; rather, it comes from ethics in general. So, what is a crime in the ethical sense can also be classified as a crime by criminal law, but criminal law is not the source for understanding what a crime is. For there are very many things that are crimes but that cannot be included in criminal law, as you will see in a moment. Thus the functioning depends on the society as a whole being intact, and not criminal. For with the criminal law, one can only deal with things under the presupposition that what a crime is, is known—and indeed correctly known—from outside the sphere of criminal law.

At this point there begins the problematic of German jurisprudence—already in the Weimar period, then under the Third Reich, and now in the Federal Republic, too. For a whole series of things have happened that without a doubt are criminal. And the question now arises, How they can be dealt with in an order of public law that cannot classify these crimes as crimes, for the good reason that all criminal law always presupposes that the society on the whole is intact? If the society as a whole commits crimes, there is indeed no one who could be a criminal lawyer, because he himself would participate in this crime and in the criminal attitude. So here is the end of this *Rechtsstaat.*

But before I go into the material, let us once again look at how the Basic Law tries to deal with this question, because it is a highly instructive matter. There the limits become visible. I singled out article 20 the last time, where it is not all that clear which of the models really underlie the idea of the *Rechtsstaat* dominating the Basic Law. And it required very complicated legal constructions, for example by the judges of the Federal Constitutional Court, to give the whole construction the sense that was really intended, namely, that we have a republic with the separation of powers. Parallel to article 20, which in this way has a key function, there is, however, article 1. It runs:

(1) The dignity of man is inviolable. To respect and protect it is the duty of all state authority.

(2) The German people therefore acknowledge inviolable and

inalienable human rights as the basis of every community, of peace and justice in the world.

(3) The following basic rights shall bind the legislature, the executive, and the judiciary as directly enforceable law.[5]

That means, first, the dignity of man is recognized. Then it is established that the state is obliged to respect and protect the dignity of man, and then it is specified how one protects the dignity of man. This is done in article 2 and following, where the fundamental rights are enumerated.

Now, if we interpret in the manner of legal positivism, then you could say that the real legal material begins with article 2, where the fundamental rights are enumerated. But this article 1 is revealing, precisely because the foundation for fundamental rights is formulated there: Fundamental rights have the purpose of protecting the dignity of man, at least against attacks from the state. But what is this dignity of man? That is not said. So all that is visible of the dignity of man is what can be protected by the fundamental rights. And that is only a very dubious part of it.

This criticism of fundamental rights runs right through the nineteenth century. If, for example, private property is protected, or the right of inheritance in article 14, it will then not be of great significance for someone who is poor or who hasn't got a rich aunt. So if it says there that property and the right of inheritance will be guaranteed, then this proposition should not be interpreted to the effect that now every federal citizen should be endowed with a share of property from some mysterious sources. The only property that will be protected is what he has. Whether he has any at all is no more guaranteed to him than is every federal citizen guaranteed a rich aunt from whom a considerable fortune can be expected. So, if he has one, then his right of inheritance is guaranteed, but if he does not, he will inherit nothing. You see that there are always inherent presuppositions that can make legal protection, as such, illusory to an extent when the substance is lacking.

Or, take article 11: "All Germans shall enjoy freedom of movement throughout the federal territory."[6] But that does not mean that if, for example, you are traveling to Hamburg, you have a claim

5. Ibid., 343–44, with slight modification of the translation.
6. Ibid., 346.

upon the state to pay for your ticket. And if you have no money, then you can't travel to Hamburg at all, although it is guaranteed to you that you have freedom of movement throughout the federal territory. Of particular interest to you as students is article 12: "All Germans have the right freely to choose their trade, occupation, or profession, their place of work, and their place of training"[7]—which naturally presupposes that the respective occupations, places of work and of training are available. But again, the state has in fact no duty to provide you with places of work and of formation. If they are there, then you can choose, but if they are not, then you can't.

It is the same, now, with the dignity of man. I have only explained that in a preliminary way so that you can see where the problem with the dignity of man lies. It is very fine if one protects the dignity of man, but what happens if men degrade themselves? Remember our preliminary concepts. It appertains to man that he is the *imago Dei.* If now someone insists that he is not the *imago Dei,* then you have the phenomenon of dehumanization. Or if he claims privileges for himself but affirms of other men, for example, Jews or Gypsies or Communists, that they are not human, that they exist outside human rights and can be killed, then he has degraded himself. There is no protection from the state against that. So if, for example, one took seriously the proposition about the dignity of man—that it is to be respected and that the state had to look after it—then all those who fall under the phenomenon of dehumanization would have to be deprived of their civil rights. And apparently that would be the case for the majority of the people, because they themselves violate their own dignity. Thus one must now subject them to a process of civic education, to ensure that they understand what dignity is and that they begin to recover the dignity, which they do not have. So here again, nothing can be done about it.

Also interesting is the third and last article of the Basic Law that we must look at, that is, article 79. It deals with the changing of the Basic Law. In its third paragraph it says:

> Amendments of this Basic Law affecting the division of the Federation into Länder, the participation in principle of the Länder in legislation, or the basic principles laid down in Articles 1 and 20 shall be inadmissable.[8]

7. Ibid., 347.
8. Ibid., 375.

So, this article 1 concerning the dignity of man and all that depends on it, along with article 20, which concerns the separation of powers, may not be amended. What does that mean? What happens if exactly that is still done? Thus you see that this requirement regarding amendment presupposes that no one will amend them. However, if there is a majority of the legislature and an approving government that can abolish the Federal Constitutional Court without further difficulties, then one can eliminate everything. The only comforting thing a jurist can say to you then is that this can no longer be grasped within the system of the provisions of the Basic Law, but that it is a revolution. So then, we have a revolution. The question of whether such a revolution occurs, and all these wise provisions of the Basic Law are simply changed, depends on whether the society as such is intact and does not carry out these changes, which, for example, in fact occurred in the transition from the constitution of the Weimar republic to the National Socialist "constitution."

At that time there was the great debate among jurists about whether the Weimar constitution, which indeed was never abolished but only changed, was in fact still the constitution of the Hitler Reich or whether a revolution had occurred. Wonderful discussions among jurists. In the meantime, people were killed. Again, that did not interest the jurists, but only whether this or that legal construction could be applied. So what matters is the moral condition of the society and not this legal construction, which really only makes sense on the presupposition that the society is intact and that it does not simply throw it on the scrap heap the next day. In terms of the law, then, one can do absolutely nothing. The topos of the *Rechtsstaat* conceals the real problem: Is the society morally intact and will it behave in accord with these legal regulations or will it not?

If it is intact, then one doesn't need all this. England, for example, can get by without a written constitution and without a list of fundamental rights. If a society is intact, one does not need fundamental laws to state the things that should not be done. They will not be done anyway. There is a similar problem at certain periods of the French constitution, where people very often invoked the 1789 declaration of human and civic rights, while in fact the constitution did not even contain it as positive law. It was only one component in the political climate that kept the society as a whole intact, but it was not a legal component in the constitution. So, if the society functions of its own accord, laws to protect fundamental rights are not needed. That such laws are formulated at all always indicates that a very serious state of degeneration already exists, which such formulations are intended to guard against. For, after all, when it is clearly formulated that they may not be changed, it is perhaps more difficult to change them than if nothing was written there. So, a purely psychological effect. That, then, is what has to be said about articles 1, 20, and 79.

§43. The Question of Morality in German War-Crime Trials

And now we pass to the problematic of crime when the society is not intact, a problematic that has come to light through the mass murder during the Third Reich. But, as I again and again emphasize, we are speaking, not about the problem of National Socialism, but about Hitler and the Germans. This problematic, which became manifest in the Third Reich and was removed not by an internal German change but by defeat in war and the occupation of foreign armies, of course still persists psychologically today. You can see in what forms it persists from the different sentences of postwar German courts for National Socialist crimes, particularly those of mass murder. I will give some examples, perhaps read out a piece or two from Langbein's investigations, *Im Namen des deutschen Volkes,* and then systematically classify the different problems. So, as a typical example of the situation:

> What was new—and also not earlier imaginable—is not only that planned and well-organized crimes were carried out that were hitherto unknown [*that is to say, these mass murders*], but also that the criminals could appeal to the fact that they were bound by the orders of their superiors. These orders to murder had, even in the Third Reich, no legal basis [*and always go back to the famous Führer's decision*]. That holds for all the campaigns of mass extermination, including the "euthanasia" murders. In the first big *Einsatzgruppen* trial, which took place in Ulm and which was paradigmatic from many viewpoints, the court explicitly stated in the grounds for the sentence:
>
>> Hitler and his helpers in the top state leadership of the Third Reich were murderers in the sense of the criminal laws valid even at that time.

> It did not trouble either those who gave the commands to murder, nor those who received them and carried them out, that they were given without any legal basis.[9]

So there you have the problem of the degeneration of the society. If someone in Hitler's position gives orders to murder—which are the instructions for a crime without any legal basis and by which he himself is a criminal in the sense of criminal law—then these orders will simply be carried out because the moral condition of the population is so low that they cannot distinguish between legality and illegality, criminality and noncriminality.

> Dr. Hans Buchheim shows that a judge who asks today whether there is a legal basis for the heinous crimes of that time is from the outset missing the perpetrators' state of consciousness. The perpetrators felt themselves on principle relieved of the need for any legal considerations. The invocation of "historical necessity" had, for them, superseded all legal questions.[10]

"Historical necessity" is put in quotation marks. You see, when reality and murder are replaced by topoi of an ideological kind, like "historical necessity"—and the same holds for the achievement of the Communist revolution, where you have the same problems—then the entire moral order comes to an end.

A new reality, that second reality about which I will have to speak later, takes the place of the first reality, where man lives morally, and an imaginary reality permits killing, which then no longer falls under the category of murder, of law, of justice, and so on. So, the entire constitution of the reality of man and of society is switched off by the dream, the fantasy, of a second reality, where things like "historical necessities" can be found. Such a second reality, of course, doesn't exist. Instead it is always a question of the man concerned being a degenerate type. Whoever is a degenerate type has historical necessities.

Let us take another few examples. In a euthanasia trial in Hamburg:

> The court recognized that the killing of children had certainly taken place; likewise, that this mass killing was objectively illegal. Only two of the doctors accused denied any cooperation. The others accused declared before the court that at that time they had believed in the

9. Langbein, *Im Namen des deutschen Volkes,* 13–14.
10. Ibid., 14.

> rightness of their action. The Hamburg judges placed them beyond prosecution and did not allow the matter even to come to a trial, since they were convinced that the evidence of guilt would not stand up in court in the trial, because the female and male doctors, while killing, had simply lacked consciousness of its illegality.[11]

Thus, if someone is lacking consciousness of illegality—that means if they are degenerate types—then they will be acquitted. There's not even a trial. Other, similar examples:

> In Ulm, the judges and the jury decided that the real perpetrators [*again, it was a matter of these mass murders*] were Hitler, Himmler, and Heydrich, and the accused, who carried out their orders, could only be punished for aiding and abetting. All other courts subsequently adopted this line of argument; the verdicts of guilt in the *Einsatzgruppen* trials from then on were pronounced on the basis of "aiding and abetting murder."[12]

Here you have a very interesting alternative for the German judiciary. If someone has himself physically committed a murder, then he was aiding and abetting or, at most, was bound by orders. However, the other one, who gave the order, had indeed himself committed no murder. Thus he cannot be incriminated at all. So everything comes to nothing. The murderer, who physically committed the murder, acts under orders; the one who gives the order committed no murder. That is to say, they are all innocent.

Of course this reaches beyond the essential problem of the *Rechtsstaat* to the problem of moral degeneracy and, further, to the comprehensiveness of criminal law. But I will speak about that later, after I have given you a few more examples. Again and again, it's a question of this reciprocal exoneration—the murderer acted under orders, and the one who gave those commands has not himself murdered. So, all are innocent. Another trial in Kassel:

> The court regarded it as proven that the accused had committed the deed. Nevertheless, it did not come to a trial, since the judges presumed in their favor that at the time they were in ignorance of the illegality of such death sentences. The court in Kassel was of the opinion that it could not have been possible for the principal accused, Wiegand, as a Nazi, to adopt his own critical viewpoint.[13]

11. Ibid., 74.
12. Ibid., 79.
13. Ibid., 106.

So, if you were a Nazi, then you could kill anyone; any German judge would acquit you.

Other trials now:

> Perhaps the reason for mitigation accepted by a court in Duisburg in December 1954 also influenced these sentences [*which have just been reviewed*]: this court had to judge the former chief of police, SA-Group Leader Franz Bauer, who, on March 11, 1945, gave the command to execute foreign workers. The Duisburg judges sentenced Bauer to six years in jail, for they held it in his favor that "for more than twenty years he had familiarized himself with the National Socialist body of ideas, which considered the value of the life of an Eastern worker to be substantially less than the value of the life of a German." This sentence was quashed by the Federal Supreme Court. [*In the new trial, Bauer was finally sentenced to only five years. And so on.*][14]

So, if you believe enough in National Socialist imbecility, you will at most be sentenced to five years in prison.

Another comment by jurists on this: If one compares the strictness of the verdicts under National Socialism with the mildness of the verdicts after National Socialism, and if

> one considers that the evident contrast between them is not to be explained in terms of a fundamental change in the personnel of the judiciary, because, as it is well known, such a change did not take place [*these are the same people who sentenced at that time and now*], then the oppressive questions force themselves on one, whether both phenomena are not, in the end, children of the same spirit. That is to say, whether the hesitant mildness of the contemporary administration of justice with regard to the National Socialist criminals is not simply a logical correlation of the merciless harshness of the administration of justice at that time toward the enemies of National Socialism. The question is whether both attitudes could not be traced back more or less to the same extensive blurring of the general consciousness of justice, which may first have made at all possible the heinous crimes of the National Socialist regime, whose atonement is what is at stake today.[15]

That is as complicated as one can possibly formulate it. It means that the judicial personnel, always disregarding exceptions, is on average also morally degenerate, and that this is why harsh verdicts

14. Ibid., 108.
15. Ibid., 128–29. Langbein is quoting from a letter of a senior public prosecutor, Dr. Gerhard Koch, in *Die Zeit,* June 22, 1962.

were pronounced against those who opposed National Socialism and why today National Socialists are not punished appropriately. That is the gist of the matter.

So that is fine material, but we are yet not finished with it. I have continually spoken of moral degeneracy; it does not exist abstractly, especially not in a society. It is, rather, a matter of this whole process of intellectual and spiritual degeneration I have already exemplified, beginning with Schramm, passing through the church, and so on, and now with these judicial decisions. To really get to the bottom of this question, one must introduce a concept, from Anglo-Saxon law, I believe. That is the concept of accessory before the fact, during the fact, and after the fact. I do not know if there is a corresponding legal expression in German for "accessory," the one who aids and abets. More concretely: one who, being absent at the time a crime is committed, yet assists, procures, counsels, incites, encourages, engages, or commands another to commit it, is accessory before the fact and just as punishable as the one who in fact committed the crime.

"During the fact" is less interesting, but "after the fact" means: one who, having full knowledge that a crime has been committed, conceals it from the authorities, or conceals the person who committed the crime or protects him from conviction, is accessory after the fact. If you apply this concept of accessory after the fact, all the judges who pronounced their verdicts, which I have just read out to you, would be accessories after the fact and, by English law, should be hanged.

This consciousness, that crime is a social matter and not necessarily a matter of individual persons, is important. Those persons who create the environment where the crime occurs and who after the crime preserve this environment so that these crimes are concealed through falsification, glossing over, distortion of legal concepts, discovery of new legal concepts that do not exist in positive law at all, such as the necessity of acting under orders—those persons participate to the same degree in the crimes that arouse immediate attention: for example, murder.

And if you reflect on this, then you will understand when Hannah Arendt in her study of the Eichmann trial says that there is no German organization that is not criminally involved in the deeds of National Socialism by standing beside and looking on, without saying a word.[16] Or through appeasing statements, for example, through the ecclesiastical ideas I have just read for you, repeatedly advocated by church representatives, that one must not lead a man into a conflict of conscience by drawing his attention to the fact that he was really committing a crime. Or by spoiling the language and by introducing, instead of concepts, topoi that have nothing to do with reality, as is quite usual in German jurisprudence, thus making it impossible to understand what law and justice is.

All of these people are accomplices. I have forgotten nobody. Remember also the generals, particularly if you read these things in Hitler's *Table Talks,* which Schramm published. In the last year of the war, when everyone knows the war is lost, field marshals like Keitel and Jodl sit together with Hitler for these evening conversations and let him give them the orders for the next day. Knowing that the war is lost, but faithful to the Führer's order, the next day some 100,000 men will be sent into battle and must die—only because these generals are degenerate types, not because of Hitler alone. So, one must get that straight in one's mind, this participation, this involvement, this sympathy.

Or the professors—I will not here, for heaven's sake, defend the professors. When in the early 1930s, after Hitler had come into power, a whole series of professors, not only Jews, were relieved of their posts, none of the others, who were not removed, ever refused to occupy with pleasure one of the posts vacated through this dismissal. Since I was myself dismissed in 1938, I have always a particularly keen eye for people who became tenured professors in Germany after 1933. So, there is this kind of aiding and abetting; one always goes along, there is no one who offers resistance and says: "No, I won't do that. Whoever is dismissed, I won't take that place." That does not happen.

Or the same thing with the generals, for example in the case of General Fritsch, who had become troublesome because of his criticism of Hitler's war plans. So Hitler and Göring devised the idea of pinning a homosexual charge on him, when they got hold of a misdemeanor committed by a completely different man, called Frisch, and asserted that Fritsch, the general, was guilty of it. Fritsch was indignant at this but said nothing and did not get involved in

16. Hannah Arendt, *Eichmann in Jerusalem: A Report on the Banality of Evil* (New York: Penguin, 1994), 18.

the scandal at all. Then an inquiry was made by a commission of generals; the falsification—that the charge had been pinned on him to put him temporarily out of action—was discovered, and then Fritsch went. But none of the other generals, who know all about this dirty trick, resigned. All cheerfully continued to cooperate.

Thus, this kind of cooperation is participation in crime, which falls under the notion of accessory. The system cannot maintain itself if people in individual situations do not cooperate but offer resistance on moral grounds. Where that does not happen, we have precisely the condition of moral degeneration. And this condition of moral degeneration cannot be grasped with the categories of criminal law in the sense of a *Rechtsstaat*. A *Rechtsstaat* functions only within a reasonably sound society. When the society is not sound, the *Rechtsstaat* ceases to exist, and if one apprehends and sentences people later, as in the Auschwitz trial, what happens to them is quite right—if they are sentenced, wrong is done to no one. But all the others, who cooperated and are now blaming the accused in the Auschwitz or the euthanasia trials and said, "But those who were in authority said that all this was nothing and that everything was fine"—they, naturally, were not apprehended, although in my opinion they were more guilty than those who had immediately committed murder. So, a president of the Supreme Court, like Bumke—who committed suicide—is without doubt more guilty of the euthanasia murders than all those doctors who carried them out, trusting that if the jurists said nothing, it would be all right. Thus, in this criminal situation, the *Rechtsstaat* runs aground.

I hope that I have now, through the examples, made the matter as clear as is possible.

Part II
Toward a Restoration of Order

7

First and Second Reality in Ancient, Post-medieval, and Modern Times of Crisis

We will now move on to more agreeable things, that is, to the questions of first and second reality. These awful situations that I have depicted for you from the different sectors of society and life have naturally not passed unnoticed. And apart from those who participated in the crimes, there are also very interesting Germans who did not. It is with these that we must concern ourselves now.

The concepts of first and second reality, which I have often used, frequently identifying second reality with ideology, were developed through the investigations of Robert Musil in his novel—which indeed is not really a novel, but has a largely essayistic character—*The Man without Qualities* (corresponding to whom are the qualities without man). These concepts were taken over and further developed intensively by von Doderer, above all in the great political novels *The Demons* and *The Merovingians.* However, the phenomenon that has been named "second reality" by those dealing with contemporary issues in our time is an older and much more general one rather than merely a German one, although it has aroused attention just now. May I characterize its principal phases in the modern period?

We have a first wave of concern with what Musil and Doderer call the second reality—as opposed to the first—from the beginning of the sixteenth century right into the seventeenth century. As opposed to the Middle Ages, where one still operated with ideas of feudalism and knightly honor, there arises a new social, economic, and political situation. At that time, that situation was just as new and requiring adaptations as modern industrial society requires adaptations when faced with older ideas and forms of existence that have become obsolete. Therefore, at the start of the sixteenth century, things like the *Utopia* of Thomas More emerge, motivated by the evil social conditions, particularly by the agrarian condition of England, in contrast to which there is now sketched a true reality of human order. So there is the situation where a once-right order, because of changed circumstances of the period and a changed economy, has decayed to a second reality no longer reflecting the true moral order. In opposition to that, a new image of the true moral order is designed, Thomas More's *Utopia.*

Another such case is Rabelais' famous work, *Gargantua and Pantagruel,* especially one part, the famous Utopia of the Abbaye de Thélème. What is sketched there, is—similar to More's opposition to the English agrarian condition—the opposition to a debased monasticism. As a satire, Rabelais sketches an abbey where all the vows, which have become debased, meaningless, and corrupt, are turned into their opposite. So, obedience, chastity, and poverty are replaced in this Abbaye de Thélème—"Thélème" means desire, will—by the opposed characteristics. Everyone does what he wants, things are by no means chaste there, both sexes are in this abbey, and there is magnificent furnishing, ostentation, and extravagance.[1] Thus, a contrasting picture is sketched in order, through satire, to lead back to reality, and through this to unmask the other as a debased, false reality.

§44. Don Quixote's Second Reality as *Divertissement*

The third great case, which for us now is of particular interest and which today I will treat in more detail, is Cervantes' *Don Quixote.*[2] Cervantes was a contemporary of Shakespeare. The first volume of *Don Quixote* was published in 1605, the second volume in 1615. This division into two volumes, however, does not give the

1. François Rabelais, *The Histories of Gargantua and Pantagruel,* trans. J. M. Cohen (Harmondsworth: Penguin, 1974), 149–60.

2. In his discussion of *Don Quixote,* Voegelin has drawn on a 1953 essay by his friend Alfred Schütz, "Don Quixote and the Problem of Reality," in Alfred Schütz, *Collected Papers,* vol. 2, ed. Arvid Brodersen (The Hague: Nijhoff, 1964), 135–58. Voegelin also develops Schütz's hints in that essay regarding formal logic and Russell's theory of classes.

complete insight into the structure of the work, for the work grew with the author and the author with it. The first part, which might originally have been *Don Quixote* but was not published separately, comprises the first six chapters. They contain Don Quixote's first expedition. Then follows the rest of the so-called first volume, including the second expedition of Don Quixote, and the second volume, with Don Quixote's third expedition.

Now these three expeditions differ from each other as follows. All were encompassed by the satire on the tale of chivalry, which is a decayed cultural value in relation to the new problematic of the nation state and its order. And within this general satire, Cervantes now distinguishes three types of tension between first and second reality. In the first expedition, Don Quixote sets out alone as a man, a traveling knight, who in the spirit of the tale of chivalry wants to help the humble to what is their right and to humble the proud. So there is the implication of an idea of justice. Since he departs alone, the matter turns out relatively well, because when he comes to this famous inn and wants to be dubbed knight there, the innkeeper and his staff enter into Don Quixote's tomfoolery and play the dubbing of a knight with him, and so on. Then he returns home highly satisfied. Thus that goes relatively well, as long as he is alone and others benevolently enter into the tomfoolery. So let the buffoon go; he is a buffoon!

The second expedition is much more complicated. For now he has a squire, Sancho Panza. Sancho Panza lives in the first reality and does not let himself be impressed by a second reality. So when it comes to the adventure of the famous fight with the windmills, Sancho Panza warns Don Quixote: Be careful, they are only windmills; they are not giants, as you believe. And a shared discourse begins, what one calls in German *ein Gespräch,* a conversation. Please note this problem of conversation. What one usually understands by conversation in Germany are always conversations between a Sancho Panza and a Don Quixote. So in this conversation, the two worlds—the first reality of Sancho Panza and the second reality of Don Quixote—must somehow be harmonized, because otherwise they cannot speak with each other. Therefore, the transformers are now introduced. These transformers from the one reality into the other are the magicians. Thus, when Don Quixote imagines that the windmills are giants and attacks them, then either the magician has changed the windmills into giants for Don Quixote so that he believes they are giants, or—if they afterward turn out really to be windmills—this magician had earlier changed the giants into windmills, although they were really giants.[3] Depending on the situation, there always enters the magician who may change things from the one reality to the other, so that both realities have their place and can get on together.

There is now the interesting social situation where Sancho Panza does not maintain his first reality but makes concessions, insofar as he at least accepts magic's transformers. He now says, perhaps a magician intervened and changed these windmills into giants or the giants back into windmills, or whatever. And the further the novel continues, the more also Sancho Panza enters into the second reality and finds highly interesting things within the second reality too. (I will later specifically comment on the climax of the second volume.) So he is the man who originally exists in first reality, but then lets himself be made an imbecile by someone of a higher social rank who has invented a second reality for himself, and gradually becomes a fellow traveler, a collaborator in the enterprise.

In the second volume of the novel, which contains the third expedition, the matter will again become much more complicated. For Cervantes continues the stories of the first volume, recounting the adventures of Don Quixote and Sancho Panza, which have been published and are known—as in fact they were—throughout Spain. And when Don Quixote leaves for the third journey, everyone already knows who he is and who Sancho Panza is. Therefore it happens that members of the Spanish nobility, a duke and a duchess, receive him and create situations, on their own initiative, where they enter into his tomfoolery and make fun of him. So, a new social factor appears, which accepts the *divertissement,* or rather makes the story a *divertissement* for an otherwise unemployed and bored nobility sitting on their estates who enter into and encourage the whole tomfoolery.

I have introduced the expression "*divertissement,*" which comes from Pascal. It is a matter of a determinate social class, which is indeed in the first reality but bored by it—that again is a condition of moral decline up to a certain level. It is now ready to fall in with a second reality under later circumstances of a revolutionary type

3. Cf. Miguel de Cervantes, *The Adventures of Don Quixote,* trans. J. M. Cohen (Harmondsworth: Penguin, 1950), pt. 1, chap. 8, pp. 68–75.

and, so to speak, to join in the intellectual playing about because it's fun. After all, this is something different from the daily routine, which has become boring.

So here you have already a whole series of differentiations of behavior with regard to the problem of first and second reality. First, the man who generally lives in and imagines a second reality, that is Don Quixote. Then the second, who joins in, and under certain circumstances enters and is dragged into, the second reality, like Sancho Panza; but for this, one still needs the transformers. And then you have the intellectual who is bored with the situation and ready to go along with ideas dished up to him that do not agree with the first reality, because that is much more stimulating than his daily work.

So that would be, for the first time, the three parts, these three expeditions, which provide a very exact distinction of types. But now, as I said, Cervantes grew within his problem. And you thus find in the second part, prepared at the end of the first part, a more detailed investigation of the problem of first and second reality. I would now like to discuss some passages from the end of the first part, so that you can see what a conversation looks like between two persons where one belongs to first, the other to second, reality.

Don Quixote is brought back in a wooden-barred cage from his second expedition, which ends at the end of part 1. Then he is let out, and in the process a conversation develops between him and the canon, who was among those escorting him home. And the canon tries to persuade him that they are all fantasies—indeed, pathological fantasies. To the canon's attempt at persuading him that he must give up his second reality in order to be a rational man again, Don Quixote answers:

> Sir, your discourse was intended, I think, to persuade me that there have never been knights-errant in the world, and that all books of chivalry are false, lying, hurtful and unprofitable to the commonwealth, and that I have done wrong to read them, and worse to believe in them, and worst of all to imitate them, in setting myself to follow the very hard profession of knight-errantry they teach. And, what is more, you deny the existence of either Amadis of Gaul or of Greece, and of all those other knights of whom the writings are full.[4]

4. Ibid., pt. 1, chap. 49, p. 437.

To which the canon replies:

> I meant precisely what you say.

And then the answer comes:

> Why then, in my opinion, it is you that are deranged and enchanted, for daring to blaspheme against an institution so universally acknowledged and so authenticated, that anyone denying it, as you do, deserves the very punishment you say that you inflict on certain books when you read them and they displease you.[5]

So, a very interesting argument is thus introduced. If there are enough people who believe some tomfoolery, then this will become a socially dominant reality, and whoever criticizes it moves into the position of the buffoon who must then be punished. Or Don Quixote's second argument:

> Books which are being printed by royal license and with the approval of those to whom they are submitted, and which are read with universal delight and applause by great and small, poor and rich, learned and ignorant, plebeians and gentlefolk—in short by all kinds of persons of every quality and condition—could they be lies and at the same time appear so much like the truth? For do they not specify the father, the mother, the family, the time, the place, and the actions, detail and detail and day by day, of this or that knight?[6]

An argument for authority is introduced. So, if it is not only generally accepted but if the relevant books go out with the king's license, then what is to be found inside must surely be true, especially if it is described in detail. Thus, the detailed description is, so to speak, the proof of truth, especially if it is accompanied by authoritative action.

Now here we have a series of criteria introduced for what second reality is. First, if tomfoolery becomes general, then it will become socially dominant; and it is particularly seen as socially dominant and correct if it is decked out with authority. Thus you have the condition of a totalitarian regime—where determinate ideologies are prescribed and propagated to those under subjection to the state, and which must therefore be OK. We are again approaching from a different angle the things I treated in earlier lectures in terms of the so-called Buttermelcher Syndrome. So, if the people who are

5. Ibid.
6. Ibid., pt. 1, chap. 50, p. 440.

in authority say it, then it surely cannot be false. Either we must all have been stupid, or we must all have been clever compared with the others and they are all stupid; and if we had believed them, then we would have been stupid, and so on. You see here, how all these phenomena, which I have empirically described, are already anticipated in Don Quixote in the analysis of the tension between first and second reality.

This tension is now brought to its conclusion in the second volume. In the first volume the analysis is only dealt with incidentally. And now we come across very interesting things, which indeed are related to various particular situations. First let me take up again a general thesis on what tomfoolery is based on. We will have to deal with this later if we concern ourselves with Novalis and Goethe.

> To make an end of the matter, I imagine all I say to be true, neither more nor less.[7]

What I imagine here is no longer reality—that is the crucial point. I believe that what I imagine is in fact really so. So, here the second reality of imagination consciously takes the place of the first reality of experience. There is now a series of collisions between this imagination and the first reality. Such a collision occurs in the second volume where Don Quixote's visions in the cave of Montesinos confronts Sancho Panza's lie, in the scene where he is allegedly conveyed into the sky on a wooden horse, to the region of fire, there to experience certain things (pt. 2, chap. 41).

This is what takes place in the cave of Montesinos: There is a cave where allegedly magicians are again at work and all possible secrets are to be learned. It is meant to be very dangerous there. Don Quixote has himself lowered down into it, then comes back up again and tells a great story of a vision he claims to have had, into which all the characters and problems of his imagination are woven (pt. 2, chaps. 22–23). Cervantes provides it with an implication: The matter is so incredible that probably the whole chapter is untrue. He wants it treated satirically and implies that that is the point where Don Quixote is no longer acting in good faith but, within his tomfoolery, consciously begins to lie.

The other scene occurs as a *divertissement* for this duke, who exploits the tomfoolery. A wooden horse is constructed on which Don

7. Ibid., pt. 1, chap. 25, p. 210.

Quixote and Sancho Panza are to be placed with their eyes covered, and they are persuaded that they are undertaking an ascent into the sky. This is accompanied with all possible aid, such as bellows, and fire, and so on, so that they should thus have some kinds of physical sensations. They come back from this trip, because the horse explodes, and recount what they have seen. This time, Don Quixote has a little less to communicate in his remarks. Rather, it is Sancho Panza who has seen the stars in the sky, and has seen that they are all little goats and has played with them, and even knows their colors.[8]

And now comes the very interesting passage, after a flow of these visions of Sancho Panza, when Don Quixote says to him, "If you want me to believe what you saw in the sky, I wish you to accept my account of what I saw in the Cave of Montesinos."[9] Thus begins the disintegration of the tomfoolery, and a preparation is made for his final return to first reality and, if you will, his dying in Christ.

However, chapter 51 is, I believe, the most interesting one in the second part. I would like to thoroughly analyze it for you, but I must first read out this scene. It too belongs to the sphere of *divertissement.* I am explicitly focusing on this because, as you will soon see, *divertissement* has received a very definite meaning. It is also *divertissement* when, at the duke's court, Sancho Panza is persuaded he is now governor of an island, and in this capacity he has to sit in the law court. And now the first case comes before him:

> The first case that came before him was a question submitted by a stranger, in the presence of the steward and the rest of the fraternity. It was this:
>
> "Sir, a deep river divides a certain lord's estate into two parts. . . . [L]isten carefully, your worship, for the case is an important one and rather difficult. I must tell you, then, that over this river there is a bridge, and at one end a gallows and a sort of courthouse, in which four judges sit to administer the law imposed by the owner of the river, the bridge and the estate. It runs like this: 'Before anyone crosses by this bridge, he must first state on oath where he is going and for what purpose. If he swears truly, he may be allowed to pass; but if he tells a lie, he shall suffer death by hanging on the gallows there displayed, without any hope of mercy.' Though they know the law and its rigorous conditions, many people cross the bridge and, as they clearly make true statements the judges let them pass freely. Now it

8. Ibid., pt. 2, chap. 41, pp. 734 f.
9. Ibid., pt. 2, chap. 41, p. 715.

> happened that they once put a man on his oath, and he swore that he was going to die on the gallows there—and that was all. After due deliberation the judges pronounced as follows: 'If we let this man pass freely he will have sworn a false oath and, according to the law, he must die; but he swore that he was going to die on the gallows, and if we hang him that will be the truth, so by the same law he should go free.' "[10]

For those who are experts in philosophy, this is a formulation of Russell's paradox; I will come back to it in a minute. But now Sancho. How does one get out of Russell's paradox? First decision:

> "I think I can resolve this business in a brace of shakes. It's like this: The man swears that he is going to die on the gallows, and if he does die his oath was true, and by the law as it stands he deserves to go free and cross the bridge. But if they don't hang him, he swore to a lie and by that same law deserves to be hanged."
>
> "The Lord Governor is quite correct . . ."
>
> "But let me continue," replied Sancho. "They must let that part of the man which swore truly cross the bridge, and hang the part that swore to a lie; and in that way the conditions of passage will be fulfilled to the letter." "Then, Lord Governor," said the questioner, "this man will have to be divided into two parts, the lying part and the truthful part; and if he's divided, he's bound to die. Thus no part of the law's demands is fulfilled, and it's absolutely necessary for us to comply with it."
>
> "Look here, my good fellow," replied Sancho, "either I'm a dolt or there's as much reason for this passenger of yours to die as to live and cross the bridge; for, if the truth saves him, the lie equally condemns him; and this being so, which it is, I think, you should tell those gentlemen who sent you to me that since the reasons for condemning him and acquitting him are equally balanced, they must let him pass freely, for it's always more commendable to do good than to do ill. This decision I would give signed with my name if I knew how to sign."[11]

So the decision is, *In dubio pro reo,* Doubt favors the accused. And thus is the problem resolved.

§45. *Divertissement*-character of Modern Logic

Let us now look at the matter, as it is constructed. I already said that the case is an example of Russell's paradox. Now Russell's paradox

10. Ibid., pt. 2, chap. 51, p. 798.
11. Ibid., pt. 2, chap. 51, pp. 798–99.

is concerned with cases of that kind, I say explicitly, of that kind. There are various other cases, too, that belong to the same kind but nevertheless have different structures. The famous example is that of the Cretan who says all Cretans lie. Is he lying, or did he tell the truth?—one cannot immediately decide that. This problem is thoroughly formulated in Russellian logic as a problem of classes of objects, which at this moment I won't further bother you with or else we would have to take on all of Russell's theory of classes. But I must deal with the solution given by Russell's theory of types for a moment. That solution can be found here completely in the consideration that statements can have different structures.

There are, first, elementary statements with regard to their terms. That means that subjects occur whose concepts can be expressed as predicates. Such elementary statements can now be generalized, and these elementary statements, along with generalized statements based on them, are called first order statements. Then there is a third type—not constituted by elementary statements and first order expressions—which are second order statements, through which statements about the first order statements are made.

So if Epimenides, who tells the story about the Cretan who lies, were to say that "all first order statements, which I affirm, are false," he affirms a second order statement, which he can affirm as true without at the same time affirming a first order statement as true. So, if I say, "I am lying," then that can mean, as a first order statement, that "usually, when I make first order statements, I am lying." But if I now make the second order statement, that is, "if I make first order statements, I am lying," then I am speaking the truth.

Thus, by means of the differentiation of classes of statements one can resolve this phenomenon. That was the solution Aristotle sought, but we need not concern ourselves further with it.[12] What is interesting is that problems of this kind repeatedly show up in

12. In some typed references for this lecture, Voegelin has included the following quotation from *De Sophisticis Elenchis* (180b3–7):

> The argument is similar, also, as regards the problem whether the same man can at the same time say what is both false and true: but it appears to be a troublesome question because it is not easy to see in which of the two connections the word "absolutely" is to be rendered—with "true" or with "false." There is, however, nothing to prevent it from being false absolutely, though true in some particular respect or relation, i.e. being true in some things, though not "true" absolutely (*Topica and De Sophisticis Elenchis*, trans. W. A.

certain political situations, and indeed always do so when losses of reality take place and language in its real function as the mediator between thinking man and reality is hollowed out into a given mold, which has its own peculiar structure and therefore is no longer related to reality—that is to say, when language itself becomes a second reality within which one operates, without having the relation to first reality. That is why these things show up. In the fifth century before Christ, with the incipient collapse of the Greek reality of the polis, the Eleatic and Megarian problems arise.

You will perhaps notice that solutions similar to Sancho Panza's for solving such conflicts of first and second reality also arise in Shakespeare's *The Merchant of Venice,* when Shylock is awarded his pound of flesh provided he does not spill a drop of blood with it. Then one must give up the whole matter, just as in Sancho Panza's story: One must let the man walk across the bridge. So here these problems occur in connection with losses of reality after the ending of the Middle Ages and the lack of new contacts with reality, when the new idea of the nation state had not yet consolidated itself.

And then the same problems reemerge at the end of the nineteenth century, with the decline of the bourgeoisie, and with what is called the New Logic, with Bertrand Russell and then Ramsey's corrections, and so on. We are in the middle of issues completely characteristic of modern logic and which revolve around conflicts between first and second reality, as exemplified in this case of the liar and in Russell's paradox. The Cervantes inquiry is of particular interest now, because it is the only one of these various situations where Russell's paradox is consciously applied to the sphere of the *divertissement,* that is to say, of second reality. If one amuses oneself with second reality, then language too becomes part of second reality, and then these problems arise, which indeed are only semantic and are resolved as soon as one starts thinking.

For example, if I say that this man is a liar, that does not mean that he lies with every breath, but that in particular situations, which are socially relevant, he lies. He does not lie, for example, when he steps out of the door in the morning and says, "Today is really a nice day." He tells the truth then. Or if he sits down at mealtime and finds the meat excellent, he is not lying then. Instead, the judgment

---

Pickard-Cambridge, ed. W. D. Ross, vol. 1, *The Works of Aristotle Translated into English* [Oxford: Oxford University Press, 1937]).

"liar" already refers to a selection of the relevance[13] of particular kinds of behavior, and if we now misunderstand this "liar," and at all costs want to understand something other than what is intended, then we arrive at the problem that the man is always lying, even when he says that he lies. But if one reestablishes reality and carries out the semantic analysis, then the semantic problems disappear. They only arise if one does not think in relation to reality, but within language itself—briefly, if the situation that Heidegger formulates arises, that is, the situation in which "language speaks." Now it is certainly not Heidegger's intention thus to characterize language as second reality, but he has in fact done that. That is to say, if language speaks, then the contact between thinking and language and between object and reality is interrupted, and these problems arise because one is no longer thinking in relation to reality.

I would like to read you a sentence of Ramsey, an English logician who applied different groups to Russell's paradox, including the following: Among the examples Russell gives as evidence of his paradox, Ramsey distinguished those that have a genuine logical character and others that are only semantic antinomies. The semantic antinomies belong to "Group B" of the examples, as Ramsey calls them, to which also belongs the case "I am lying." And Ramsey says:

> But the contradictions of Group B are not purely logical, and cannot be stated in logical terms alone; for they all contain some reference to thought, language, or symbolism, which are not formal but empirical terms. So they may be due not to faulty logic or mathematics, but to faulty ideas concerning thought and language.[14]

So you see that logic is in itself a closed system of relations in a given system. But if the system contains semantic errors, this is not a logical problem; rather, one is referred back to thinking. And now you have expressed the very interesting development of the *divertissement*-character of modern logic, for logic has nothing to do with thinking. If one is thinking, then one is no longer formally within logic, but related to empirical reality, and here it is a question

13. The notion of "relevance" is a key category in Alfred Schütz's work, for example in his posthumous publication, *Reflections on the Problem of Relevance* (New Haven: Yale University Press, 1970).

14. Frank P. Ramsey, *The Foundations of Mathematics,* ed. R. B. Braithwaite (London: Routledge and Kegan Paul, 1931), 20–21.

of semantic problems that can be empirically resolved. Where one does not think, but only establishes objective relations between symbols, there is the area of formal logic and mathematics. That is to say, logic is no longer an instrument of thought, but an objective sphere between relation and time. Most of second reality is no longer related to first reality at all. However, the cases of Russell's paradox that occur here still have a relation to first reality insofar as they introduce thought symbols from the empirical sphere, and the mistakes are to be sought in the thought symbols. And they can then be resolved through the methods we have indicated.

Thus it pertains to the collapse of a society, when loss of reality and lack of contact with reality occur, that certain problems of the type of Russell's paradox appear as *divertissement,* in the sense that the playing about with paradoxes can and will become a *divertissement* because the intellectual contact of man with reality is interrupted.

I have, then, cited three examples for you. The Eleatic problems, within the phenomena of the disintegration of the Greek polis in the fifth century B.C. Then these very interesting cases in Cervantes, where that disintegration again becomes acute. (There are also some interesting cases in the Middle Ages with the decline of the medieval order and the emergence of nominalism.) And then in the modern period, with the decline of the bourgeoisie, where also, after these problems had been long forgotten, they again came into question semantically in logic in the nineteenth century. Thus the conflicts between two realities, through which the problem of *divertissement* became a problem in terms of experience and also a social problem.

With this, we have arrived at the point where we unfortunately must break off from the question of how that appeared to Musil and Doderer. However, I must do that in the next lecture. *The Man Without Qualities* requires somewhat more time.

(Tenth Lecture)

Certain phenomena of the second reality always emerge at times of social crises. For example, during the Eleatic period there was the collapse of the polis and the Cretan paradox; at the end of the Middle Ages, there was Cervantes' Don Quixote, and in the modern period, the example of Russell and Wittgenstein indicate that concern with the logical problems of the second reality runs parallel to symptoms of social decline.

The loss of reality expresses itself in the loss of contact of words. Words acquire their own existence; language becomes an independent reality in itself. This symptom can first be seen in the Romantic period. Father of gymnastics Jahn coined the term "*Volkstums*" in the first place to purify language; it was to replace the foreign word "nationality." But later, *Volkstum* was understood as "the essence of a *Volk*."

There have been many cases of language's becoming independent in the twentieth century. For example, in his lecture on Armin the Cherusker,[15] Moeller van den Bruck constructs a reality out of words that is no longer supported by first reality. What followed from this was highly concentrated imbecility. Such highly concentrated imbecility is a specific literary genre in Germany. It can be found also in Gottfried Benn, for example in the essays "Probleme der Lyrik" and "Dorische Welt." However, this phenomenon is not a constant factor in him. From time to time he breaks out of the artificial linguistic reality, the concentrated imbecility, and looks reality in the eye, as in his essay, "Zum Thema Geschichte," where he portrays German academic life.[16]

Still, the highly concentrated imbecility of the second reality of an independent language has so penetrated the German language that the question can be asked whether today such a thing as a "German language" still exists. With his characterization of Goebbels, Kraus in *Die Dritte Walpurgisnacht* has compiled a horrifying dunghill from clichés of the second reality. Apart from this cliché language, there's nothing else available.

§46. Musil and Doderer on the Refusal to Apperceive Reality

The problem deepens with a new literary flowering in the twentieth century. Kraus, Musil, Broch, and Doderer in particular worked

15. Armin(ius), or Hermann (17 B.C.–21 A.D.), prince of the Germanic tribe of the Cherusker, overwhelmingly defeated three Roman legions under Varus in the battle of the Teutoburg forest in 9 A.D. In the nineteenth century he was celebrated as the mythical ancestor of the German nation.

16. Gottfried Benn, *Essays, Reden, Vorträge,* ed. Dieter Wellershoff (Wiesbaden: Limes Verlag, 1965), 262–94, 494–532, 371–88.

out the problems of first and second reality. In Robert Musil's *The Man Without Qualities,* the man without qualities is contrasted with the qualities without the man. The hero lives in a shadowy relationship with himself. He doesn't recognize his qualities as his own because they operate as qualities of a particular role and not as the qualities of a man. The qualities are classified within specific contexts. The "man without qualities" can do this and that; he merely carries out different roles. The qualities are defined in terms of their social function. But no man belongs to them. In this context, the expression "spirit" has become meaningless; there's no longer any meditative experience. The hero finds out that he doesn't love himself. Aristotle had defined *nous* as the core of personality. If man doesn't love this core, and thus his own self, he has lost contact with reality. This self-love, of course, is not the same as selfishness. Self-love is a core problem not only for Aristotle but also within Christianity. The self-love implicit in "Love your neighbor as yourself" also implies love of the divine. But in Musil, the hero doesn't love himself because he doesn't have a self, and so the world becomes an apparent reality. Musil thus has performed a decisive analysis of the breakdown of contact with reality.

Heimito von Doderer, too, in his short stories continually takes up the phenomenon of blindness toward reality. Thus he gives important descriptions of the basic factual situation of modern politics: of ideologists who don't see reality but want to force something through somewhere, for example, a revolution. As a result, other people fall under the wheels, with disastrous consequences. For example, the application of the principle of self-determination in the Eastern European countries after the First World War led to the setting up of weak states that were conquered first by National Socialism, then by Communism. Or in the Congo in 1959–1960, where chaos was caused in the name of freedom. Fools want to rule even if those who are harmed don't want anything to do with them.

Let us now take another look at *Don Quixote.* Here the problem is grasped historically, in terms of the obsolescence of chivalry. But we should also note that Don Quixote is indeed a fool but aims at interesting goals: He wants to eliminate injustice from the world. That is to say, we have here a second reality that maintains itself at an ethical level but that, as folly, causes mischief.

Two figures of the Spanish renaissance at the end of the nineteenth century wrote about *Don Quixote.* In 1897 Ángel Ganivet concluded his essay *Idearium español* with a treatment of Don Quixote. For Ganivet, Odysseus was the basic figure in the comparison. He portrayed Odysseus as the representative type of the Greek, uniting cunning intelligence with exalted aims. Ganivet relates him to figures like Robinson Crusoe, Faust, and particularly Don Quixote. He regarded Don Quixote and Sancho Panza as, in a certain way, one whole figure that is explained in terms of the two characters in the novel.[17]

Miguel de Unamuno, in "The Tomb of Don Quixote,"[18] places Sancho Panza on the side of reality. But this first reality becomes the debased reality of the petit bourgeoisie. So in that context, Don Quixote undergoes a reevaluation. Unamuno carries out an interesting reversal: The folly of Don Quixote becomes true reality in contrast to the debased reality of the bourgeoisie. With Ganivet and Unamuno, bourgeois culture has become reduced to second reality (with Cervantes, the culture of chivalry). The basic problem however, has still not received analytic clarification.

Doderer has pushed ahead with such an analysis principally in his novels, *The Demons* and *The Merovingians.* His penetration of the problematic of the second reality is grounded in a deep knowledge of history. Doderer has thoroughly acquainted himself with the Merovingian period and the end of the Middle Ages. Both epochs were periods of decline, as has been that of the nineteenth and twentieth centuries. To set up an analogy to the modern period of decline, Doderer in *The Demons* turns back to the late Middle Ages. Witchcraft is often assigned to the Middle Ages; in fact, it's a phenomenon of the late Middle Ages and particularly of the modern era. The first outbreaks of witchcraft occur in 1434 to 1445 and in the 1480s; then in the sixteenth and seventeenth centuries, with occurrences as late as the nineteenth century. Witchcraft is an outbreak of the second reality. There's a continuum from witchcraft to National Socialism, which is what Doderer is grappling with. In the article "Witchcraft" in the *Encyclopedia Britannica,* you can read that witchcraft didn't exist in the High Middle Ages. In a Christian society, one believes in God, not in witches. Whoever

17. Ángel Ganivet, *Idearium español* (1897; reprint, Buenos Aires: Espasa-Calpe Argentina, 1943), 151–52.

18. Miguel de Unamuno, "El sepolcro de Don Quijote" (first published in 1906), in *Nuevos ensayos,* ed. Manuel Garcia Blanco, vol. 3 of *Obras completas* (Madrid: Escelicer, 1968), 51–59.

believes in witches is a heretic. Belief in witches first became possible through the development of an extensive demonology.

This is the general background material, in terms of which Doderer develops his ideas:

(1) The notion of the "second reality": The construction of a second reality comes from the desire to have the beyond in this life. One does not have a genuine relation to the transcendent, which becomes rather an object to be possessed. Political conviction is understood as a kind of slit in an armored car through which one glimpses only arbitrary facets of reality.

(2) The notion of a worldview (*Weltanschauung*): The worldview takes the place of reality. The worldview is the expression of a systematic refusal to apperceive reality (*Apperzeptionsverweigerung*). The one who represents a worldview is beyond rational discussion. The refusal to apperceive reality is, not sheer ignorance, but a deliberate desire not to understand. A worldview is a concupiscent fantasy. A worldview can apply to every sector of reality, for example to sexuality and eroticism (a particularly interesting phenomenon), but also to the areas of law, language, and order in general. In all of these areas, the worldview can produce constructs in conflict with reality.

There is also the problem of the raging ructions. If the concupiscent fantasy is disappointed, outbursts of rage can occur. The outburst of rage reveals a radical lack of contact with reality. (This links Doderer to Musil's analysis of stupidity.) From a worldview that is still contemplative there can be a shift toward active outbursts of rage.

At the end of *The Merovingians,* Doderer places a conversation between the novel's chronicler, Dr. Döblinger, and a reader, Mr. Aldershot. In order to justify the disempowerment of Childerich III through castration, Dr. Döblinger cites Heidegger, to which Mr. Aldershot retorts, "Murderous imbecility," and Dr. Döblinger agrees: "What else is it but imbecility?! All nonsense."[19] That should mean that the language of second reality must be castrated,

19. Heimito von Doderer, *Die Merowinger oder Die totale Familie* (Munich: Deutscher Taschenbuch Verlag, 1981), 307.

its virility struck down, pulled out by the roots. The representation of the problem is played out in the novel as a farce. Doderer repeatedly makes this point, that one should not get involved in discussions with imbecility. Faced with a corrupt society, all that's possible is the boycott—the refusal to get involved with it—or its adequate representation in literature, that is, the transmogrification of imbecility into farce (which is not the same as satire).

That was an unresolved problem for Karl Kraus. The reality of the Third Reich was so corrupt for him that he could not go beyond it by means of satire. "I can't think of a thing to say about Hitler."[20] So he doesn't begin with Hitler. There's no more first reality. But in Kraus's attitude there's also a certain incapacity. Kraus definitely sees the problem, but he only states exactly what the situation is. Doderer and Musil go deeper, insofar as they represent the problem as farce. It all depends on the character of the second reality that is to be presented as imbecility. If you want to clarify the problems of the corrupt society, you have to represent them as farce.

Doderer has provided one characteristic of the revolutionary in *The Demons.* A revolutionary is "someone who wants to change the general situation because of the impossibility or untenability of his own position," or rather, of "the fundaments of life in general." The fact is, however, that

> A person who has been unable to endure himself becomes a revolutionary; then it is others who have to endure him. The abandoned, highly concrete task of his own life . . . has of course to be consigned to oblivion, and along with it the capacity for remembering in general.[21]

From which it follows directly that the revolution carries out a systematic falsification of history. And from here on, Doderer proceeds to the analysis of aggression and force.

If the second reality becomes dominant in a society, there is indeed formally still a community made up of members of that society. But such a society perpetrates the highest betrayal of humanity. And in this kind of society anyone who is not alienated from the first reality can only commit high treason.

20. Karl Kraus, *Dritte Walpurgisnacht* (Frankfurt: Suhrkamp, 1989), 12.

21. Heimito von Doderer, *The Demons,* trans. Richard and Clara Winston (New York: Knopf, 1961), 491.

8

The Greatness of Max Weber

§47. Unmasking of Passions of the Age by Marx, Nietzsche, Freud, and Weber

(Eleventh Lecture)

In the German history of spirit a stylistic break occurs during the thirties of the nineteenth century.[1] It was preceded by the period of idealism in philosophy, of classicism and Romanticism in literature, coming to an end with the death of Hegel (1831) and of Goethe (1832). Through its spiritual achievements it can be understood and chronologically determined as a meaningful period. After it there begins a time that has so little meaningful shape that it can hardly be grasped as an intelligible period of spirit. Indeed there exist categories for this age—we speak of the epoch of '48, of the time of the foundation of the empire, of the Wilhelmine period—but these categories focus on the political events, on the significant expressions of the exercise of power. The spiritual illumination from within and the self-image are lacking. Not that the age was impoverished in the sense of significant achievements in the natural sciences, the positive sciences of history, or in the theory of knowledge; but, on the whole, it is negatively characterized as a time of epigones, of historicism and relativism. And politically its ominous negativity flows into the catastrophe of the First World War, which is again followed by the even greater catastrophes of National Socialism and the Second World War. The age, it would appear, has no countenance that is characterized by the spirit.

1. The tape recording and part ms. of this lecture have been transcribed as "Die Größe Max Webers," in Eric Voegelin, *Ordnung, Bewußtsein, Geschichte,* ed. Peter J. Opitz (Stuttgart: Klett-Cotta, 1988), 78–98.

Or is this only in appearance?

For precisely in this time without recognizable character, Germany produced four figures of world rank: Karl Marx (1818–1883), Friedrich Nietzsche (1844–1900), Sigmund Freud (1856–1939), and Max Weber (1864–1920). Four figures of world rank—that is certainly not a few. And it would be odd if four men of surpassing stature emerged in a society within a period of fifty years without their appearance being the expression of a meaningfully characterizable situation. We may therefore ask: Are there not recognizable traits in the intellectual attitudes of these men that were essentially common to all? Do not these four great thinkers give that opaque, blurred, epigonic age a signature by which it would become an understandable period of the spirit?

The question is to be answered in the affirmative, for in their thinking common traits can in fact be recognized.

What they agree on above all else is that man, and his action, is to be understood from the perspective of power, of conflict, and of instinct. They concentrate their attention on that level of existence that, in classical and Christian ethics, fell under the heading of the *passiones*, the *concupiscentiae*, the *libidines*; the level that had been declared to be the nature of man by Hobbes and that now, after the destruction of classical ethics through German idealism, had become socially dominant within the climate of the abandonment of reason and of spirit. Such an attempt at interpreting man from the perspective of reduced humanity required new symbols. The four thinkers therefore became linguistically creative and propagated a whole new realm of expressions that displaced the language of philosophy with ecumenical success: Marx with the class struggle, Nietzsche with the will to power, Freud with the libido, Max Weber with the rational expediency of action as the *Ananke* of politics and history.

In the second place: They all have the common concern to uncover values as masks for interests, conflict, and instinct. The undertaking of unmasking requires, further, two series of expressions whose correlation has received little attention up to now. First, the symbols, through which reason and spirit become masks of the sphere of instinct. So we hear of ideology as determined by class and situation; of culture as the superstructure of the relations of production; of the ethical justification of action as a rationalization of desires and interests; and of the spirit as the sublimation of instinct. Correlative to the first, however, there must be developed the second series of expressions, which is intended to displace the rational language of the goods and virtues in ethics and politics. I am speaking of the praxeology of values, of value judgments beyond rational verification, of value-related method and of value-free science. Without the willed opacity of this second series of symbols there would be nothing to uncover; for in the language of philosophy, the motivations of action through the passions are just as transparent as the orientation of action through love for the divine being.

In the third place: Common to all of them is aversion—one might even say hatred—toward the citizen in his variety from financier and industrialist down to petit bourgeois, and also toward the narrow-minded bourgeois morality of property and sexuality. And corresponding again to this hatred was an aristocraticism of attitude that rebelled against the spiritual and intellectual, and consequently ethical, corruption of the age.

However, if the traits we have mentioned as common are recognizable, why are these four men not recognized and acknowledged as those who have given the age their signature? Why do we not speak of a period, characterized through them, that follows the period of German idealism, of the classics and Romantics? Or more precisely: Why do we lack the linguistic expression for indicating a period that indubitably possesses recognizable characteristics?

The answer is to be sought in the antirationalism of the newly created linguistic expressions. It is true indeed that the common traits—the concentration on the sphere of the *concupiscentiae*, which had become socially dominant, the aversion to values as concealing and opaque, and the aristocraticism of attitude—may be recognized as a reaction against the decline of the age. However, the reactive behavior does not find a language suitable for that decline in the spirit of the Platonic *andreia*. The age is so profoundly corrupted that it has also discredited the experience of reason and its symbolization. To the spiritual-reactive attitude we find in each of the four, therefore, there corresponds no common language in which the commonness of attitude could be articulated and communicated. Each one developed a separate language as expression of his specific reaction and thereby increased the linguistic confusion that had come about through the loss of philosophical language and that could only be removed by its restoration. Since the swamp of the age had also sucked into itself the linguistic means of criticism, the age was stronger than the strongest who tried to resist it. As a result, the reactive behavior is really a hybrid: It wishes to set up a philosophically critical distance from the age, but it lacks the philosophical distance to carry out that intention. It wishes to lead the struggle against the decline of the age, but it must carry this out with the language of the decline. The hybrid nature of this distanceless distance is probably the reason for the emergence of the trait of aggressive self-assurance and self-portrayal that today strikes us as remarkable in the four thinkers struggling against the age. None of them seems to have been troubled by mistrust of himself and his work—by that malaise of mistrust that distinguishes the independent thinker.

The reactive attitude without spiritual articulation causes the separate languages, which in turn make the achievement of the four thinkers intellectually opaque. Neither can the common traits be portrayed in the language of any one of them—we cannot render intelligible the work of any of the others in the language, respectively, of Marx, Nietzsche, Freud, or Weber—nor will the work of any one of them become transparent if we make use of their own language to interpret it. The plurality of private languages in the nineteenth and early twentieth centuries must first be overcome through the restoration of the public language of philosophizing, in order to make intelligible for reason the common traits of the age of decay and rebellion against it. With the restoration of the common language, however, the problem of periodizing the age without a period becomes clear, insofar as it again becomes possible critically to overcome the decay of the age through the distance of reason and of spirit. Through this new situation, in which we are no longer constrained to put up with the dominance of power, of conflict, and of instincts in terms of their own vocabulary, a new period is constituted. Looking back from this new period, the age of decay and of the reactive attitudes on the other hand can also be seen to constitute an intelligible period of the spirit.

At the beginning we spoke of a stylistic break in the German history of spirit. In conclusion we should again refer to this point in order to prevent a possible misunderstanding, for the stylistic break should not be understood as a break in the continuity of the spirit and its history. In that meaningfully intelligible, brilliant period of German idealism, of the classics and Romantics, this opaque, difficult to characterize age that followed it was prepared. So that the age of brilliance was therefore not quite as brilliant, perhaps, as it appeared to the citizens in the periods after it, even up to today. We must deal with the period of the four great thinkers, and with Max Weber's place in it.

§48. Nonexperience of Transcendence Leading to Dehumanization

Let us characterize the period further.

We notice that there occurs within it a remarkable shifting of the accent in the representation of what is reality. The reality of reason and spirit, which reveals itself in noetic and pneumatic experiences, fades away, and in its place the accent is transferred to the experience of the world of things in space-time existence. This has various consequences—some dubious, some gratifying. The period itself is dubious, insofar as all reality that does not have the manner of being of world-immanent existing things sinks to nonreality. The period is gratifying for us in the new situation of philosophizing, insofar as the energetic contraction of the expression "existence" to the manner of being of world-immanent things fits well into exact concept-formation and so should be adopted. In this way we gain the freedom of speaking with precision of the realms of reason and the spirit as nonexistent reality. At all events, this manner of speaking seems actually clearer than Heidegger's attempt to claim the expression "existence" for the transcending being of man and, further, to connect it with the problem of historicity, since this attempt at a compromise will not do justice to the world-immanent existing things, to our experiences of transcendence, or to history.

But let us remain with the period we are discussing. Within it, the accent of reality shifted toward immanent being, and in this period the expressions "science" and "experience" were monopolized for this realm; the science of experience became the science of world-immanent things. On the other hand, with regard to the nonexistent reality of reason and spirit, the symbols of philosophy and revelation, in which the experiences of transcendence are interpreted, became opaque for their experiential content. And this increasing opacity was further limited by the atrophy of experience in the sense of the denial of the meditative interest and of the energy for the articulation of the nonexistent realms of reality. There was no further living meditative reality, and consequently the language of reason and spirit became obscured to the point of the famous value-judgments, which from the viewpoint of world-immanent experience had no basis in critical experience. The *episteme* in the classical sense was dead.

Yet even if the life of the spirit sinks to the level of enlightened reason, to bourgeois morality, and to liberal or nonliberal *Weltanschauungen,* and even if the symbols of transcendence are subjected to serious deformations of their meaning and become discredited, nevertheless these occurrences leave the order of being itself utterly unchanged. Even if Hegel, Marx, and Nietzsche thoroughly murder God and explain him away as dead, divine being remains eternal and man must still get on with living his life sealed by his creatureliness and by death. When concupiscent fantasy shifts the accents of reality, it then superimposes a false image on reality. We speak of this fantasy image as the second reality. And when man tries to live in this second reality, when he attempts to transform himself from the *imago Dei* into an *imago hominis,* then conflicts arise with the first reality, whose order continually exists. Characteristic for the period, then, are the phenomena of friction between second and first reality—even if their very beginnings reach further back in time. For us the most interesting frictions are those that emerge at the point of fracture with the realms of the nonexistent realities of reason and spirit, which have been discredited and explained away as nonreal. I will enumerate some of these phenomena:

(1) Since nonexistent reality cannot be abolished, the empty space arising from its discrediting must be refilled with the symbolism of the second reality. Among other phenomena, this requirement is served by the world-immanent apocalypses of history created by Kant, Condorcet, Comte, and Marx. Because the new images of history originate in the world-immanent concupiscence of action, progressive and revolutionary activism belong essentially to them, along with revolutionary consciousness.

(2) With the sinking of nonexistent reality to the status of nonreality, there arises the phenomenon of disillusionment, accompanied by the feeling of obligation to live one's life without the illusions of transcendence. The denial of the spirit produces the suffering of Godforsakenness. We can

think of the suffering of Nietzsche, who had learned through Pascal's example what faith meant but did not want to submit himself to its discipline.

(3) The denial of the nonexistent reality of transcending toward divine being destroys the *imago Dei.* Man becomes dehumanized. The suffering from the meaninglessness of a Godforsaken existence leads to outbreaks of concupiscent fantasy, to the grotesque creation of a "new man"—of Marx's and Nietzsche's supermen.

(4) Since statements regarding the mystery of the ground of being must no longer emerge as exegesis of noetic and pneumatic experience, they become for Nietzsche masks of the world-immanent "deep spirit." The quest for the meaning of life degenerates to aesthetic operations with symbols of transcendence, to a game with masks of nonobligatory obligation. Going beyond the case of Nietzsche one can say in general: The world-immanent phenomena of power, conflict, instinct, class, nation, and race were laden with the meaning of nonexistent realities and thereby became masks of transcendence. We notice as characteristic the phenomenon of a despairing affirmation of the world-immanent game of life that takes up the problem of transcendence and loads this world-immanent game of life with a meaning it in fact does not have. Nietzsche formulated this loading in a brilliant saying. He speaks of the life-affirming man, "who not only has learned to put up with and get on with what was and is, but who wants to have it again *as it was and is* to all eternity, insatiably calling out *da capo,* not only to himself but to the whole piece and play, and not only to a play, but basically to him who needs precisely this play—and who makes it necessary . . . What? And would this not be—*circulus vitiosus deus*?"[2] The divine eternity is transposed into an everlasting, self-repeating game of immanence. The hiddenness of the ground becomes the superficiality of the game, and in the hiddenness proceeds the man who plays it. But is he

2. Friedrich Nietzsche, *Jenseits von Gut und Böse* (Berlin: De Gruyter, 1968), 73. Translated by R. J. Hollingdale as *Beyond Good and Evil: Prelude to a Philosophy of the Future* (London: Penguin, 1990), 82, here used with slight changes.

still human? For "all that is deep, loves the mask," and the antithesis and contradictions of the masks are "the correct disguise for the shame of a God."[3] In fact: *circulus vitiosus deus.* The game of the masks that Nietzsche's God-man plays takes the place of Plato's "serious play" of life.

§49. Weber's Unresolved Tension toward Transcendence

What about the phenomenon of friction in Max Weber?

It emerges in a much more subdued way or not at all.

This youngest of the four great thinkers stands at the frontier of the new. Above all, with him there is no ideology, no revolutionary apocalypse, no revolutionary activism, no revolutionary consciousness. His image of history recalls the Enlightenment idea of unending progress toward rationality—sometimes the formulations approach those of Kant's "History from a Cosmopolitan Viewpoint." However, it differs from it insofar as he does not understand the progression toward rationality optimistically, in the spirit of the Enlightenment, as an approaching of the final reign of reason, but rather as a necessity, an *Ananke* of history, which is a heavy burden of man. And since for Weber, unlike Kant, the idea of progress is not balanced by belief in the true fulfillment of the meaning of life in the beyond, it remains to be feared that the tension of the soul will lead to the breakdown of man. The realities of the industrial society and its rationality, of the mass society and its rational administration through bureaucracies, will become a tunnel of immanent occurrences from which no one can escape. And there is no escape, because the praxis of life has no dimension of the *vita contemplativa.* The life of reason has sunk to nonreality, replaced by the world-immanent activism of science, where the achievements of a scholar, however significant they may be, will be superseded in thirty to forty years at most. The meaninglessness of the immanent process defeats science, too. The psychic atmosphere of progress had, in relation to the eighteenth century Enlightenment, essentially changed, and in fact when Max Weber dealt with this issue, he gave as his authority, not Kant, but

3. Nietzsche, *Jenseits von Gut und Böse,* 53. Cf. Hollingdale trans., *Beyond Good and Evil,* 69.

Tolstoy. However, he permitted himself neither Tolstoy's flight into "primitive Christianity" nor Nietzsche's game—or should one say, playing around?—with the *circulus vitiosus deus.* The illusionlessness of immanence was taken with unflinching seriousness.

So, for Weber, there was also no fantasy of the superman. Perhaps something of that could be found in his concepts of charisma and the charismatics. However, Weber's association of charisma with the nobility of being betrays rather his closeness to Stefan George—from whom, still, he again ironically distanced himself when he called him his "consecrated Stefan" occasionally among friends. Weber's attitude to the question of the superman may be more exactly determined through comparison with G. B. Shaw's. For the idea of the superman developed by Shaw in his *Man and Superman* (1904) more or less coincides with Weber's charismatics—Caesar, Luther, Cromwell, Napoleon, Goethe, were given as examples. The symbol of the superman was adopted, but its eschatological meaning was rejected by common sense. Shaw's superman can clearly, much more clearly than Weber's charismatic, be recognized as descended from Aristotle's *spoudaios.* Shaw thought that only when all members of society are of such a high spiritual and intellectual rank—as only rarely exemplified for us in history—can all the drawbacks be overcome that otherwise, because of the relationships between the various ranks of men in society, lead inevitably to revolution. When he speaks of the breeding of the superman, he is dreaming of what George Santayana called the society of patrician plebeians, and this dream again fits into the classic context of Aristotle's politics—along the lines of J. Stuart Mill's "improvement" of man and his progress toward a free, rational society. For Shaw, therefore, who was able to distinguish between dream and reality very precisely, it was clear in the real situation of the time that, on the one hand, revolutions were inevitable, and that, on the other hand, they did not lead to the state of perfection the revolutionaries hoped for: "Revolutions have never lightened the burden of tyranny: they have only shifted it to another shoulder."[4] A proletarian democracy would therefore only bring a new domination, burdened with the same defects, rooted in human nature, as those just overcome.

4. From George Bernard Shaw, *The Revolutionist's Handbook,* referred to in, and printed after, the text of the play *Man and Superman: A Comedy and a Philosophy* (London: Constable, 1929), 180.

How close these thoughts are to Max Weber may be gauged by the fact that this previous sentence could have been written by him. In his late speech "Politics as a Vocation," Weber speaks of this. He says that revolutionary socialists, Bolsheviks and Spartacists, would give up their undertakings if it could be made clear to them that through their revolution they would only arrive at a new bourgeois industrial society stripped of some feudal and dynastic elements, and that this goal was not worth the enormous bloodshed.[5] The parallel is almost word for word—and yet it marks the point where Weber radically differs from the realism of a Shaw. For Shaw permits himself the dream of a society of supermen precisely because, in view of the reality of man and society, he considered the blindness of the attempt at resolution of the problem through force to be inevitable. It never occurred to him to believe that, through his better insight into the disappointing consequences of the revolution, he could hold it back. His common sense always remained open to the divine ground, even if—in tribute to the age—he called it evolution. Twenty years after *Man and Superman* he therefore consistently transformed the comedy of the superman into the tragic chronicle of the saint; and *Saint Joan* concludes with the lament: "O God that madest this beautiful earth, when will it be ready to receive Thy saints? How long, O Lord, how long?"[6] Max Weber, on the contrary, in the ardor of his immanence, thought he possessed the recipe for the solution of evil: The insights of a value-free social science should and could educate the revolutionaries to a sense of responsibility by making them aware of the consequences of their action. When we consider that, in the concrete situation, the very best social science has no more to offer than any man with common sense, as for example Bernard Shaw, even without knowing it, then the remarkable blind spot in Max Weber's attitude becomes obvious to us.

Weber sees that these flights into apocalypse do not work; he knows that reality does not have an apocalyptic structure. But he does not understand—and here again lie the limits of his understanding of transcendence—that these men in fact are in a false attitude toward transcendence that cannot be shaken by rational

5. See Max Weber, "Politics as a Vocation," in *From Max Weber: Essays in Sociology*, trans. H. H. Gerth and C. Wright Mills (New York: Oxford University Press, 1947), 77–128, esp. 119.

6. George Bernard Shaw, *Saint Joan* (London: Constable, 1924), 114.

considerations of a scientific sort, precisely because it is a matter of a specific attitude toward transcendence, even if of a deformed kind. As one of the great ones at the level of spirit, Weber had to struggle with the problem, as many great men have, that he regarded the others as his equal. Bernard Shaw once formulated this problem excellently when he wrote in *The Revolutionist's Handbook:* From the viewpoint of the important man, his distance from the other, less important people, is slight; which is why he can regard them as equals. However, on the other hand, from the viewpoint of those less important, the distance is enormous.[7]

Let us emphasize again that for Weber there is no "superman," no "illusion." His vocabulary is made up of expressions like "disenchantment of the world," "dedivinization"; his writings are characterized by resignation that the great ages of the openness of the spirit and of prophecy are over, that we no longer live in an age of prophecy—rather, that we are reduced to the sobriety of responsibility in world-immanent action. So, for a man like Max Weber there is no play with masks like Nietzsche, nor a play with masks of any other kind, such as was developed by other men in similar situations. One can think of a Picasso and of the sequence of phases in his style—a play with masks concealing a Spanish mystic. Or one can consider a Bertrand Russell, whose philosophy one does not really know, since in the various phases of his life he passed through so many different ones that one can get support for every philosophical position in his work. Yet with him too, behind that, there is a mystical attitude.

Max Weber, on the contrary, is quite different. He is characterized by the constancy of his attitude and his style; this is where his difference from the other great thinkers can be observed. According to the evidence of Marianne Weber and of others who knew him well, his attitude and style were settled by his mid-twenties at the latest. His personality and his vocabulary were formed in the decade between his fifteenth and twenty-fifth years; later, nothing further essentially changed them. Still this constancy of attitude and style does not resolve anything. If Weber had neither illusions nor any escapes such as others were able to use—in ideologies, in fantasies

7. A paraphrase from George Bernard Shaw's *Maxims for Revolutionists*, printed after *The Revolutionist's Handbook*, in *Man and Superman*, 236. The maxim reads: "The difference between the shallowest routineer and the deepest thinker appears to the latter trifling; to the former, infinite."

of supermen—yet he had to pay for this sobriety and for his knowing why that was the case, with what was called his "breakdown."

Here a few dates must be set down briefly: Weber received his habilitation[8] in 1895 in Freiburg; in 1896 came the call to Heidelberg; in 1898, exhaustion and breakdown; in 1899 he retired from his position at his own request; and after a renewed attempt between 1903 and 1904, he finally resigned his professorship.

He has no profession in which he can fully occupy himself. This state of affairs tends now to be explained as a psychopathological phenomenon—unjustly, it seems to me, for I do not believe this to be the case even if the external symptoms were perhaps similar to those of some kind of psychopathological phenomena. Because this breakdown was preceded by a frantic absorption in work, which indicated his unrest. In this frenzy of working lay the real cause that brought about his external breakdown. And as his health stabilized after this breakdown, there began the great period of creative achievement through which Weber became the one whose one hundredth birthday we are celebrating today.

In other words, that outer breakdown is a bourgeois category. In the economy of the spirit the breakdown manifested itself in the preceding frenzy of working; and as soon as this frenzy came to a halt, he recovered. Even then, there always remained something of that earlier tension; there was no final resolution of the problematic of the breakdown. For the work Weber left behind him has a completely fragmentary character, while being encyclopedic at the same time. The tremendous unrest was still there, but directed now toward the comprehension of the entire materials of the history of mankind in order to elaborate something like a philosophy of humanity: the fate of its *ratio,* the ascent towards rationalism—from the rationalism of ancient Judaism through Puritanism to the rationalism of the industrial society. However, everything remained fragmentary. There are just a few points where something like a completion of his work can be seen, one of them, as Weber himself stated, being the section on natural law in *Economy and Society.*[9]

8. In the German university system the "Habilitation" is the qualification necessary for tenured professorship.

9. Max Weber, *Economy and Society: An Outline of Interpretative Sociology,* ed. Guenther Roth and Claus Wittich (Berkeley: University of California Press, 1978), 2:865–80.

Let us summarize our characterization. For Weber, unlike the others, treating the world-immanent situation with radical seriousness is characteristic. Weber does not permit himself any escape from the *Ananke* of action in the world. Nonetheless—or, in fact, because of this—he suffers from the false attitude, which he is unable to resolve but which, as a man bound up with the situation of an age from which he can no more fully break out than the others, he has to put up with. This expresses itself in his political behavior through a passionate interest in politics along with, however, a withdrawal in decisive situations where possibilities for political involvement open up to him, for example as a parliamentary representative or state secretary. In his scientific work this suffering shows itself in his feeling that scientific activity is cognitively meaningless in the sense that its present level is superseded in one generation at the latest. This is the problem that Kant, long before Weber, already addressed in his analysis of progress: Where will this continual progress of science lead us? What is the benefit to us men here and now from the fact that in the future others will live in a more perfect realm of *ratio*? Our life will be unaffected by that. This last meaninglessness, which aroused Kant's sense of "strangeness," can only be resolved by openness to transcendence in the sense of life's opening toward meaning. It does not lie in the world. Weber was very conscious of this meaninglessness, and this should partly explain the fragmentary character of his work.

As a result we find in him an extreme spiritual sensitivity, which recognizes the falsity and wishes to resolve the tension, but no definitive breakthrough. The deformation of the idea of science into a science of world-immanent action by the society as a power organization in the form of a nation state remains unchanged. Plato and Aristotle and the philosophy of order are rejected as superseded by the rationality of immanence. The Weberian ideal remains that of post-Galilean science. Yet in all of these, the situation in which he found himself is clearly illuminated. And precisely because of this, there is no return to Max Weber nor even behind Max Weber. He clearly outlined the problematic; we have to go from there in the direction of the openness to transcendence and the restoration of those symbols by which the experiences of reason and spirit can interpret themselves. Max Weber has overcome this situation for us. We must in our age restore reality again.

Let me conclude this part of my talk with an anecdote from

Baumgarten's work on Max Weber. Baumgarten relates that Weber showed calm courtesy to others not only after his illness but also during the most serious moments of that illness. When Marianne Weber experienced the low point where her husband, despite her inner resistance and her grief, handed in his resignation, then the sick one consoled his wife, who passionately rebelled against his fate, with a statement as kind as it was irrepressibly self-conscious: "Some time I will find a hole, out of which I rush up again into the heights."[10] That is the symbolism of the activist, who sits in the night, but as activist, like a rocket through a hole, rushes out from the cave again up into the heights. Beside this, one thinks of the Platonic parable of the cave and of the man who is open to transcendence and feels himself compelled to turn himself around in order to carry out the *periagoge* and ascend toward the light. Quite differently Max Weber: He rushes like a rocket out of the hole. The symbol for that age and for its unresolved tension could hardly be more characteristic.

§50. Weber as Intellectual Mystic

It is possible throughout Max Weber's entire vocabulary to show this tension I have spoken of, for example in the categories under which he deals with politics as a field determined by passion, responsibility, and a sense of proportion.

As I conclude, let me deal with this point briefly. What does Weber mean by "passion"? A glance at the synonyms he uses leads further: He uses the expression "objectivity" as synonymous with "passion"; and again synonymous with "objectivity" he uses the expression "taming of the soul." "Passion" therefore means precisely the opposite of what is usually meant by this concept: not to give in to the passions but to tame the soul and to concentrate completely on the matter in hand. Or what does Weber mean by "responsibility"? This too is responsibility in relation to the situation, and this responsibility is the guiding star of action. It too is a formulation that recalls the classic problem of the highest good and of openness to this highest good. Or, finally, let us consider the word "proportion." For Weber it means distance from things

10. Eduard Baumgarten, *Max Weber: Werk und Person. Dokumente ausgewählte und kommentiert von Eduard Baumgarten* (Tübingen: J. C. B. Mohr, 1964), 638.

and men. That is perhaps the most revealing formulation, because distance requires that a person must himself stand somewhere. The entire immanent reality of being is the reality from which one must have distance. Still, where can one find this distance, if not in the nonexistent reality of reason and of spirit?

Everywhere, then, where these words are employed in discourse, the use of synonyms makes it possible to establish that Weber in fact sets out his ethics in exactly the same form as a classic philosopher, as an Aristotle would formulate it in his *Politics.* No difference can be discovered, and as a result the most astounding parallels can be found. One could well say that certain of Weber's investigations—for example on the nature of the modern party system or on bureaucracy—in their brilliant analysis, in their distantiation with regard to the genuine problematic of politics, are absolutely to be placed beside the Aristotelian discussion on revolution, the *stasis* in Book V of the *Politics.* This is the height at which Weber moves when he engages in political investigations from a distance.

With regard to this distance, then, arise the mortal sins committed by the excited intellectuals through their lack of distance. Under this category falls all that is to be found in the ideologies of the time, especially in the revolutionary time of 1918: the vanity and irresponsibility, for—I am now continually using Weber's vocabulary to make clear how transcendence is again restored by him—all these activities are superficial in comparison to the meaning of human action. So he knows what that is, and this meaning is the knowledge of the tragic, in which all action is entangled. Tragic, that is, in the classic sense of the word. Objectivity in behavior toward the world and its sphere of power is a requirement of human dignity. The one motivated by the ethics of responsibility, as Weber calls it, is the bearer of this dignity. His task is to oppose evil. The opposite to him is the one motivated by the ethics of intention[11]—exemplified for Weber by pacifists, but also by the Sermon on the Mount, linked with an undignified attitude, but again with the proviso, undignified only for whoever is not a saint. Weber completely

11. Using Voegelin's own translation of *Gesinnungsethik* as "ethics of intention" rather than the more usual "ethics of conviction" in his *The New Science of Politics: An Introduction* (Chicago: University of Chicago Press, 1987), 16. See, however, *Autobiographical Reflections,* ed. Sandoz, 11–13.

acknowledges the saint and the grounds on account of which he is a saint, in the sense of the sanctification of life. Here we have a similar situation with Weber, as in general with his relation to Christianity and Judaism. He understands what is involved, but from a final incapacity he is himself denied from being able to break through the closure and to turn back to openness toward transcendence. This could lead to an understanding of the whole problematic of intention for the one motivated by the ethics of responsibility.

Finally, allow me to indicate one other point: Since Weber was a man fully conscious of the transcendent—even if not openly so, nor articulated in his language—as a scientist he had to translate into world-immanent types everything whose meaningful content required that it be interpreted by the symbolism of reason and of spirit. That is, he had to develop, from world-immanent social processes, ideal-types that would reflect the order of spirit and of reason. In this context can also be seen the significance of his splendid section on the natural law. The natural law—that of the Stoa as much as the modern revolutionary natural law—fascinated him. For in this natural law the pragmatic paradigms of right order indeed manifest themselves—with a rightness that is determined by the openness to transcendence, where the nature of man finds its adequate structuring in institutions and orders within society. The natural law for Weber, to use his own language, is one of the ideal types of right order. In this way he includes in his considerations right order along with natural law. And this inclusion, in the case of the natural law, is the general principle in his development of historical ideal-types. He had already explicitly established in his early investigation of the methods of the social sciences that these ideal-types were in no way value free, since they are indeed produced by the ideas of men who have lived in the orders of the past. And each of the orders that manifested itself as typical in the context of these ideas now gave rise to the setting up of ideal-types, through which they are grasped.

However, the orders of those times included, indeed, in contrast to Weber's own age, openness to transcendence and the order of reason and spirit. This inclusion of the order of reason and spirit within ideal-types is characteristic for the entire work of Max Weber and particularly for the project of a philosophy of history. Such a project is not simply a philosophy of the history of progress or of materialism. In it the problem of the *ratio* is to be understood in the context of the Puritan's rational conduct of life, which again refers back to the rationality of Judaism and particularly of prophetism, as well as to the rationality of monasticism. All are instances of the rationality of the conduct of life, which through the distance of transcendence reaches the immanent order, and Weber wants to make this rationality his continuous leading image in relation to the ideal-type for the consideration of history.

Instead of employing further examples, I will end with an anecdote that, again, is related by Baumgarten, although it cannot be given an exact date. It goes like this: Before going to bed, Max and Marianne Weber often sat in the living room of their house in Heidelberg on the Ziegelhäuserstraße, mostly in silence, he with a cigar that glowed in the dark with little flashes of light to and fro. All at once through the large, silent room, he said to her over at the window: "Tell me, could you imagine that you are a mystic?" Marianne Weber, who had a lot of common sense, replied: "That would definitely be the last thing I would ever think of. Could you imagine this, perhaps, for yourself?" To which Max Weber replied: "I suppose it could be that I am one. Since I have dreamed more in my life than one should really allow oneself to do, I am also nowhere at home with complete certainty. It is as if I could and would also completely withdraw myself from everything."[12] That is a splendid formulation of the Pauline *hos me,* the as-if-not, of the Christian counsel, "Be in the world, but not of it. Live in the world as if you did not live in it and belong to it" (cf. 1 Cor. 7:29–31). And now, again with this formulation, which is not completely Christian but only expresses the possibility that one could withdraw oneself from the world, Weber is close to another thinker who lived at the beginning of this time of tension—Thomas More. In his *Utopia,* the wanderer, who in his wandering all over the earth is seeking true order and the meaning of life, says to his friend in the dialogue: "Wherever I am in my wandering it turns out that I am always equally far from God."[13]

12. Baumgarten, *Max Weber: Werk und Person,* 677.

13. Translated more exactly in *The Complete Works of St. Thomas More,* vol. 4, *Utopia,* ed. Edward Surtz and J. H. Hexter (New Haven: Yale University Press, 1965), 51, as "From all places it is the same distance to heaven."

Index

Abendzeitung (Munich), 67
Accessory to crime, 234–36
Achreios, 89
Adenauer, Konrad, 11*n*26, 12, 66–67, 66*n*25
Administrative model, 216
Agnoia, 34. *See also Nous* 34
Aion, 179–80, 181
Alethos pseudos, 34
Alibi, 91–96
Allgemeine Staatslehre (Krüger), 214
Althaus, Paul, 167
Amathes, 89
Amathia, 89, 98
Ambros, Otto, 68
Amery, Carl, 102–5
Anamnesis, 18, 28, 32, 34, 37, 40
Anamnesis (Voegelin), 18, 28
Ananke, 136, 258, 264, 269
"Anatomy of a Dictator" (Schramm), 29, 53–63, 110–54
Andreia, 259
Anstand (propriety), 103
Anthropological principle, 25–29, 37
Antiquarian history, 33
Anti-Semitism: and Catholic Church, 189–92; Cologne synagogue defacement, 14, 174; in Evangelical Church, 171–77; and Holocaust, 39–40; in West Germany in 1950s–1960s, 14. *See also* Jews
Apperzeptionsverweigerung (refusal to apperceive reality), 255
Aquinas. *See* Thomas Aquinas
Archontes (municipal authorities), 180
Arendt, Hannah, 4, 7, 11, 26–27, 38, 39, 64, 64*n*19, 65, 234–35
Aristotle: on corruption, 157; on *homonoia,* 32, 180; on human nature, 26, 29, 88–89, 96; logic of, 248; on *nous,* 73, 253; politics of, 205–6, 265; rejection of, by Weber, 269; on slavery, 89, 96–97; on *spoudaios,* 265; on *stasis,* 85; on virtues, 180
—Works: *De Sophisticis Elenchis,* 248*n*12; *Nicomachean Ethics,* 88; *Politics,* 206, 271
Armin the Cherusker, 252, 252*n*15
Augstein, Rudolf, 61, 62
Augustine, Saint, 36
Auschwitz (Naumann), 39
Auschwitz concentration camp, 67–68
Auschwitz trials, 63–65, 63*n*18, 105, 213, 236
Authoritarian state, 221–22
Authority: in *Don Quixote,* 244; Justinian on, 79–80; in Romans 13, 178–83

Baptism, 31. *See also* Sacraments
Basic Law of Federal Republic of Germany, 216–19, 220, 222–23, 226–30
Baumgarten, Eduard, 270, 273
Bea, Augustine, 201
Beck, Ludwig, 174
Benn, Gottfried, 95, 95*n*25, 252
Bergmann, Ernst, 163, 163*n*14
Bergneustadt Conference, 176–77
Berning, Wilhelm, 194, 195
Bertram, Adolf, 160, 160*n*6
Besson, Waldemar, 58, 58*n*10, 60, 89
Bible. *See* specific books of Bible
Biedermann und die Brandstifter (Frisch), 100, 106
Bierce, Ambrose, 169
Bismarck, Otto von, 78

Bodenschatz, Karl, 118
Bodin, Jean, 73, 215, 222, 223
Bölsche, Wilhelm, 137, 137*n*50
Bonhoeffer, Dietrich, 17, 165, 174, 196
Bormann, Martin, 118, 133
Bourgeois culture, 102–5, 254, 259, 262
Braun, Eva, 135
Breiden, Hugo, 64
Britain. *See* Great Britain
Broch, Hermann, 26, 26*n*72, 28, 252
Brzezinski, Zbigniew K., 11
Buber, Martin, 206
Buchheim, Hans, 231
Bullock, Alan, 61, 125, 147, 149, 150–54
Bultmann, Rudolf, 16, 167–68, 167*n*28, 169–71
Bumke, Erwin, 66, 236
Bütefisch, Heinrich, 67–68
Buttermelcher Syndrome, 26, 58, 60, 64, 81, 89, 244–45

Caesar, 265
Carstens, Karl, 12*n*26
Catholic Church: advances and regressions of, in differentiation of knowledge of presence under God, 204–9; in Austria, 188; and concentration camps, 194–96; and conscientious objectors, 192–93; as *corpus mysticum,* 211; dehumanized response of, to state authority and those outside church, 188–94; Delp's resistance to dehumanization, 17, 174, 196–99, 201; and Fourth Commandment, 178, 200; "guidelines" for German clerics and theologians, 199–201; intellectual and spiritual decline of, in Germany, 157–62; and *Kristallnacht,* 192; and murder of Catholics in 1934, 188–89; and race question, 189–92; and research into ancestry to establish Jewish origin, 192; and resistance against Hitler, 174, 188, 193–94, 196–99, 221; response to National Socialism by, 31, 74, 160–62, 178, 185–212, 221; as social institution, 155, 201–4; as supranational institution, 155; tension between church as social institution and as community of universal humanity under Christ, 201–4
Catholic Church and Nazi Germany (Lewy), 160, 162
Central Office of State Administrations for the Prosecution of National Socialist Crimes, 13–14
Cervantes, Miguel de, 32, 184, 240–47, 251
"Character of consciousness," 34
Charisma and charismatics, 149, 265
Christ. *See* Jesus Christ
Christianity: and Haeckel, 126, 128–29; and Hitler, 121–29; and Pauline *hos me* (as-if-not), 273; and presence of God in society and history, 204–5; and science, 124–25; and Trinity, 204–5; and Weber, 272. *See also* Catholic Church; Church; Evangelical Church
Christliche Ständestaat (Vienna), 188
Church: as *corpus mysticum,* 23, 31, 156, 178, 200, 201–4, 211; corruption of, in corrupt society, 157–58; intellectual and spiritual decline in German churches, 157–62; lack of theoretical articulation of, 155–57; and representation of universal humanity, 209–12; as social institution versus *corpus mysticum,* 201–4. *See also* Catholic Church; Christianity; Evangelical Church
Churchill, Winston, 84, 84*n*8
Cicero, 208
Circulus vitiosus deus, 265
Clemens, Detlev, 1–21
Coch, Friedrich, 165
Cold war, 9–10
Collective guilt, 5–7, 5–6*n*12, 9–11, 75–82
Communism, 78, 157, 159, 222, 253
Comte, Auguste, 126, 262
Concentration and extermination camps, 5*n*12, 6, 19, 40, 67–68, 94, 158, 160*n*3, 194–96
Concupiscentia, 107, 258, 259
Conditio humana, 72
Condorcet, Marie Jean Antoine Nicholas de Caritat, Marquis de, 262
Confessio Germanica (Bergmann), 163, 163*n*14
Congar, Yves, 190
Conscientious objectors, 192–93
Constitution: and England, 229; of Federal Republic of Germany, 216–19, 220, 222–23, 226–30; in France, 229–30; Weimar constitution, 229
Contemplation, 108–9
Contra legem, 216

Corinthians, First Epistle to, 169, 169*n*33, 273
Corpus mysticum, 23, 31, 200, 201–4, 211, 218
Corpus mysticum Christi, 156, 178
Cretan paradox, 248, 251
Crimes. *See* War-crime trials
Criminal law, 225–26
Critical history, 33
Critique of Pure Reason (Kant), 73
Cromwell, Oliver, 265

Darwin, Charles, 143–45
Dasein (existence), 86
Death of God, 262
Dedivinization, 27, 87, 96
Defensor fidei (defender of the faith), 80
Dehumanization, 16, 20, 27, 87, 107, 153, 163, 173, 188–94, 196–99, 261–64, 263
Delp, Alfred, 17, 174, 196–99, 201
Democracy, 83–85, 84*nn*8–9, 265
Demons (Doderer), 29, 30, 32, 239, 254
Denazification, 3–8, 5*n*11, 9*n*21, 10, 11
Denzinger, Henricus, 198, 198*n*31
Derealisierung (unrealization), 19
Des deutschen Spießers Wunderhorn (Meyrinck), 106
De Sophisticis Elenchis, 248*n*12
Destruction of the European Jews (Hilberg), 68
Detwiler, Donald S., 110*n*1
Devils (Dostoevsky), 30
Devil's Dictionary (Bierce), 169
Dialectic, 146
Diary of Anne Frank, 19
Dibelius, Otto, 162, 181–82, 181–82*n*52
Dichtung und Wahrheit (Goethe), 148, 149
Dietrich, Otto, 118
Dignity, loss of, 87
Disillusionment, 262–63
Divertissement, 242–51
Doctor Faustus (Mann), 30–31
Doderer, Heimito von: as representative of intact spirit and morality, 17; on second reality, 102, 108, 184, 239, 252–56
—Works: *Demons,* 29, 30, 32, 239, 254; *Die Merovingians,* 100, 239, 254–56
Dönitz, Karl, 154
Donne, John, 153, 177, 200
Don Quixote (Cervantes), 240–47, 249, 251, 253–54
"Dorische Welt" (Benn), 252
Dostoevsky, Fyodor, 30
Dritte Walpurgisnacht, Die (Kraus), 30, 91–98, 91*n*15, 122, 131–32, 189, 195–96, 252

East Germany. *See* German Democratic Republic
Ecclesia (church), 202, 203, 204
Ecumenic Age (Voegelin), 22, 23, 35–36
Eichmann, Adolf, 14, 64, 65, 234–35
Einsatz commandos, 210
Einsatzgruppen trials, 13, 14, 213, 214, 214*n*1, 230–31
Eleatic problems, 249, 251
Elert, Werner, 167
Eliot, T. S., 30, 73
Enabling Law of 1933, 106, 106*n*44
England. *See* Great Britain
Enlightenment, 264
Epimenides, 248
Episteme, 262
Esse gratiae (grace), 202
Esse naturae (natural existence), 202
Esser, Hermann, 133
Euthanasia trials, 63, 63*n*18, 65–66, 213, 230–32, 236
Evangelical Church: anti-Semitic tendencies in, 171–77; intellectual and spiritual decline of, in Germany, 157–62; participation of, in nationalistic-*völkisch* ideology, 162–65; anti-Semitism in, 173–77; response to National Socialism, 31, 74, 155–83, 185–86; as social institution, 155; theological opinions of, on race laws, 165–71; and theoretical inquiry into Romans 13, 178–83
Existential representation, 80–81
Existenz (existence), 86
Existenzlüge (lie of existence), 34–35
Existenzmacht (power of existence), 107, 117
Experience, 261–62
Extermination camps. *See* Concentration and extermination camps
Ezekiel, 75, 200

Faulhaber, Michael von, 16, 189–91, 190*n*8, 192, 193
Federal Constitutional Court, 217–19, 226, 229
Federal Republic of Germany: amendments to constitution of, 228–29; anti-Semitism in 1950s–1960s, 14; beginning of, 3; and cold war, 9–10; and collective

guilt, 9–11, 75–82; and collective silence about Nazi past, 8, 11, 13; compensation payments by, to individual victims, 9; constitution of, 216–19, 220, 222–23, 226–30; as countermodel to East Germany, 10; as countermodel to Nazi regime, 9, 10; and denazification, 3, 8, 10, 11; economic and political success of, 10; former Nazis in government of, 9*n*21, 11, 11–12*n*26; and individual guilt for Nazi past, 6–8, 7*n*14, 12–13, 15; and memory suppression about Nazi regime, 19; and "policy of the past," 13; presence of past in, 2–3; German laxity toward former Nazis, 63–69; and prosecution of Nazi crimes in 1950s–1960s, 13–14; and rehabilitation of "victims of denazification," 13, 13*n*31; reintegration of Nazi party members in, 12–13, 13*n*31; and *Spiegel* affair, 52*n*1; and Sudetenland, 78; Voegelin's challenges toward, regarding Nazi past, 14–18

Feudalism, 239

Fichte, Johann, 24, 107

First reality, 108–9, 241–44, 246, 252–64

Fleischer, Josef, 193

Forsthoff, Ernst, 220

Fourth Commandment, 178, 200

France, constitution of, 229–30

Frank, Hans, 93*n*19

Freedom, 227–28

Freisler, Roland, 197

Freud, Sigmund, 258–60

Friedrich, Carl J., 11

Frings, Joseph, 201

Frisch, Max, 100, 106

Fritsch, Werner von, 235–36

Fundamental rights, 226–28, 229

Galen, Clemens August von, 162, 185, 185*n*1, 194

Ganivet, Aacutengel, 253–54

Gargantua and Pantagruel (Rabelais), 240

GDR. *See* German Democratic Republic (GDR)

Gebhardt, Friedrich, 164

Gehrlich, Fritz, 189

George, Stefan, 265

Gerade Weg, Der (Munich), 189

German Democratic Republic (GDR), 9*n*21, 10, 78

German Folkdom (Jahn), 159*n*2

German National People's Party, 175*n*45

Germany: and Bismarck, 78; bourgeois "propriety" in, 102–5; collective guilt of, 5–7, 5–6*n*12, 9–11, 75–82; denazification of, 3–8, 5*n*11, 9*n*21, 10, 11; and Enabling Law of 1933, 106, 106*n*44; extermination of Poles by, 210; Holocaust memorial in, 20–21; illiteracy in, 90–91; and Law for the Restoration of the Civil Service, 164–65; and "mastering of the past," 2, 3, 11–12, 14, 17, 18, 24, 70–74; and "mastering of the present," 2–3, 19, 70–74; partitioning of, 76; postwar collective silence about Nazi past, 8, 11, 13; reunification of, 76; spiritual decline of, 15–17, 25–28, 153; and stupidity of individuals and society, 25–28, 55–63, 81, 89–90, 93, 97; "unrealization" and "orientation toward the unreal," 19; Voegelin's lectures on treatment of Nazi past by Germans, 1–21; Weimar republic in, 11, 78, 157, 186, 222, 224, 226, 229; withdrawal from League of Nations, 172. *See also* Federal Republic of Germany; German Democratic Republic (GDR)

Gesinnungsethik (ethics of intention), 271*n*11

Gespräch (conversation), 241–42

Gestapo, 187

Giordano, Ralph, 12

Gisevius, Hans Bernd, 58, 58*n*10, 60

Globke, Hans, 11*n*26, 66–67, 66*n*25

God: and Israel, 86, 207; and just war, 210; as mystery, 86; Nietzsche on death of, 262; "presence under God," 70–75, 204–9, 212

Godforsakenness, 262–63

Goebbels, Joseph, 57, 132, 252

Goethe, Johann Wolfgang von, 30, 42, 136, 148–49, 184, 245, 257, 265

Goldhagen, Daniel J., 20, 39

Goldschmidt, Dietrich, 161–62

Gollwitzer, Helmut Hans, 175–76, 201

Gorgias (Plato), 25, 71, 146

Göring, Hermann, 235

Great Britain, 10, 10*n*23, 229

Greek philosophy, 205–6. *See also* Aristotle; Plato; specific terms

Greek tragedy, 36*n*98

Greiner, Helmut, 118–19, 118*n*16

Gröber, Konrad, 189, 189*n*5, 191

Grundgesetz (German Basic Law), 216–19, 220, 222–23, 226–30

Guilt: Broch's "guilt of the guiltless," 26, 26*n*72, 28; collective guilt of Germans, 5–7, 5–6*n*12, 9–11, 75–82; individual guilt of Germans, 6–8, 7*n*14, 12–13, 15; Jaspers on categories of, 7*n*14
Guiltless (Broch), 26, 26*n*72, 28
Gürtner, Franz, 171
Gymnastic movement, 159*n*2

Haeckel, Ernst, 124–28, 137*n*50, 138, 139, 145
Harvard University, 18, 29
Hasselbach, Hanskarl von, 133, 134
"Hebraism," 207
Hefelman, Hans, 65
Hegel, G. W. F., 9, 73, 82–83, 257, 262
Heidegger, Martin, 95, 100, 250, 261
Hellas, 22, 86. *See also* Greek philosophy; Greek tragedy
Helldorf, Wolf Heinrich Graf von, 196
Heraclitus, 27, 28, 32, 141–43, 145, 181
"Herrschaftslehre" (Voegelin), 36
Hesiod, 26, 88, 89
Hierarchical legal systems, 215–19, 222–25
Hilberg, Raul, 68
Hilfrich, Antonius, 191
Hillesum, Etty, 40
Himmler, Heinrich, 32, 104
"Historical necessities," 231
Historikerstreit, 39
Historiography: in early postwar period, 10–11; German neo-Kantian school of, 139; "revisionist" German historiography, 12; Voegelin's exploration of, 22, 29–30
History: antiquarian history, 33; critical history, 33; Eliot on, 30; linear view of, 71; monumental history, 33; Nietzsche on, 33; Voegelin on "History I" and "History II," 24–25, 35–36, 37, 40
"History from a Cosmopolitan Viewpoint" (Kant), 264
Hitler, Adolf: appearance of, 55, 116–17; attempted assassination of, 58*n*10; attitude of, toward Germans and foreigners, 82; "aura" of, 114–21, 123–24; Bullock on, 61, 150–54; as charismatic leader, 149–50; and Christianity, 121–29; core problem of, 88; demonization of, 11, 38, 58–59; and election of 1933, 175, 175*n*45; and Enabling Law of 1933, 106, 106*n*44; as enigmatic, 115–16, 123–24; entourage of, 118–19, 133–36, 235; Greiner on, 118–19; and irrational, 150–51; Kraus on, 256; libido or existence-power of, 107–8, 117–18, 151; Mann on, 120–21, 126–27; *Mein Kampf* by, 137–40, 172, 196; planetarium planned by, 125, 126; pneumopathology of, 150–51; as politician, 62–63, 81–82; power of, 80–81; reading by, 136–42; reasons for rise of, 15–16, 25–28, 51–53, 77–78; relationship with generals and admirals, 123–24, 235–36; resistance against, 174, 188, 193–94, 196–99, 221; Schramm on, 16, 16*n*35, 26, 53–55, 107, 110–54; Schramm's conceptual and stylistic incomprehension of, 26, 102, 107, 110–14; Schramm's spiritual illiteracy on, 147–49; social Darwinism of, 142–47; as strong willed, 107; as *stultus* (fool) or idiot, 60–61, 89; and stupidity of German individuals and German society, 25–32, 55–63, 81, 89–90, 93, 97; success of, 62–63, 81–82; and Sudetenland, 78; suicide of, 30*n*84, 154; *Table Talks* of, 16, 53, 82, 110*n*1, 111–14, 124, 141, 146, 235; Voegelin's characterization of, 15–16; and withdrawal of Germany from League of Nations, 172; and women, 129–32, 134, 135; Wucher on, 54–55. *See also* National Socialism
"Hitler and the Germans" lectures: anamnetic method of, 29; on anthropological principle versus radical stupidity in individuals and in society, 25–28; antipathy aroused by, 1, 1*n*1, 18; by Voegelin at Munich University, 1–3, 17–18; on diagnosing radical stupidity, 28–32; editing of, for publication, 41–42; on Germans' treatment of Nazi past, 1–21; importance of, 18–21; layout of, 184; on overcoming radical stupidity in the present, 33–40; philosophical context of, 21–40; on restoration of order, 33–40; typescript of, 41–42; on universal humanity versus closed racial society, 21–25; Voegelin's decision not to publish, 17–18
Hitler's Willing Executioners (Goldhagen), 20, 39
Hobbes, Thomas, 258
Hoffmann, Heinrich, 133
Holocaust, 19, 39–40. *See also*

Concentration and extermination camps
Holocaust memorial in Germany, 20–21
Holy Sonnets (Donne), 177
Homologein, 32
Homonoia, 32, 180
Honnêteté (decency), 103
Hossenfelder, Joachim, 163–64
Human nature: Aristotle on, 88–89, 96; Freud on, 258–59; Greek philosophers on, 205–6; Hesiod on, 88, 89; Hobbes on, 258; and *imago Dei,* 205, 228, 262, 263; and *imago hominis,* 262; Marx on, 258–59; Nietzsche on, 258–59; philosophical and biblical understanding of, 85–91, 96; as theomorphic, 87; Weber on, 258–59. *See also* Dehumanization
Hupka, Herbert, 59
Huxley, Aldous, 90, 90*n*13

Idearium español (Ganivet), 254
Ideologies, 72–73, 102, 157, 222, 239, 258–59, 271
Illiteracy, 90–91, 93, 97, 147–49
Imago Dei, 40, 87, 205, 228, 262, 263
Imago hominis, 262
Im Namen des deutschen Volkes (Langbein), 230–33
Inability to Mourn (Mitscherlich and Mitscherlich), 19
In Search of Order (Voegelin), 35
Institute for Contemporary History, 10
Irrational, 150–51
I Shall Bear Witness (Klemperer), 34
Israel, 22, 86, 164, 190, 206–7, 208
Italy, fascism in, 221

Jahn, Friedrich Ludwig, 31, 159, 159*n*2, 164, 167, 170, 200, 252
Jaspers, Karl, 6–7, 7*n*14, 8, 14, 17, 156–57
Jeremiah's Lamentation, 30–31
Jesus Christ: as head of *corpus mysticum,* 200, 201–4, 211; as Jew, 191; Jews as not guilty for crucifixion of, 176–77; as Savior, 202
Jews: anti-Semitism against, 14, 39–40, 171–77, 189–92; Catholic Church's views on, 189–92; and Cologne synagogue defacement, 174–76; conference on depiction of, in teacher training and schoolteaching, 176–77; elimination of, from civil service, 165; Evangelical Church's views on, 164, 165–77; Jesus as Jew, 191; and *Kristallnacht,* 192; as not guilty for crucifixion of Jesus, 176–77; persecution of, as secret, 66–67; and rationality of Judaism, 273; and research into ancestry to establish Jewish origin, 192; statistics on, in Germany, 156. *See also* Concentration and extermination camps
Jodl, Alfred, 115, 118, 119, 134, 235
John, First Epistle of, 202
Judaism. *See* Jews
Judentum (Jewry), 168
Just war, 210
Justinian, 79–80, 79–80*n*3
Justitia (intellectual virtue), 80

Kairos, 181
Kant, Immanuel, 73, 179, 262, 264, 269
Kapitulation oder deutscher Katholizismus heute, Die (Amery), 102–5
Katholische Kirche und die Rassenfrage, Die (The Catholic Church and the Race Question) (Congar), 190
Katholische Kirche und National-sozialismus (Müller), 162
Keitel, Wilhelm, 118, 134, 235
Kelsen, Hans, 32
Khrushchev, Nikita, 125
Kiesinger, Kurt Georg, 11–12*n*26
King Lear (Shakespeare), 106
Kingship, 206–7
Kirchentag, 174, 201
Kirchentum, 170
Kirchentümer (churchdoms), 167–68
Kirchenvolk (church people), 156
Klausener, Erich, 189
Klemperer, Viktor, 34
Kogon, Eugen, 6, 12
Kollektivschuld (collective guilt), 5–7, 9–11, 75–82
Kölnische Volkszeitung, 194
Kosmos (Bölsche), 137
Kraus, Hans-Joachim, 161–62
Kraus, Karl: on Christianity and Hitler, 122; on concentration camps, 19, 194–96; on Hitler, 122, 256; on National Socialism's lies and propaganda, 91–98, 109; on Oberammergau Passion play, 123; on "rabble," 26; Voegelin's portrayal of, 17; on women under National Socialism, 130–32
—Works: *Die Dritte Walpurgisnacht,* 30, 91–98, 91*n*15, 122, 131–32, 189,

195–96, 252; *Last Days of Mankind,* 91*n*14
Krausnick, Helmut, 58, 58*n*10, 59, 60
Kreuz und Hakenkreuz (Neuhäusler), 160
Krima (judgment), 179
Kristallnacht, 192
Krüger, Herbert, 214, 218

Lactantius, 208
Langbein, Hermann, 230–33
Last Days of Mankind (Kraus), 91*n*14
Law: conflict between hierarchical legal systems and separation of powers, 215–19, 222–23; criminal law, 225–26; German Basic Law, 216–19, 220, 222–23, 226–30; historical background to closed legal systems, 223–25; judge-made law in Anglo-Saxon countries, 220; Justinian on, 80; natural law, 208, 209, 225–30, 268, 272; positive law, 219–22, 225–30; study of, 127–28. *See also Rechtsstaat*
Law for the Restoration of the Civil Service, 164–65
League of Nations, 172
Lebensraum, 210
Legal education, 127–28
Leibniz, Gottfried Wilhelm von, 86
Leiden an Deutschland (Suffering from Germany (Mann), 120–21, 126
Leiturgoi (servants), 179
Lewy, Guenter, 160, 161, 162, 190, 193
Libidines, 258
Libido, 27, 107–8, 151, 258
Lichtenberg, Bernhard, 192, 192*n*14
Liénart, Achille, 177
Lie of existence, 34–35
Lies: and Cretan paradox, 248, 251; and propaganda of National Socialism, 91–98, 109; and Russell's paradox, 247–51
Life of the Mind (Arendt), 26–27
Logic, 247–52
Love (in revelation and philosophy), 253
Luther, Martin, 178, 179, 265

Malthus, Thomas, 144
Man and Superman (Shaw), 265, 266
Mann, Golo, 53
Mann, Thomas: on Hitler, 120–21, 126–27; on "rabble," 26; as representative of intact spirit and morality, 17; Voegelin's lecture on, 42, 184; on Voegelin's *Political Religions,* 36–37
—Works: *Doctor Faustus,* 30–31; *Leiden an Deutschland (Suffering from Germany),* 120–21, 126
Man without Qualities (Musil), 32, 98, 108, 239, 253
Marx, Karl, 108, 109, 209, 258–63
Marxism, 23
Masks, 264, 267
"Mastering of the past," 2, 3, 11–12, 14, 17, 18, 24, 70–74
"Mastering of the present," 2–3, 19, 70–74, 82
Matthew, Gospel of, 24
May, Karl, 136, 136*n*49
Megarian problem, 249
Meier, Charles, 39
Meinecke, Friedrich, 10*n*24
Mein Kampf (Hitler), 137–40, 172, 196
Merchant of Venice (Shakespeare), 249
Merovingians, The (Doderer), 100, 239, 254–56
Metanoia, 37
Methexis, 87
Meyrinck, Gustav, 106
Middle Ages, 239, 251, 254–55
Mill, John Stuart, 265
Mitscherlich, Alexander, 19
Mitscherlich, Margarete, 19
Moeller van den Bruck, Arthur, 252
Moltke, Count Helmuth James von, 196
Monasticism, 240, 273
Monism, 126–28, 137*n*50
Monumental history, 33
More, Thomas, 240, 273
Morell, Theodor, 133
Moses, 206
Müller, Hans, 162
Müller, Ludwig, 163, 164
Munich University, 1–3, 1*n*1, 17
Murderers Are among Us (Staudte), 6
Musil, Robert von: on second reality, 108, 184, 239, 252, 253; on simple and intelligent stupidity, 62, 98–102, 255; Voegelin's lecture on, 42
—Work: *Man without Qualities,* 32, 98, 108, 239, 253
Mystici Corporis Christi (Pius XII), 211
Mythus des 20. Jahrhunderts (Rosenberg), 187

Napoleon Bonaparte, 265
National Democratic Party (NPD), 14
Nationalistic-*völkisch* ideology, 162–65
National Socialism: Catholic Church's response to, 31, 74, 160–62, 178,

185–212, 221; and denazification, 3–8, 5*n*11, 9*n*21, 10, 11; early postwar research on, 10–11; and election of 1933, 175, 175*n*45; and Enabling Law of 1933, 106, 106*n*44; Evangelical Church's response to, 31, 74, 155–83, 185–86; as farce, 36*n*98, 100; German historiography on, 10–11; Germans' postwar collective silence about, 8, 11, 13; as "Hitlerism," 11, 38; intentionalist versus structuralist interpretations of, 38; Kraus on, 91–98, 109; and Law for the Restoration of the Civil Service, 164–65; lies and propaganda of, 91–98, 109; "Luciferic" attractiveness of, 23–24; and outbreak of Second World War, 11; German laxity toward former Nazis, 63–69; and reasons for Hitler's rise to power, 15–16, 25–28, 51–53, 77–78; recrudescence of, 14; resistance against, 174, 188, 193–94, 196–99, 221; as "satanic," 23–24, 36, 36*n*100; and Schramm, 110; and stupidity of individuals and society, 25–28, 55–63, 89–90, 93, 97; Voegelin's lectures on Germans' treatment of Nazi past, 1–21; and witchcraft, 30; women's role under, 130–31. *See also* Hitler, Adolf

National state: and closed legal system, 223–25; definition of, 223. *See also* *Rechtsstaat;* State

Natural law, 208, 209, 225–30, 268, 272

Natural selection, 143–44

Nature of the Law (Voegelin), 32

Naumann, Bernd, 39

Nazism. *See* National Socialism

Neo-Kantian school of historiography, 139

Neopaganism, 187

Neuere Entwicklung des Rechsstaates in Deutschland, Die (Scheuner), 215

Neuhäusler, Johann, 16, 160–61, 160*n*3

New Logic, 249

New Science of Politics (Voegelin), 28, 80, 271*n*11

New Testament, 164, 176–77, 208. *See also* specific books of New Testament

Nicomachean Ethics (Aristotle), 88

Niemöller, Martin, 16, 166, 166*n*23, 171, 172–73, 186

Nietzsche, Friedrich, 33, 37, 107–9, 258–65, 267

"Nietzsche, the Crisis, and the War" (Voegelin), 37

Nihilism, 37

Nolte, Ernst, 39

Notre Dame University, 18

Nous, 32, 73, 86, 88, 253. *See also* *Agnoia*

Novalis, 27, 42, 88, 184, 245

NPD. *See* National Democratic Party (NPD)

Nuremberg Laws, 67

Nuremberg trials, 3–4, 67, 68, 149

Oberammergau Passion play, 121–23

Objectivity, Weber on, 270, 271

Odysseus, 254

Old Testament, 30–31, 164, 176, 190, 191, 200, 202, 206–7. *See also* Israel

On the Advantage and Disadvantage of History for Life (Nietzsche), 33

Order and History (Voegelin), 18, 22

Order *Pour le Mérite,* 16, 154, 154*n*80

Origin of Species (Darwin), 143–45

Origins of Totalitarianism (Arendt), 38, 64*n*19

Osservatore Romano, 186

Pan aristos, 88

Participatio, 87

Pascal, Blaise, 109, 242, 263

Passion, Weber on, 270

Passiones, 258

Paul, Saint, 24, 31, 169, 179, 180, 273

Periagoge, 34, 35, 37, 270

Persil-Scheine, 5

Philia, 180

Philia politike, 180

Philosophy of Law (Hegel), 82–83

Picasso, Pablo, 267

Pius XII, Pope, 211

Planck, Max, 120–21

Plato: and *amathia,* 89; on *andreia,* 259; anthropology of, 29; on "being-under-judgment," 71–72; on corruption, 157; and *nous,* 73; and parable of the cave, 270; and *periagoge,* 33–34, 35, 37; and pneumopathology, 102; and polis, 25, 72; politics of, 205; rejection of, by Weber, 269; on "serious play" of life, 264; spiritual realism of, 24; and *zetema,* 87

—Works: *Gorgias,* 25, 71, 146; *Politeia,* 35, 71; *Republic,* 25

Pneuma, 74

Pneumopathology, 101–2, 108, 109, 150–52, 155

Poland, 210

Polis, 25, 72, 180, 205–6, 249, 251

Politeia (Plato), 35, 71
Political Religions (Voegelin), 36–37
Politics: of Aristotle and Plato, 205–6, 265; Weber on "politics as a vocation," 35, 266
Politics (Aristotle), 206, 271
"Politics as a Vocation" (Weber), 35, 266
Polus, 25, 26
Polybius, 24
Positive law, 219–22, 225–30
Praeter legem, 216
"Presence under God," 70–75, 204–9, 212
Preysing, Konrad Graf von, 162, 162*n*13, 185, 192*n*14
Prima causa (first cause), 87
Private property rights, 227
"Probleme der Lyrik" (Benn), 252
Pröbst, Adalbert, 189
Progress, 264, 269
Propaganda of National Socialism, 91–98, 109
Property rights, 227
Propheticism, 273
Proportion, Weber on, 270–71
Propriety, 102–5
Purcell, Brendan, 21–40
Puritans, 207, 273

Question of German Guilt (Jaspers), 7*n*14, 14

"Rabble," 26, 32, 89, 97, 119, 121, 219
Rabelais, François, 32, 184, 240
Race question and race laws, 23, 164–71, 189–92
Raeder, Erich, 115, 123
Rahner, Karl, 210–11, 212, 218
Ramsey, Frank P., 249, 250
Ratio, 268–69, 272–73
Rationalism, 268, 272–73
Raubal, Angela, 135*n*48
Raubal, Geli, 135*n*48
Rauschning, Hermann, 149–50, 152
Reality: first reality, 108–9, 241–44, 246, 262–64; frictions between first and second reality, 262–64; loss of, 87–88, 105–9; nonexistent reality, 262, 263. *See also* Second reality
Reason, 86, 107
Rebellion, 88, 104–5
Rechtsstaat: and conflict between hierarchical legal systems and separation of powers, 215–19, 222–23; and historical background to closed legal systems, 223–25; and legal positivism, judge-made law, and authoritarian rule, 219–22; and positive law and natural law, 225–30; problems of, 31–32, 65, 94, 213–15, 218–19, 221–23; and question of morality in German war-crime trials, 230–36; as second reality, 31–32, 231; as untranslated term, 65*n*22
Reinisch, Franz, 193
Relevance, 250, 250*n*13
Religiosissimus iuris, 79–80, 79–80*n*3
Representation, 28, 75–76, 79–82, 209–12
Republic (Plato), 25
Resistance, 174, 188, 193–94, 196–99, 221
Responsibility, Weber on, 270
Revolutionist's Handbook (Shaw), 267
Rights, 226–28, 229
Romans, Epistle to, 31, 162, 178–83, 200
Romanticism, 88, 159, 252, 257
Rosenberg, Alfred, 187
Russell, Bertrand, 249, 267
Russell's paradox, 247–51

Sacraments, 211–12. *See also* Baptism
Saint Joan (Shaw), 266
Saints, 266, 271–72
Santayana, George, 84, 265
Schaub, Julius, 133
Schelling, Friedrich von, 101, 101*n*35, 102, 141
Scheuner, Ulrich, 215
Schindler's List (Spielberg), 19
Schlegelberger, Franz, 65–66
Schlußstrich (bottom line), 11
Scholder, Klaus, 31
Scholl siblings (Hans and Sophie), 104
Schramm, Percy E.: on "aura" of Hitler, 114–21; biographical information on, 16*n*35, 53*n*2; as chancellor of Order *Pour le Mérite,* 16, 154, 154*n*80; on Christianity and Hitler, 121; conceptual and stylistic incomprehension of Hitler, 26, 102, 107, 110–14; on Darwin, 143–45; on entourage of Hitler, 133–36, 235; on Hitler as strong willed, 107; and National Socialism, 110; on psychopathology, 102; reactions to "Anatomy of a Dictator," 53–63, 110, 111; on reading by Hitler, 137; on social Darwinism of Hitler, 142–47; spiritual illiteracy of, on Hitler, 147–49; Voegelin's criticism of, 16, 234; on women and Hitler, 129–32

—Work: "Anatomy of a Dictator," 29, 53–63, 110–54
Schütz, Alfred, 240*n*2, 250*n*13
Science, 124–25, 212, 261, 264, 269
Second reality: criteria for, 244–45; Doderer on, 102, 108, 184, 239, 252–56; of *Don Quixote,* 240–47, 251, 253–54; frictions between first reality and, 262–64; and "historical necessities," 231; and language, 250–52; Musil on, 108, 184, 239, 252, 253; phases of, in modern period, 239–40, 251–52; *Rechtsstaat* as, 31–32; and Russell's paradox, 249–50; and system, 108–9
Seebohm, Hans-Christoph, 78, 78*n*2
Self-determination, 253
Self-love, 253
Separation of powers, 217–19, 223
Shakespeare, William, 106, 240, 249
Shaw, George Bernard, 265–67, 267*n*7
Slavery, Aristotle on, 89, 96–97
Social Darwinism, 142–47
Social Democrats, 209
Socialist Unity Party of Germany, 78*n*1
Soden, Hans von, 167
Spencer, Herbert, 144
Spiegel, Der 52, 52*n*1, 53, 57, 61
Spielberg, Steven, 19
Spirit, 86, 107
Spiritual sickness, 101–2, 108, 109
Spoudaios, 96, 265
Stalin, Josef, 125
State: cliché of, 82–83; closed legal system in national state, 232–25; definition of national state, 223; Hegel on, 83
Staudte, Wolfgang, 6
Stoics, 179, 208
Strauss, Franz Josef, 52*n*1
Stultus (fool), 60–61, 89–90
Stupidity: as act of abuse, 99–100; criminal stupidity and loss of experience of reality in disordered society, 105–9; definition of, 98; and fool *(stultus),* 60–61, 89–90; of German individuals and society, 25–32, 55–63, 81, 89–90; and illiteracy, 90–91, 93, 97; Musil on simple and intelligent stupidity, 62, 98–102, 255; in relation to social and historical context, 99
Stürmer, Der, 132
Süddeutsche Zeitung, 53–63, 53–54*nn*4–5, 110
Sudetenland, 78
Summa theologiae (Thomas Aquinas), 201–2, 208
Superman, 265–68
Supreme Court, U.S., 220
Survival of the fittest, 143–44

Table Talks (Hitler), 16, 53, 82, 110*n*1, 111–14, 124, 141, 146, 235
Theo-morphes, 158
Theopolity, 206
Third Witches' Sabbath (Kraus). *See Dritte Walpurgisnacht* (Kraus)
Thomas Aquinas, 23, 31, 73, 89, 201–3, 208, 211
Timothy, First Epistle to, 202
Tolstoy, Leo, 265
Totalitarianism, 21–22, 221
Transcendence: nonexperience of, 261–64; Weber's unresolved tension toward, 264–70, 272
Transcendental representation, 80–81
Trials. *See* War-crime trials
Trinity, 204–5
Turgot, Anne-Robert Jacques, 24
Turnbewegung (gymnastic movement), 159*n*2
Twain, Mark, 84–85, 84*n*9

Unamuno, Miguel de, 254
Ungekündigte Bund, Der (The Unbroken Covenant) (Goldschmidt and Kraus), 161–62, 164, 176–77
United States: and denazification, 10, 10*n*23; Supreme Court in, 220; Voegelin in, 17, 18
University of Mainz, 53*n*4
"Unmastered past" versus "presence under God," 70–75
"Unmastered present," 70–71
"Unrealization," 19
Unrechtsstaat (state of injustice), 221
Utopia (More), 240, 273

Varus, 252*n*15
Vergangenheitsbewältigung (mastering of the past), 2, 3, 11–12, 14, 17, 24, 70–74
Vergangenheitspolitik ("policy of the past"), 13
Virtues: Aristotle on, 180; bourgeois "propriety," 102–5
Vita contemplativa, 264
Voegelin, Eric: antipathy toward, at Munich University, 1, 1*n*1, 18; decision not to publish "Hitler and the Germans" lectures, 17–18; dismissal from University of Vienna

in 1938, 235; emigration from Austria, 17; "German University" address of, 30–31, 33; "Immortality: Experience and Symbol" lecture by, 29–30; lectures on Hitler and Germans at Munich University, 1–3, 1*n*1, 17; methodological approach of, 28–29; students' response to, 1–2; in United States, 17, 18. *See also* specific titles of works
Völkisch, 156, 167–68
"Volksbildung, Wissenschaft und Politik" (Voegelin), 36
Volkstum, 159, 159*n*2, 163–64, 167–68, 170, 252
Voluntas (will), 107, 151
Vondung, Klaus, 42

Wagner, Adolf, 133
War as just war, 210
War-crime trials, 3–4, 63–68, 63*n*18, 105, 149, 213–14, 214*n*1, 230–36
Wasserman, Jakob, 120
Weber, Marianne, 267, 270, 273
Weber, Max: academic career of, 268, 268*n*8; aristocraticism of, 259; and bourgeois culture, 259; "breakdown" of, 268, 270; centenary of, 42; on charisma and charismatics, 265; and Christianity, 272; constancy of attitude and style of, 267–68; ethics of intention, 271, 271*n*11; on human nature, 258–59; as intellectual mystic, 270–73; language of, 259–60; and nonexperience of transcendence leading to dehumanization, 261–64; and recovery of experience of transcendence, 32; and unresolved tension toward transcendence, 32, 264–70; Voegelin's lecture on, 170, 184
—Works: *Economy and Society*, 268; "Politics as a Vocation," 35, 266
Weidling, Helmuth, 154
Weimar republic, 11, 78, 157, 186, 222, 224, 226, 229
Weltanschauung (worldview), 255, 262
Welträtsel (Haeckel), 124–28
Wessel, Horst, 196
West Germany. *See* Federal Republic of Germany
Wilhelm II, 137
Will: classical and Christian sense of, 107; as libido, 107, 151
Will to power, 107, 258
Witchcraft, 30, 254–55
Wittgenstein, Ludwig, 251–52
Wolff, Christian, 73
Wolff, Karl, 118
Works and Days (Hesiod), 88
Worldview, 100, 128, 129, 137, 138, 139, 221, 255
Wucher, Albert, 53, 53*n*4, 54–56, 58, 60, 62
Wurm, Theophil, 171–72, 171*n*39

Xynon, 27

Zahn, Gordon C., 192
Zech-Nenntwich affair, 68–69
"Zum Thema Geschichte" (Benn), 252